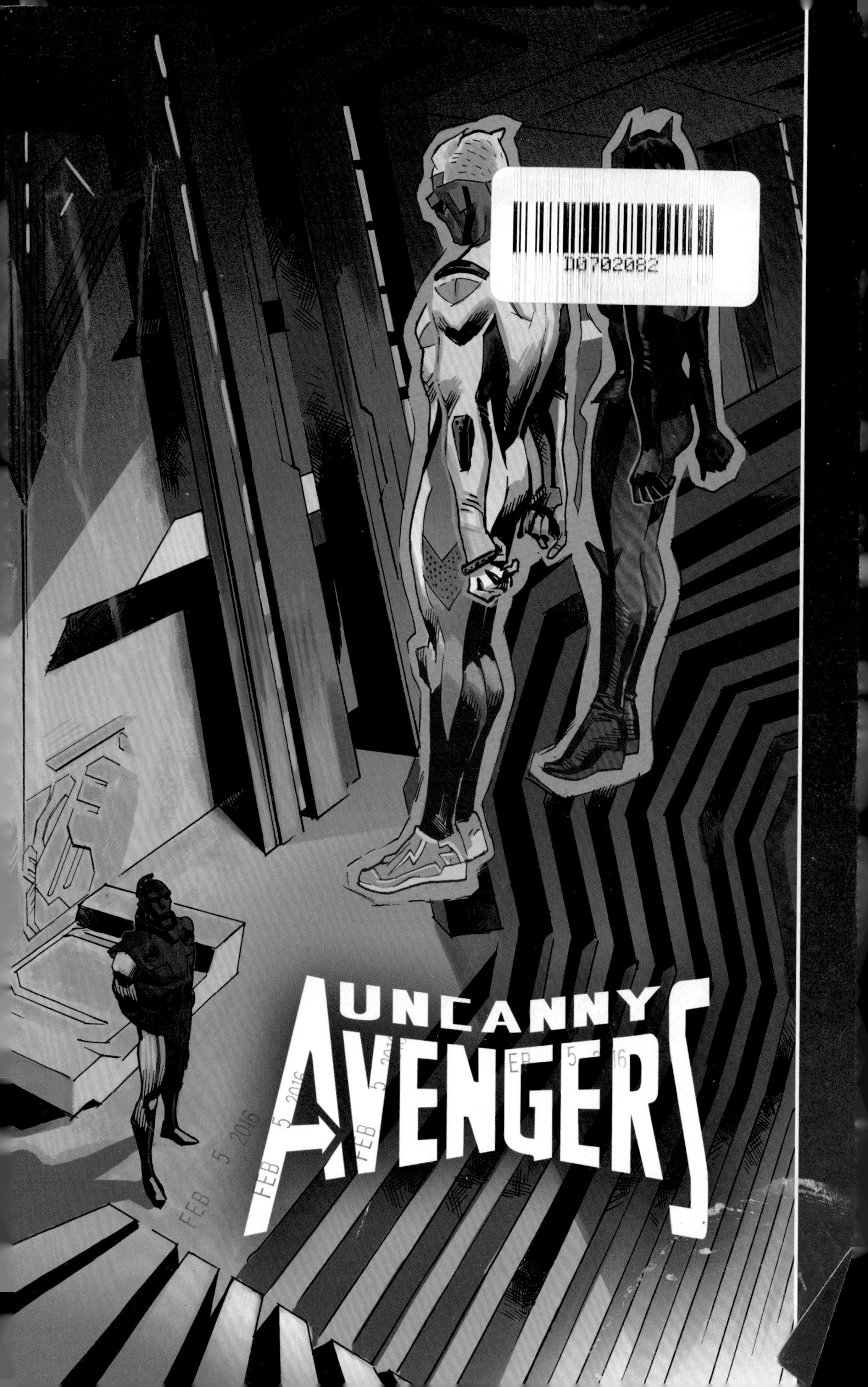
UNCANNY
AVENGERS

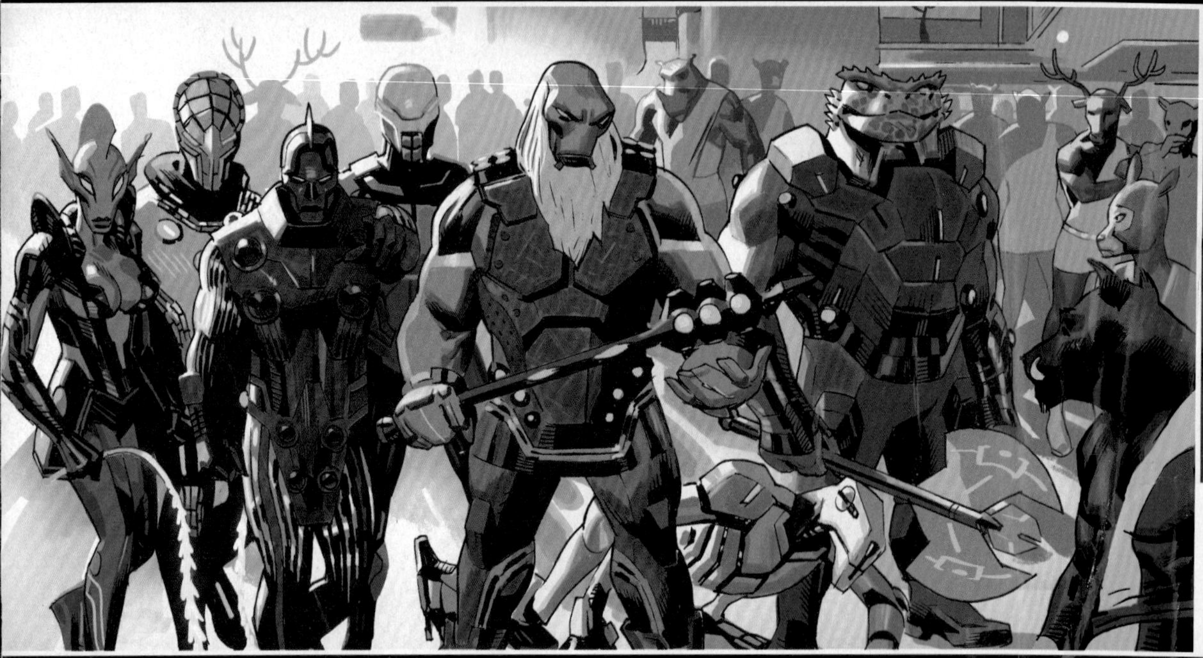

COUNTER-EVOLUTIONARY

JENNIFER GRÜNWALD COLLECTION EDITOR

SARAH BRUNSTAD ASSISTANT EDITOR

ALEX STARBUCK ASSOCIATE MANAGING EDITOR

MARK D. BEAZLEY EDITOR, SPECIAL PROJECTS

JEFF YOUNGQUIST SENIOR EDITOR, SPECIAL PROJECTS

UNCANNY AVENGERS

AS A JOINT TEAM OF AVENGERS AND X-MEN, THE AVENGERS UNITY SQUAD'S MISSION IS TO DEMONSTRATE TO THE WORLD THAT MAN AND MUTANT CAN WORK HAND IN HAND. MOST RECENTLY, THIS MEANT COMBATING LONGTIME AVENGERS FOE RED SKULL. WHILE THEY ULTIMATELY OVERCAME THEIR ADVERSARY, NOT EVERYONE RETURNED TO THEIR FORMER LIVES UNSCATHED: THE VILLAINOUS SABRETOOTH'S BLOODLUST WAS REPLACED WITH REMORSE FOR THE REPREHENSIBLE DEEDS OF HIS PAST, AND TWINS QUICKSILVER AND SCARLET WITCH MADE THE STARTLING DISCOVERY THAT MAGNETO MAY NOT BE THEIR TRUE FATHER AFTER ALL.

SEARCHING FOR ANSWERS, QUICKSILVER AND SCARLET WITCH TRAVELED TO COUNTER-EARTH—A DOPPLEGANGER PLANET SITUATED ON THE OPPOSITE SIDE OF THE SUN, HOME OF THE ENIGMATIC HIGH EVOLUTIONARY. CONCERNED FOR WANDA'S SAFETY, ROGUE RALLIED THE UNITY SQUAD TO FOLLOW. BUT WHEN DOCTOR VOODOO'S TELEPORTATION SPELL WAS INTERRUPTED, THE AVENGERS FOUND THEMSELVES SCATTERED ACROSS UNFAMILIAR TERRAIN...WITH SABRETOOTH FALLING RIGHT AT THE FEET OF THE HIGH EVOLUTIONARY HIMSELF.

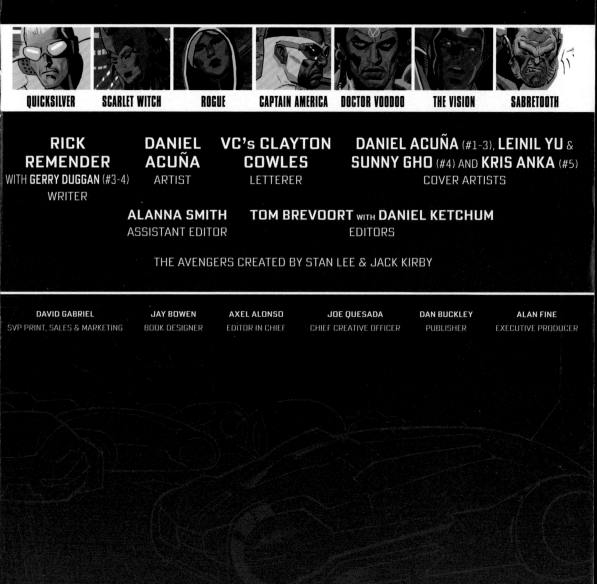

| QUICKSILVER | SCARLET WITCH | ROGUE | CAPTAIN AMERICA | DOCTOR VOODOO | THE VISION | SABRETOOTH |

RICK REMENDER
WITH **GERRY DUGGAN** (#3-4)
WRITER

DANIEL ACUÑA
ARTIST

VC's CLAYTON COWLES
LETTERER

DANIEL ACUÑA (#1-3), **LEINIL YU** & **SUNNY GHO** (#4) AND **KRIS ANKA** (#5)
COVER ARTISTS

ALANNA SMITH
ASSISTANT EDITOR

TOM BREVOORT WITH **DANIEL KETCHUM**
EDITORS

THE AVENGERS CREATED BY STAN LEE & JACK KIRBY

DAVID GABRIEL
SVP PRINT, SALES & MARKETING

JAY BOWEN
BOOK DESIGNER

AXEL ALONSO
EDITOR IN CHIEF

JOE QUESADA
CHIEF CREATIVE OFFICER

DAN BUCKLEY
PUBLISHER

ALAN FINE
EXECUTIVE PRODUCER

UNCANNY AVENGERS VOL. 1: COUNTER-EVOLUTIONARY. Contains material originally published in magazine form as UNCANNY AVENGERS #1-5. First printing 2015. ISBN# 978-0-7851-9237-4. Published by MARVEL WORLDWIDE, INC., a subsidiary of MARVEL ENTERTAINMENT, LLC. OFFICE OF PUBLICATION: 135 West 50th Street, New York, NY 10020. Copyright © 2015 MARVEL. No similarity between any of the names, characters, persons, and/or institutions in this magazine with those of any living or dead person or institution is intended, and any such similarity which may exist is purely coincidental. **Printed in Canada.** ALAN FINE, President, Marvel Entertainment; DAN BUCKLEY, President, TV, Publishing and Brand Management; JOE QUESADA, Chief Creative Officer; TOM BREVOORT, SVP of Publishing; DAVID BOGART, SVP of Operations & Procurement, Publishing; C.B. CEBULSKI, VP of International Development & Brand Management; DAVID GABRIEL, SVP Print, Sales & Marketing; JIM O'KEEFE, VP of Operations & Logistics; DAN CARR, Executive Director of Publishing Technology; SUSAN CRESPI, Editorial Operations Manager; ALEX MORALES, Publishing Operations Manager; STAN LEE, Chairman Emeritus. For information regarding advertising in Marvel Comics or on Marvel.com, please contact Jonathan Rheingold, VP of Custom Solutions & Ad Sales, at jrheingold@marvel.com. For Marvel subscription inquiries, please call 800-217-9158. **Manufactured between 7/3/2015 and 8/10/2015 by SOLISCO PRINTERS, SCOTT, QC, CANADA.**

10 9 8 7 6 5 4 3 2 1

UNCANNY AVENGERS #1

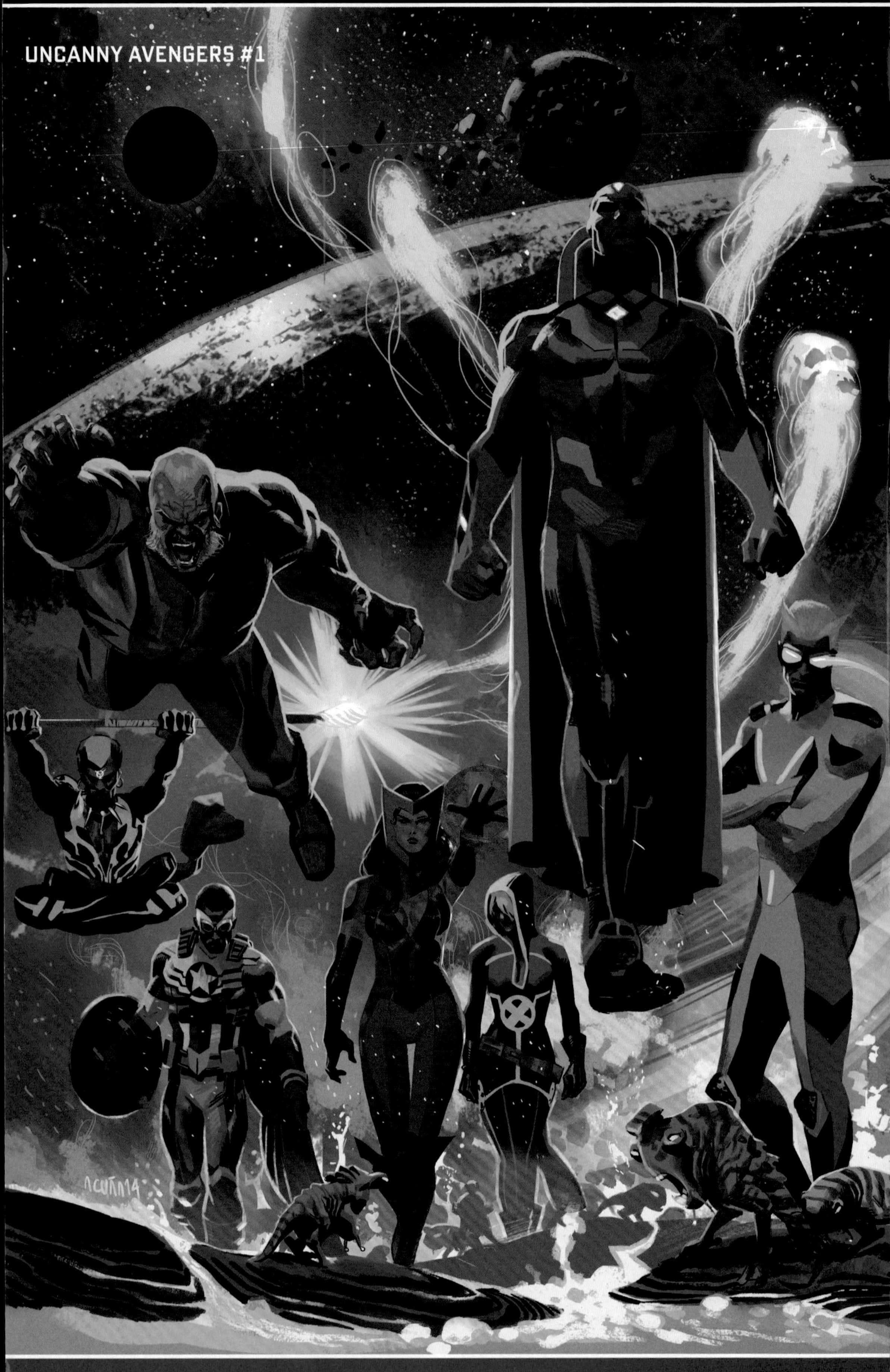

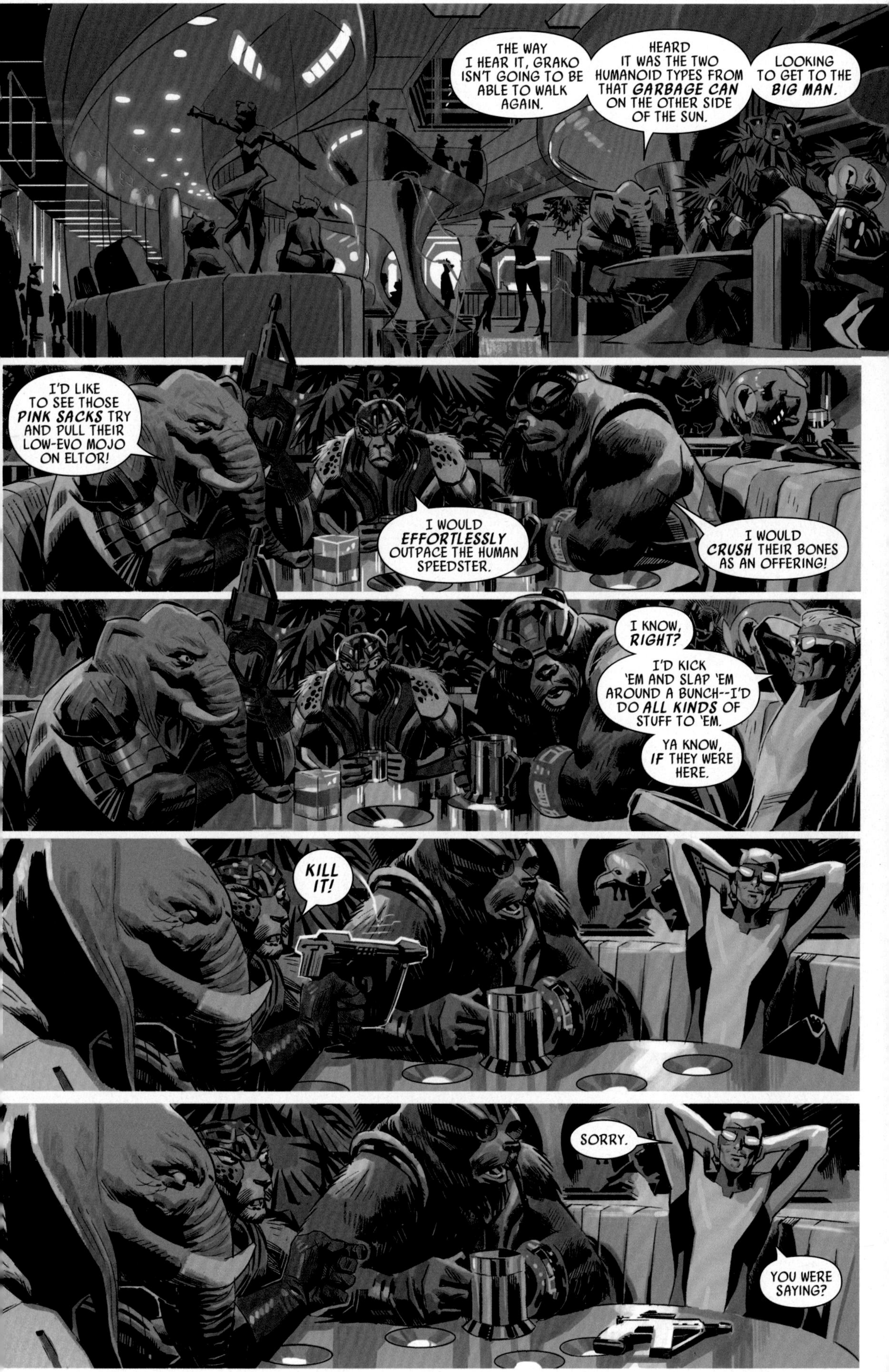
THE WAY I HEAR IT, GRAKO ISN'T GOING TO BE ABLE TO WALK AGAIN.
HEARD IT WAS THE TWO HUMANOID TYPES FROM THAT GARBAGE CAN ON THE OTHER SIDE OF THE SUN.
LOOKING TO GET TO THE BIG MAN.
I'D LIKE TO SEE THOSE PINK SACKS TRY AND PULL THEIR LOW-EVO MOJO ON ELTOR!
I WOULD EFFORTLESSLY OUTPACE THE HUMAN SPEEDSTER.
I WOULD CRUSH THEIR BONES AS AN OFFERING!
I KNOW, RIGHT?
I'D KICK 'EM AND SLAP 'EM AROUND A BUNCH--I'D DO ALL KINDS OF STUFF TO 'EM.
YA KNOW, IF THEY WERE HERE.
KILL IT!
SORRY.
YOU WERE SAYING?

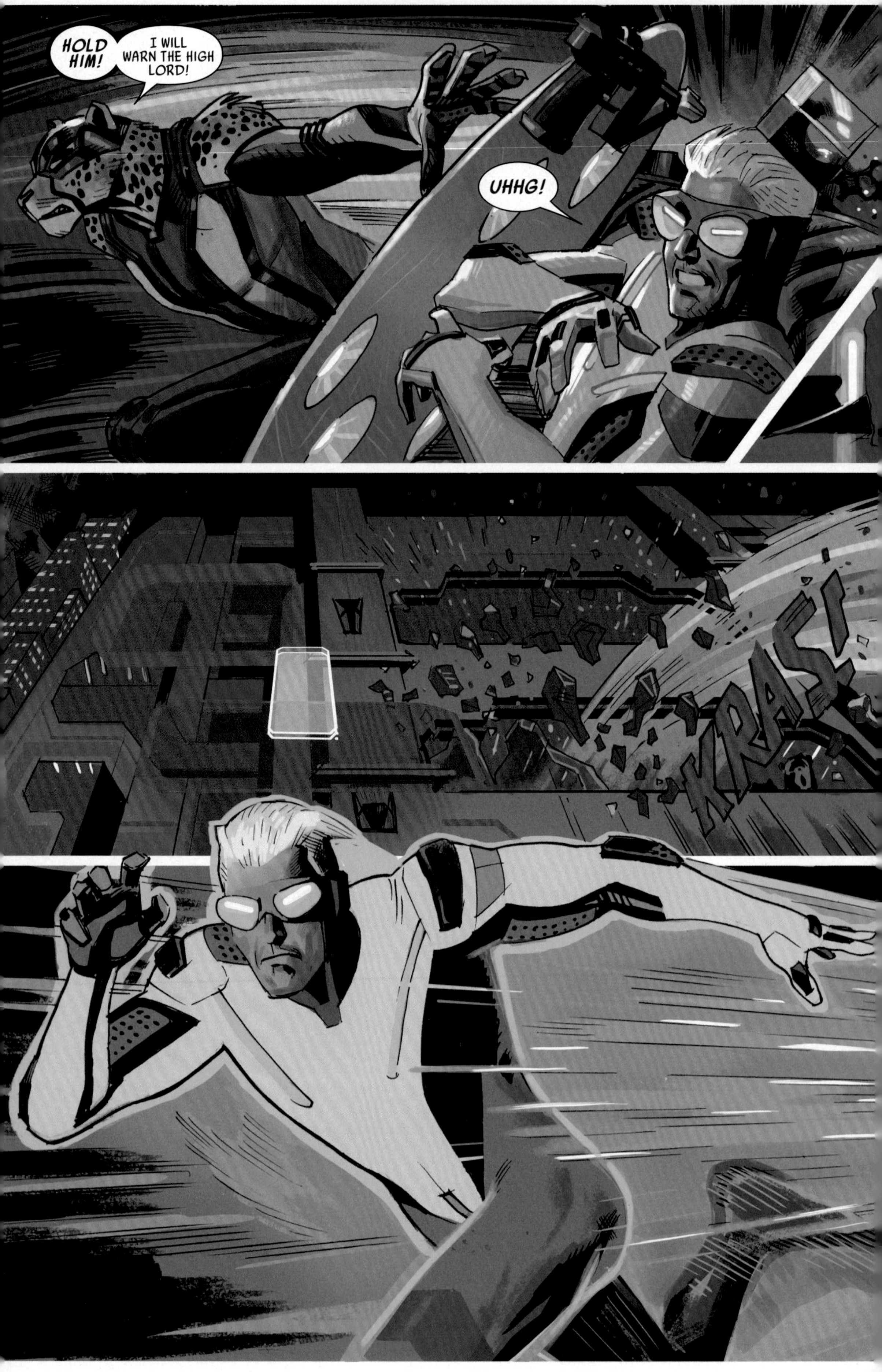
HOLD HIM!
I WILL WARN THE HIGH LORD!
UHHG!
KRASH!

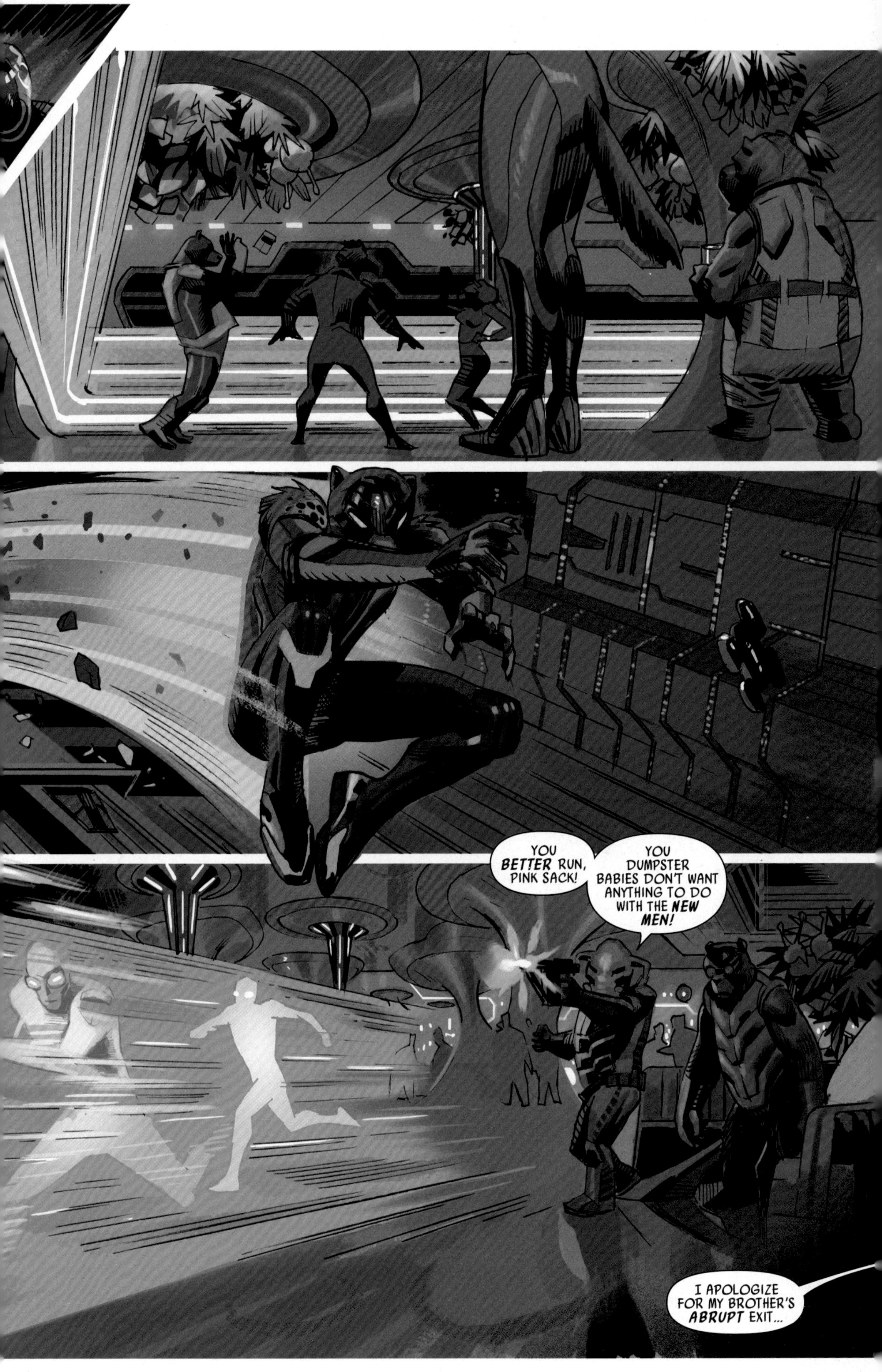
YOU BETTER RUN, PINK SACK!
YOU DUMPSTER BABIES DON'T WANT ANYTHING TO DO WITH THE NEW MEN!
I APOLOGIZE FOR MY BROTHER'S ABRUPT EXIT...

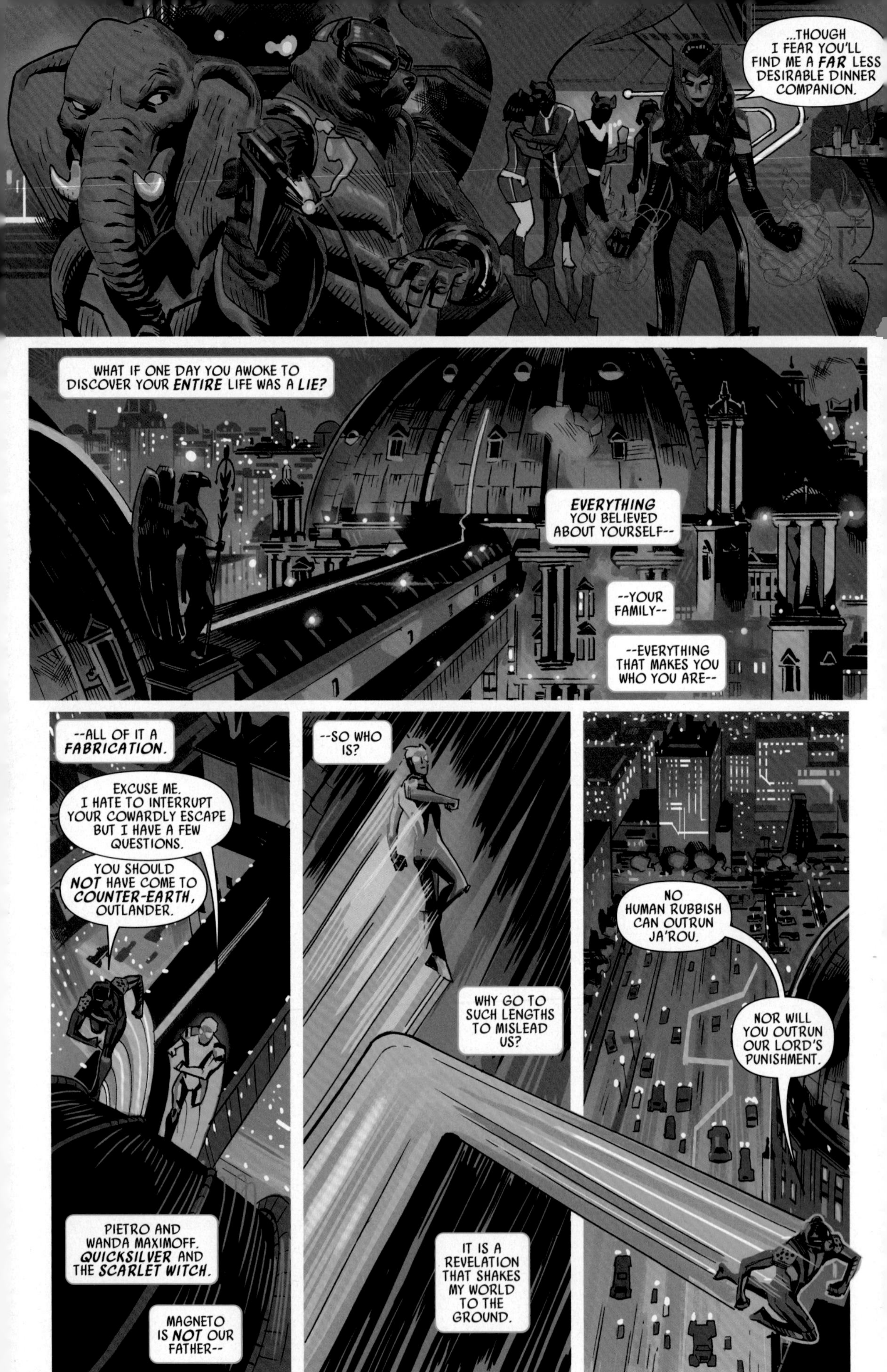
...THOUGH I FEAR YOU'LL FIND ME A FAR LESS DESIRABLE DINNER COMPANION.
WHAT IF ONE DAY YOU AWOKE TO DISCOVER YOUR ENTIRE LIFE WAS A LIE?
EVERYTHING YOU BELIEVED ABOUT YOURSELF--
--YOUR FAMILY--
--EVERYTHING THAT MAKES YOU WHO YOU ARE--
--ALL OF IT A FABRICATION.
EXCUSE ME. I HATE TO INTERRUPT YOUR COWARDLY ESCAPE BUT I HAVE A FEW QUESTIONS.
YOU SHOULD NOT HAVE COME TO COUNTER-EARTH, OUTLANDER.
PIETRO AND WANDA MAXIMOFF. QUICKSILVER AND THE SCARLET WITCH.
MAGNETO IS NOT OUR FATHER--
--SO WHO IS?
WHY GO TO SUCH LENGTHS TO MISLEAD US?
IT IS A REVELATION THAT SHAKES MY WORLD TO THE GROUND.
NO HUMAN RUBBISH CAN OUTRUN JA'ROU.
NOR WILL YOU OUTRUN OUR LORD'S PUNISHMENT.

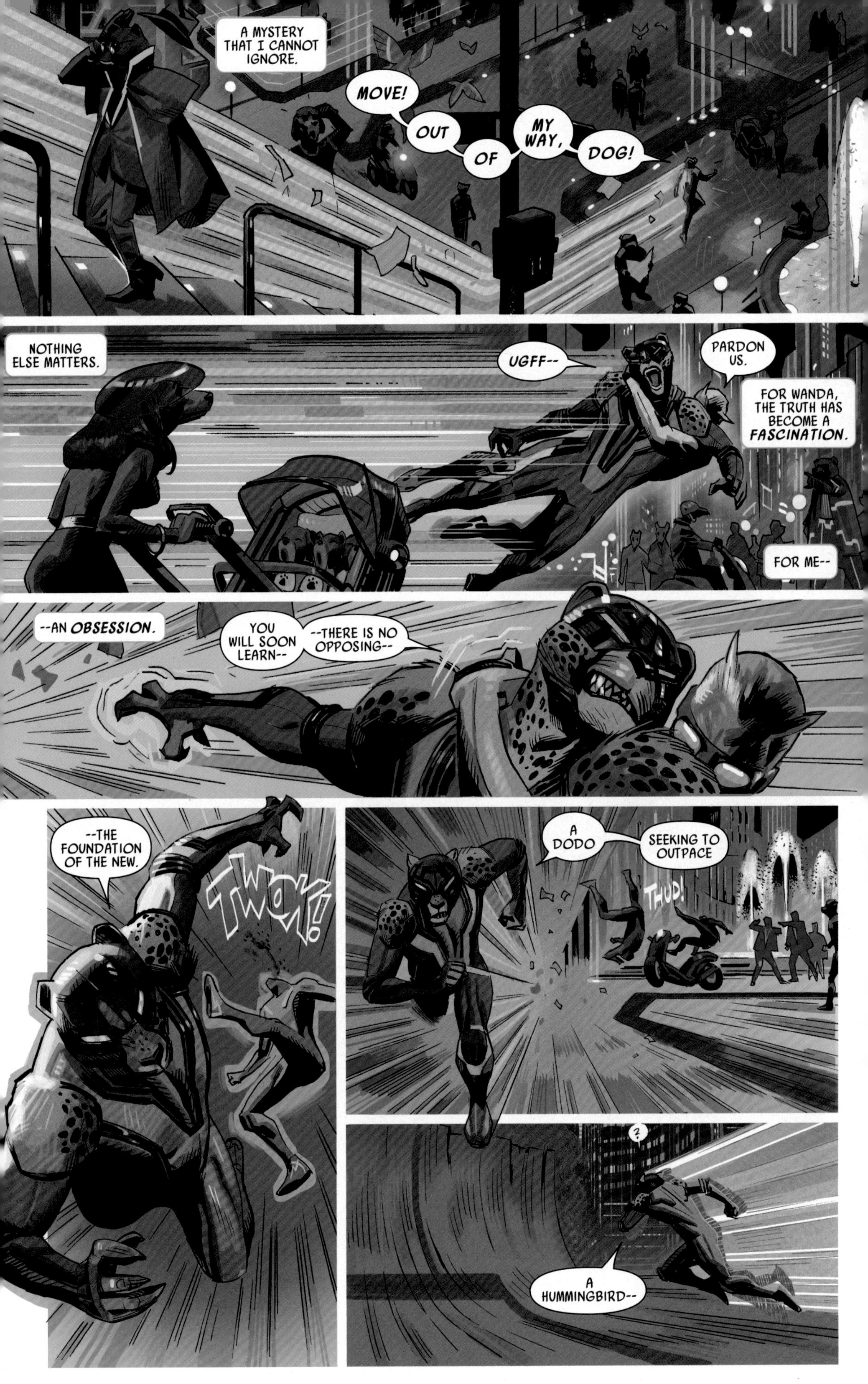

A MYSTERY THAT I CANNOT IGNORE.
MOVE!
OUT
OF
MY WAY,
DOG!
NOTHING ELSE MATTERS.
UGFF--
PARDON US.
FOR WANDA, THE TRUTH HAS BECOME A FASCINATION.
FOR ME--
--AN OBSESSION.
YOU WILL SOON LEARN--
--THERE IS NO OPPOSING--
--THE FOUNDATION OF THE NEW.
TWOK!
A DODO
SEEKING TO OUTPACE
THUD!
?
A HUMMINGBIRD--

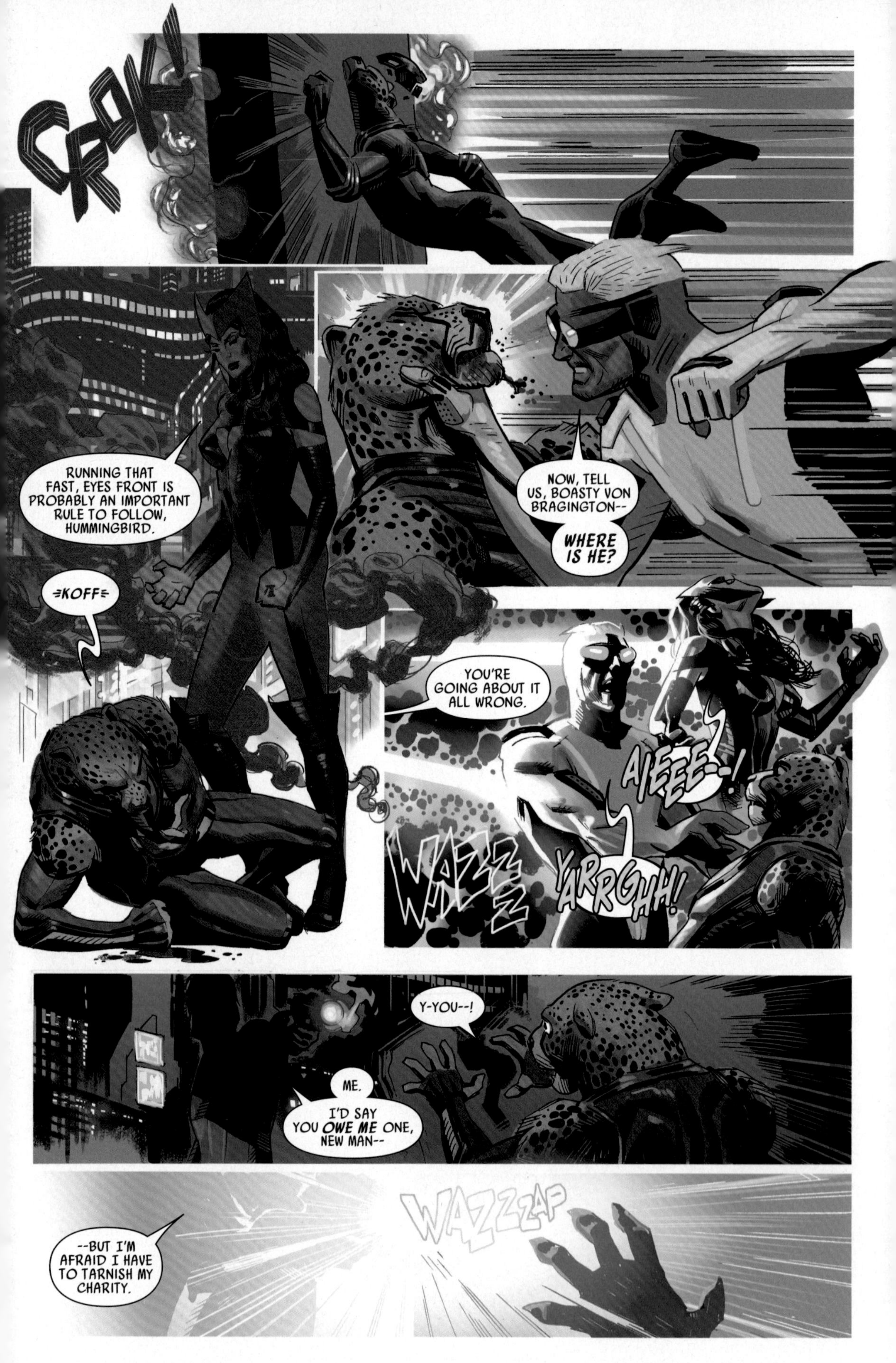
CROK!
RUNNING THAT FAST, EYES FRONT IS PROBABLY AN IMPORTANT RULE TO FOLLOW, HUMMINGBIRD.
NOW, TELL US, BOASTY VON BRAGINGTON--
WHERE IS HE?
=KOFF=
YOU'RE GOING ABOUT IT ALL WRONG.
AIEEE--!
WAZZZ
YARRGHH!
Y-YOU--!
ME.
I'D SAY YOU OWE ME ONE, NEW MAN--
WAZZZAP
--BUT I'M AFRAID I HAVE TO TARNISH MY CHARITY.

COUNTER-
EVOLUTIONARY

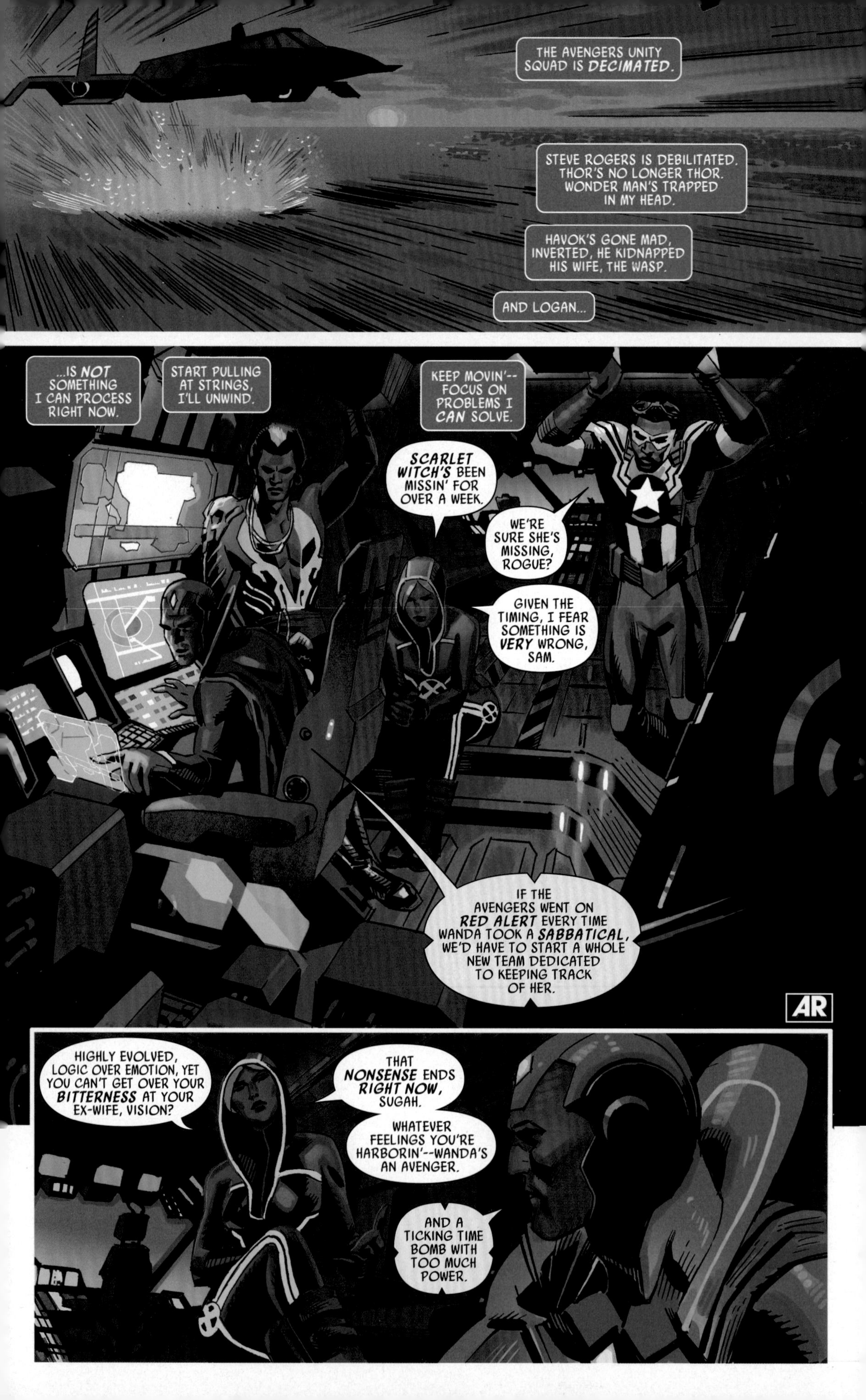

THE AVENGERS UNITY SQUAD IS DECIMATED.
STEVE ROGERS IS DEBILITATED. THOR'S NO LONGER THOR. WONDER MAN'S TRAPPED IN MY HEAD.
HAVOK'S GONE MAD, INVERTED, HE KIDNAPPED HIS WIFE, THE WASP.
AND LOGAN...
...IS NOT SOMETHING I CAN PROCESS RIGHT NOW.
START PULLING AT STRINGS, I'LL UNWIND.
KEEP MOVIN'-- FOCUS ON PROBLEMS I CAN SOLVE.
SCARLET WITCH'S BEEN MISSIN' FOR OVER A WEEK.
WE'RE SURE SHE'S MISSING, ROGUE?
GIVEN THE TIMING, I FEAR SOMETHING IS VERY WRONG, SAM.
IF THE AVENGERS WENT ON RED ALERT EVERY TIME WANDA TOOK A SABBATICAL, WE'D HAVE TO START A WHOLE NEW TEAM DEDICATED TO KEEPING TRACK OF HER.
HIGHLY EVOLVED, LOGIC OVER EMOTION, YET YOU CAN'T GET OVER YOUR BITTERNESS AT YOUR EX-WIFE, VISION?
THAT NONSENSE ENDS RIGHT NOW, SUGAH.
WHATEVER FEELINGS YOU'RE HARBORIN'--WANDA'S AN AVENGER.
AND A TICKING TIME BOMB WITH TOO MUCH POWER.

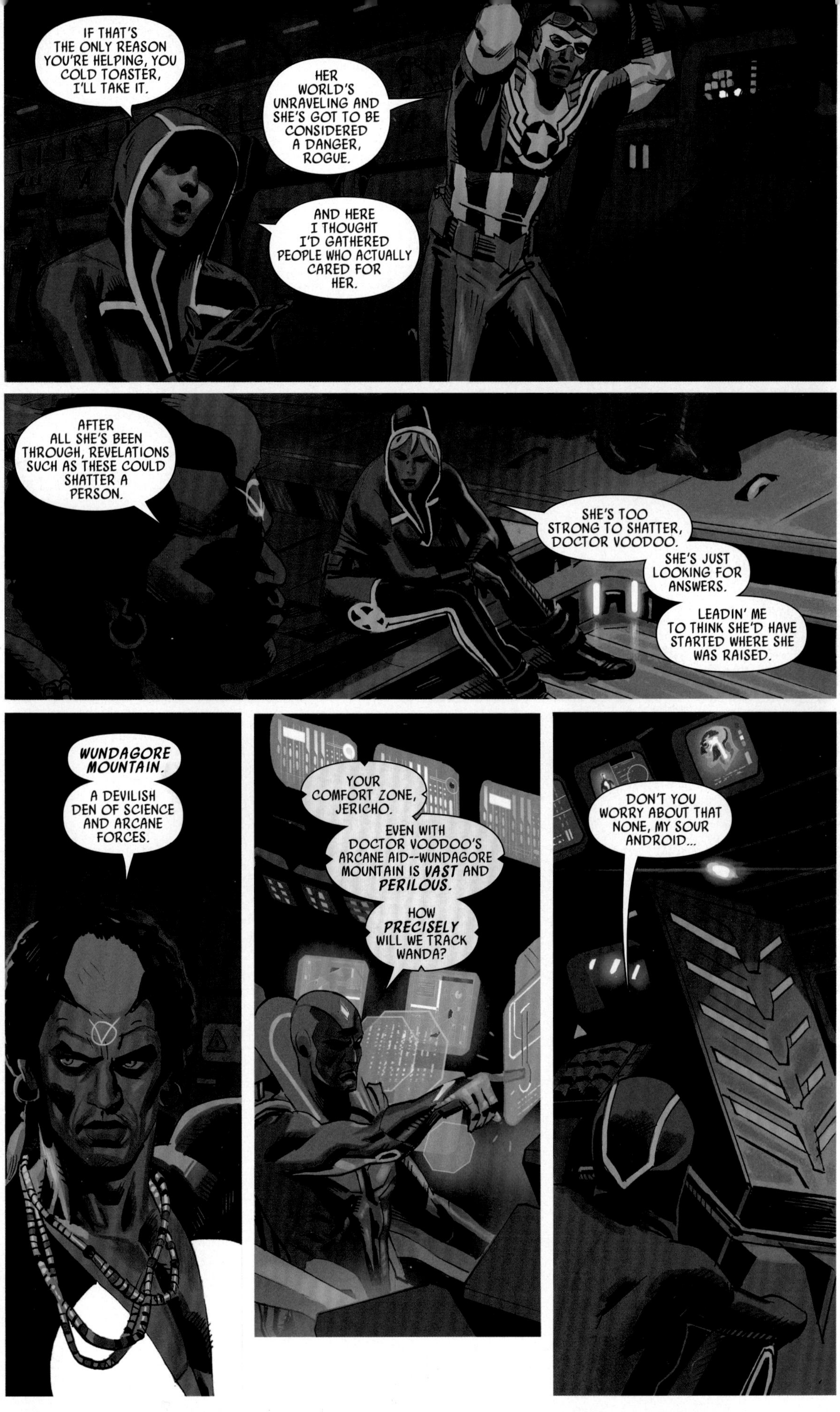
IF THAT'S THE ONLY REASON YOU'RE HELPING, YOU COLD TOASTER, I'LL TAKE IT.
HER WORLD'S UNRAVELING AND SHE'S GOT TO BE CONSIDERED A DANGER, ROGUE.
AND HERE I THOUGHT I'D GATHERED PEOPLE WHO ACTUALLY CARED FOR HER.
AFTER ALL SHE'S BEEN THROUGH, REVELATIONS SUCH AS THESE COULD SHATTER A PERSON.
SHE'S TOO STRONG TO SHATTER, DOCTOR VOODOO.
SHE'S JUST LOOKING FOR ANSWERS.
LEADIN' ME TO THINK SHE'D HAVE STARTED WHERE SHE WAS RAISED.
WUNDAGORE MOUNTAIN.
A DEVILISH DEN OF SCIENCE AND ARCANE FORCES.
YOUR COMFORT ZONE, JERICHO.
EVEN WITH DOCTOR VOODOO'S ARCANE AID--WUNDAGORE MOUNTAIN IS VAST AND PERILOUS.
HOW PRECISELY WILL WE TRACK WANDA?
DON'T YOU WORRY ABOUT THAT NONE, MY SOUR ANDROID...

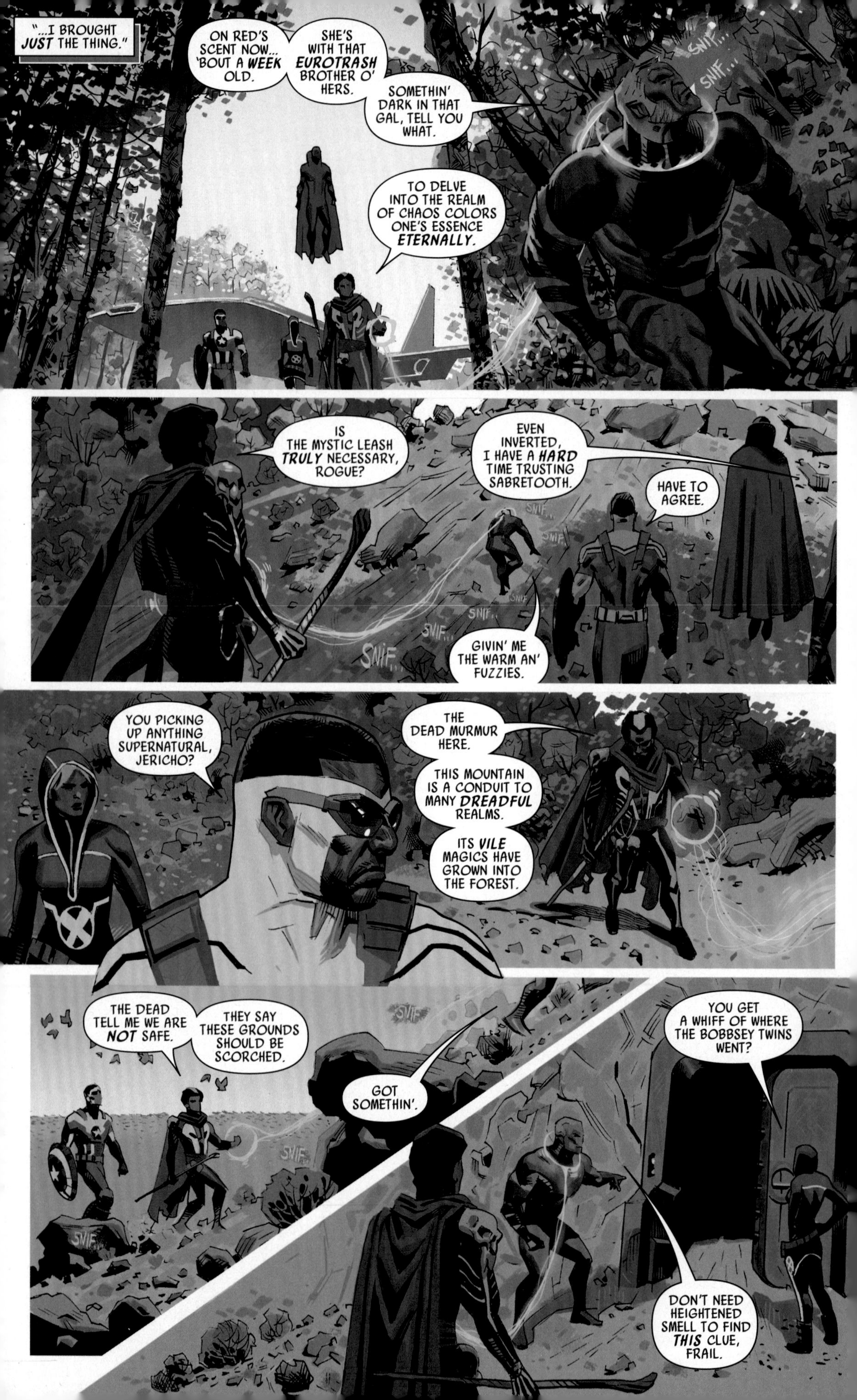
"...I BROUGHT JUST THE THING."
ON RED'S SCENT NOW... 'BOUT A WEEK OLD.
SHE'S WITH THAT EUROTRASH BROTHER O' HERS.
SOMETHIN' DARK IN THAT GAL, TELL YOU WHAT.
SNIF... SNIF...
TO DELVE INTO THE REALM OF CHAOS COLORS ONE'S ESSENCE ETERNALLY.
IS THE MYSTIC LEASH TRULY NECESSARY, ROGUE?
EVEN INVERTED, I HAVE A HARD TIME TRUSTING SABRETOOTH.
HAVE TO AGREE.
SNIF... SNIF... SNIF... SNIF... SNIF... SNIF...
GIVIN' ME THE WARM AN' FUZZIES.
YOU PICKING UP ANYTHING SUPERNATURAL, JERICHO?
THE DEAD MURMUR HERE.
THIS MOUNTAIN IS A CONDUIT TO MANY DREADFUL REALMS.
ITS VILE MAGICS HAVE GROWN INTO THE FOREST.
THE DEAD TELL ME WE ARE NOT SAFE.
THEY SAY THESE GROUNDS SHOULD BE SCORCHED.
SNIF
GOT SOMETHIN'.
SNIF...
SNIF...
YOU GET A WHIFF OF WHERE THE BOBBSEY TWINS WENT?
DON'T NEED HEIGHTENED SMELL TO FIND THIS CLUE, FRAIL.

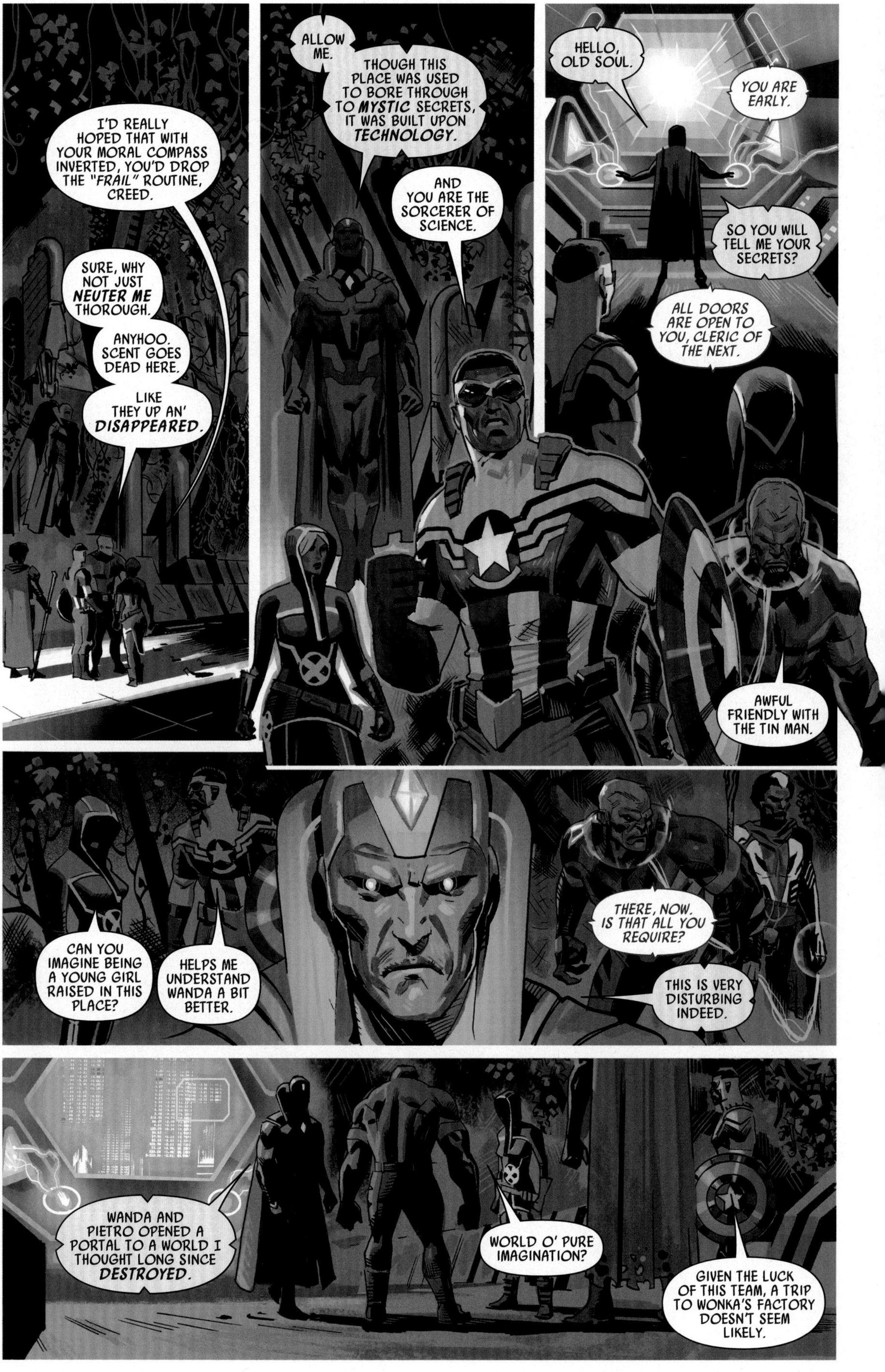
I'D REALLY HOPED THAT WITH YOUR MORAL COMPASS INVERTED, YOU'D DROP THE "FRAIL" ROUTINE, CREED.
SURE, WHY NOT JUST NEUTER ME THOROUGH.
ANYHOO. SCENT GOES DEAD HERE.
LIKE THEY UP AN' DISAPPEARED.
ALLOW ME.
THOUGH THIS PLACE WAS USED TO BORE THROUGH TO MYSTIC SECRETS, IT WAS BUILT UPON TECHNOLOGY.
AND YOU ARE THE SORCERER OF SCIENCE.
HELLO, OLD SOUL.
YOU ARE EARLY.
SO YOU WILL TELL ME YOUR SECRETS?
ALL DOORS ARE OPEN TO YOU, CLERIC OF THE NEXT.
AWFUL FRIENDLY WITH THE TIN MAN.
CAN YOU IMAGINE BEING A YOUNG GIRL RAISED IN THIS PLACE?
HELPS ME UNDERSTAND WANDA A BIT BETTER.
THERE, NOW. IS THAT ALL YOU REQUIRE?
THIS IS VERY DISTURBING INDEED.
WANDA AND PIETRO OPENED A PORTAL TO A WORLD I THOUGHT LONG SINCE DESTROYED.
WORLD O' PURE IMAGINATION?
GIVEN THE LUCK OF THIS TEAM, A TRIP TO WONKA'S FACTORY DOESN'T SEEM LIKELY.

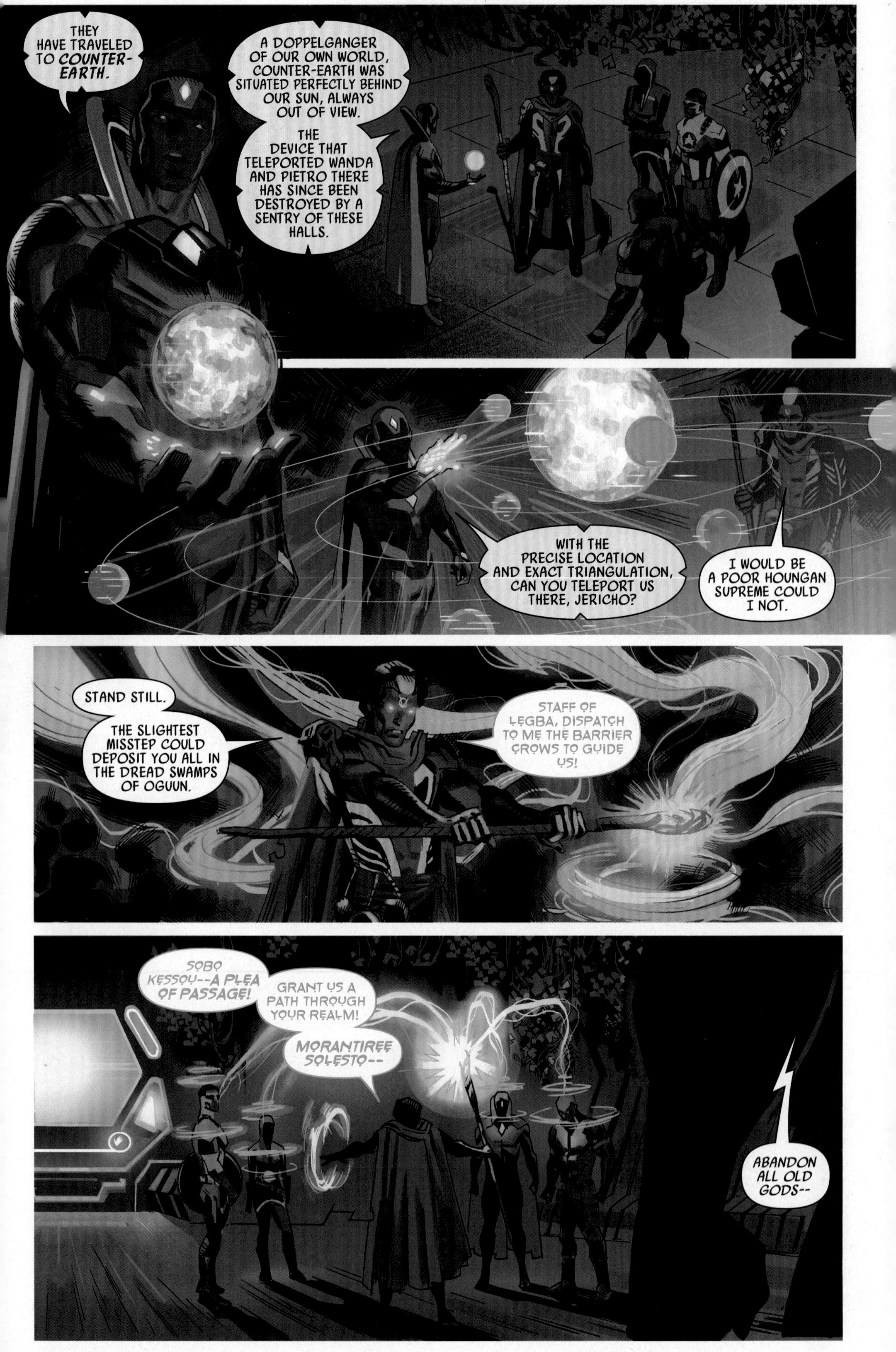
THEY HAVE TRAVELED TO COUNTER-EARTH.
A DOPPELGANGER OF OUR OWN WORLD, COUNTER-EARTH WAS SITUATED PERFECTLY BEHIND OUR SUN, ALWAYS OUT OF VIEW.
THE DEVICE THAT TELEPORTED WANDA AND PIETRO THERE HAS SINCE BEEN DESTROYED BY A SENTRY OF THESE HALLS.
WITH THE PRECISE LOCATION AND EXACT TRIANGULATION, CAN YOU TELEPORT US THERE, JERICHO?
I WOULD BE A POOR HOUNGAN SUPREME COULD I NOT.
STAND STILL.
THE SLIGHTEST MISSTEP COULD DEPOSIT YOU ALL IN THE DREAD SWAMPS OF OGUUN.
STAFF OF LEGBA, DISPATCH TO ME THE BARRIER CROWS TO GUIDE US!
SOBO KESSOU--A PLEA OF PASSAGE!
GRANT US A PATH THROUGH YOUR REALM!
MORANTIREE SOLESTO--
ABANDON ALL OLD GODS--

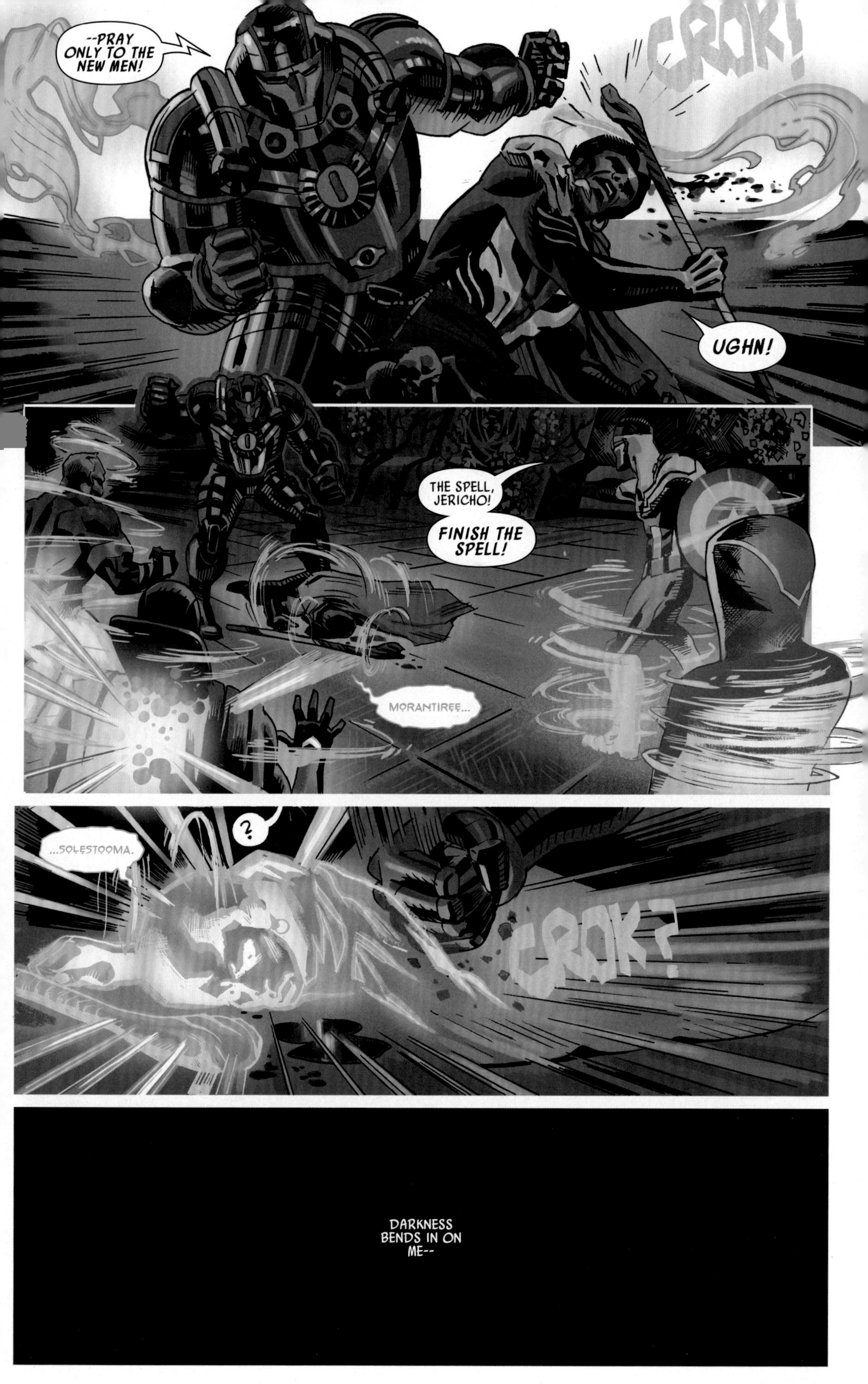
--PRAY ONLY TO THE NEW MEN!
CROK!
UGHN!
THE SPELL, JERICHO!
FINISH THE SPELL!
MORANTIREE...
...SOLESTOOMA.
?
CROK?
DARKNESS BENDS IN ON ME--

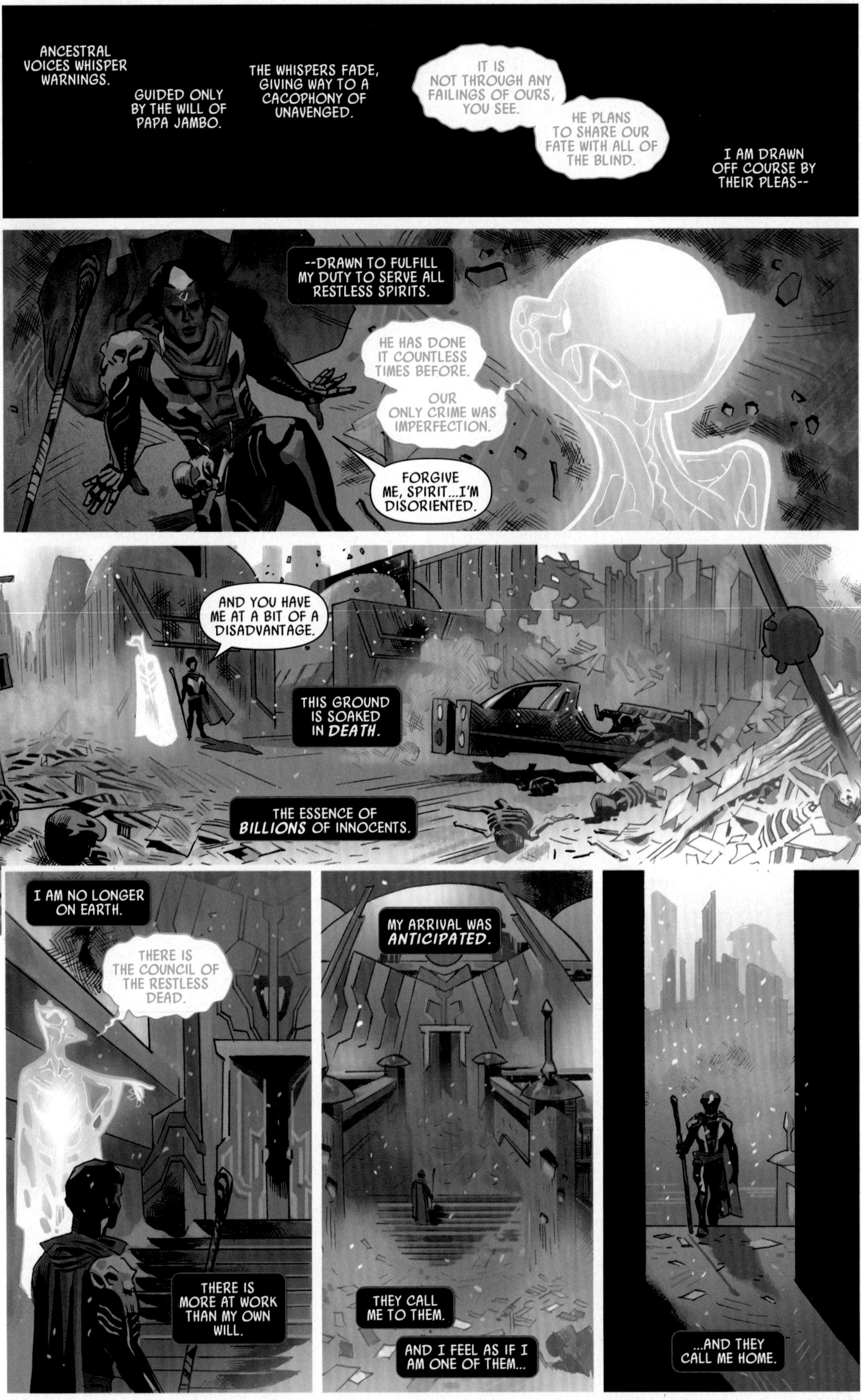
ANCESTRAL VOICES WHISPER WARNINGS.
GUIDED ONLY BY THE WILL OF PAPA JAMBO.
THE WHISPERS FADE, GIVING WAY TO A CACOPHONY OF UNAVENGED.
IT IS NOT THROUGH ANY FAILINGS OF OURS, YOU SEE.
HE PLANS TO SHARE OUR FATE WITH ALL OF THE BLIND.
I AM DRAWN OFF COURSE BY THEIR PLEAS--
--DRAWN TO FULFILL MY DUTY TO SERVE ALL RESTLESS SPIRITS.
HE HAS DONE IT COUNTLESS TIMES BEFORE.
OUR ONLY CRIME WAS IMPERFECTION.
FORGIVE ME, SPIRIT...I'M DISORIENTED.
AND YOU HAVE ME AT A BIT OF A DISADVANTAGE.
THIS GROUND IS SOAKED IN *DEATH*.
THE ESSENCE OF *BILLIONS* OF INNOCENTS.
I AM NO LONGER ON EARTH.
THERE IS THE COUNCIL OF THE RESTLESS DEAD.
THERE IS MORE AT WORK THAN MY OWN WILL.
MY ARRIVAL WAS *ANTICIPATED*.
THEY CALL ME TO THEM.
AND I FEEL AS IF I AM ONE OF THEM...
...AND THEY CALL ME HOME.

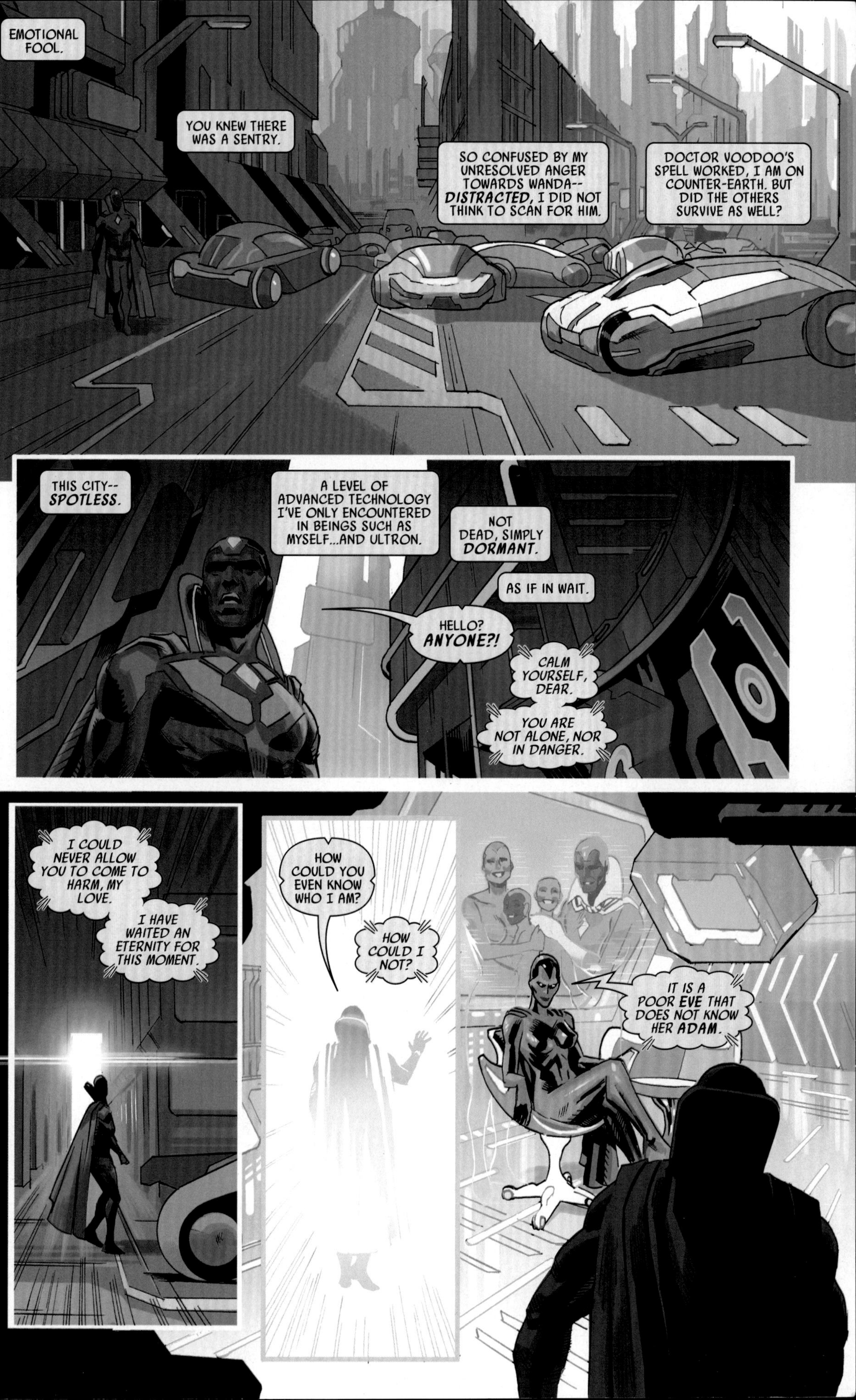
EMOTIONAL FOOL.
YOU KNEW THERE WAS A SENTRY.
SO CONFUSED BY MY UNRESOLVED ANGER TOWARDS WANDA-- DISTRACTED, I DID NOT THINK TO SCAN FOR HIM.
DOCTOR VOODOO'S SPELL WORKED, I AM ON COUNTER-EARTH. BUT DID THE OTHERS SURVIVE AS WELL?
THIS CITY-- SPOTLESS.
A LEVEL OF ADVANCED TECHNOLOGY I'VE ONLY ENCOUNTERED IN BEINGS SUCH AS MYSELF...AND ULTRON.
NOT DEAD, SIMPLY DORMANT.
AS IF IN WAIT.
HELLO? ANYONE?!
CALM YOURSELF, DEAR.
YOU ARE NOT ALONE, NOR IN DANGER.
I COULD NEVER ALLOW YOU TO COME TO HARM, MY LOVE.
I HAVE WAITED AN ETERNITY FOR THIS MOMENT.
HOW COULD YOU EVEN KNOW WHO I AM?
HOW COULD I NOT?
IT IS A POOR EVE THAT DOES NOT KNOW HER ADAM.

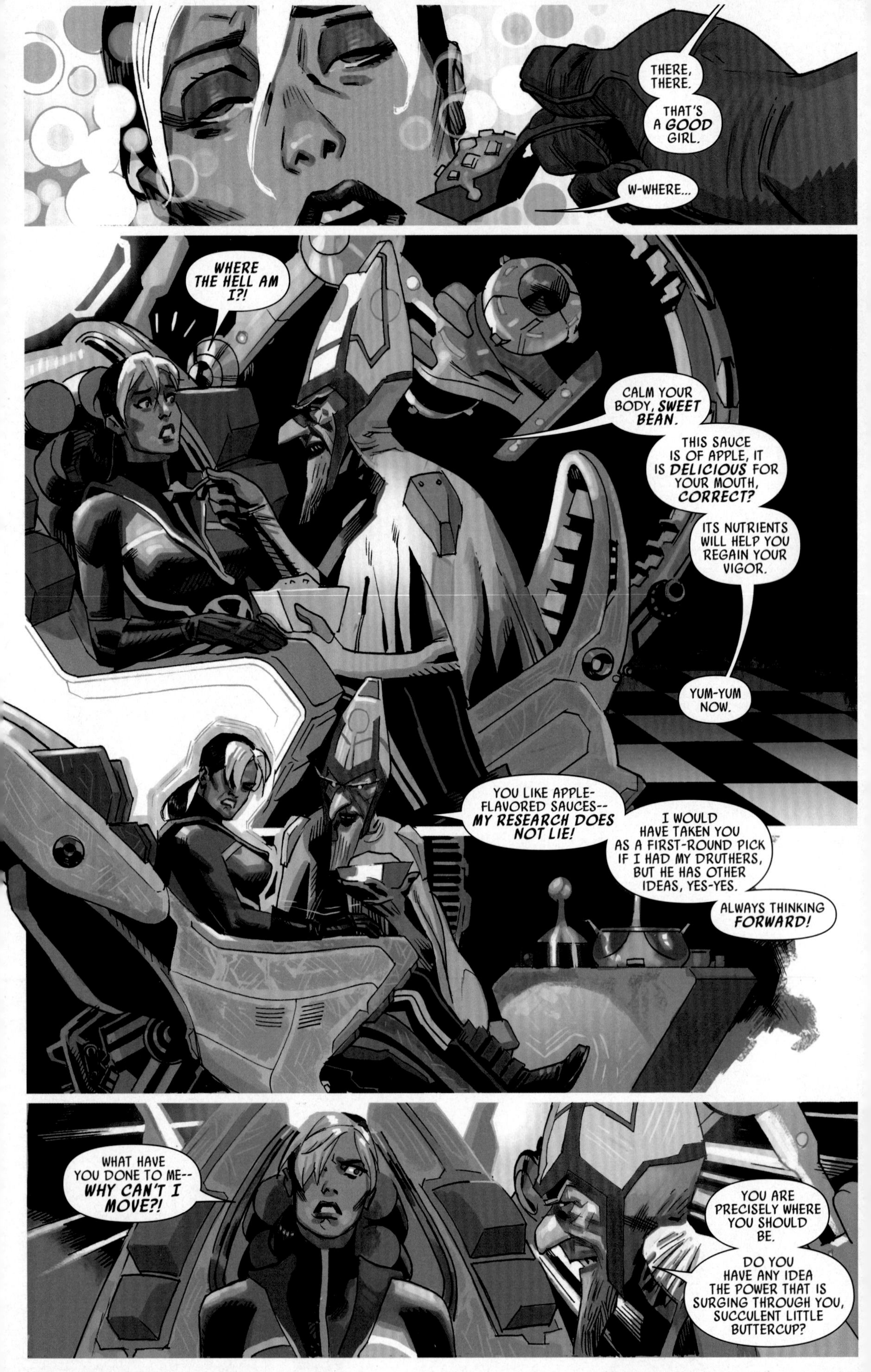
THERE, THERE.
THAT'S A GOOD GIRL.
W-WHERE...
WHERE THE HELL AM I?!
CALM YOUR BODY, SWEET BEAN.
THIS SAUCE IS OF APPLE, IT IS DELICIOUS FOR YOUR MOUTH, CORRECT?
ITS NUTRIENTS WILL HELP YOU REGAIN YOUR VIGOR.
YUM-YUM NOW.
YOU LIKE APPLE-FLAVORED SAUCES-- MY RESEARCH DOES NOT LIE!
I WOULD HAVE TAKEN YOU AS A FIRST-ROUND PICK IF I HAD MY DRUTHERS, BUT HE HAS OTHER IDEAS, YES-YES.
ALWAYS THINKING FORWARD!
WHAT HAVE YOU DONE TO ME-- WHY CAN'T I MOVE?!
YOU ARE PRECISELY WHERE YOU SHOULD BE.
DO YOU HAVE ANY IDEA THE POWER THAT IS SURGING THROUGH YOU, SUCCULENT LITTLE BUTTERCUP?

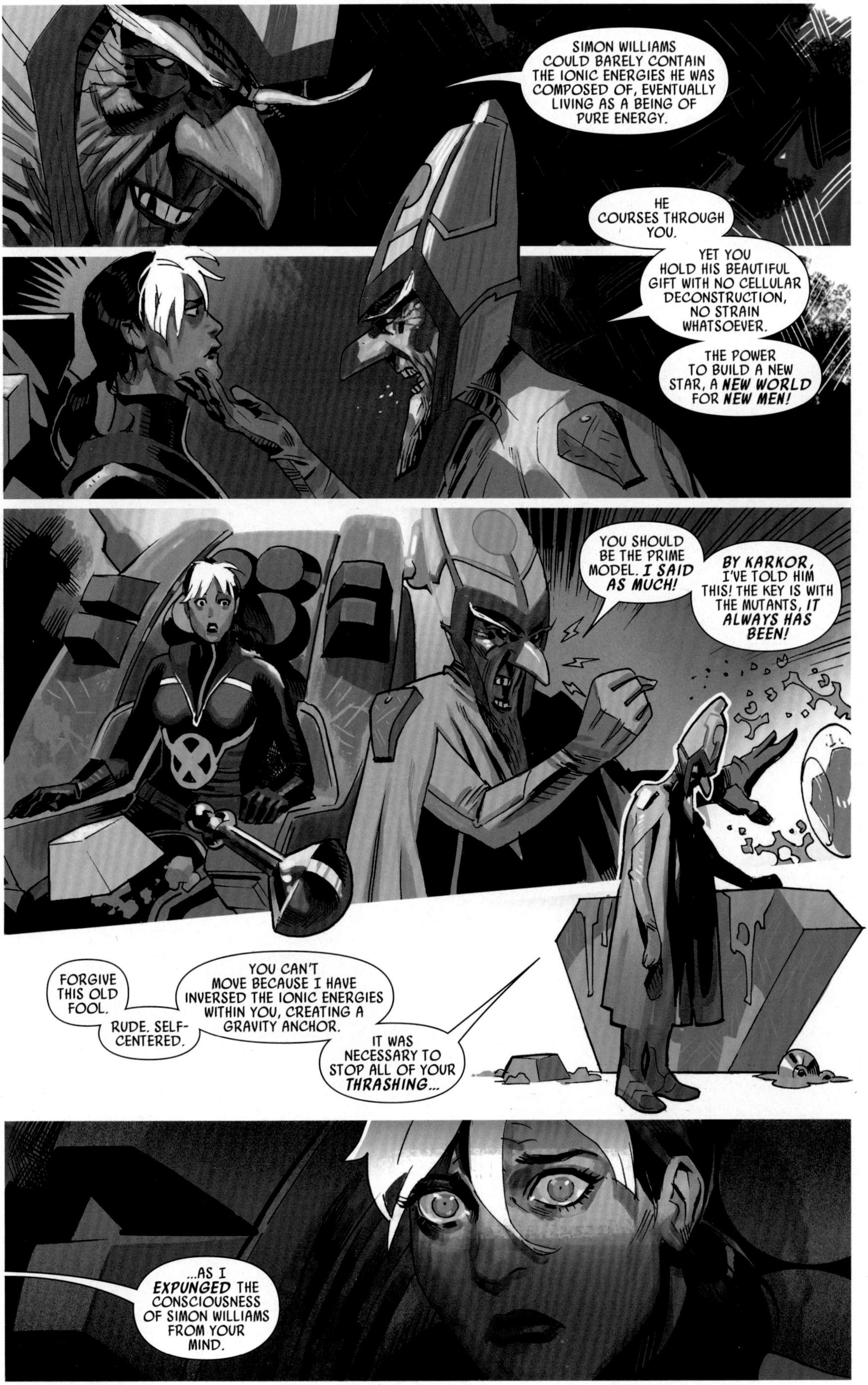
SIMON WILLIAMS COULD BARELY CONTAIN THE IONIC ENERGIES HE WAS COMPOSED OF, EVENTUALLY LIVING AS A BEING OF PURE ENERGY.
HE COURSES THROUGH YOU.
YET YOU HOLD HIS BEAUTIFUL GIFT WITH NO CELLULAR DECONSTRUCTION, NO STRAIN WHATSOEVER.
THE POWER TO BUILD A NEW STAR, A **NEW WORLD** FOR **NEW MEN!**
YOU SHOULD BE THE PRIME MODEL. **I SAID AS MUCH!**
BY KARKOR, I'VE TOLD HIM THIS! THE KEY IS WITH THE MUTANTS, **IT ALWAYS HAS BEEN!**
FORGIVE THIS OLD FOOL.
RUDE. SELF-CENTERED.
YOU CAN'T MOVE BECAUSE I HAVE INVERSED THE IONIC ENERGIES WITHIN YOU, CREATING A GRAVITY ANCHOR.
IT WAS NECESSARY TO STOP ALL OF YOUR **THRASHING...**
...AS I **EXPUNGED** THE CONSCIOUSNESS OF SIMON WILLIAMS FROM YOUR MIND.

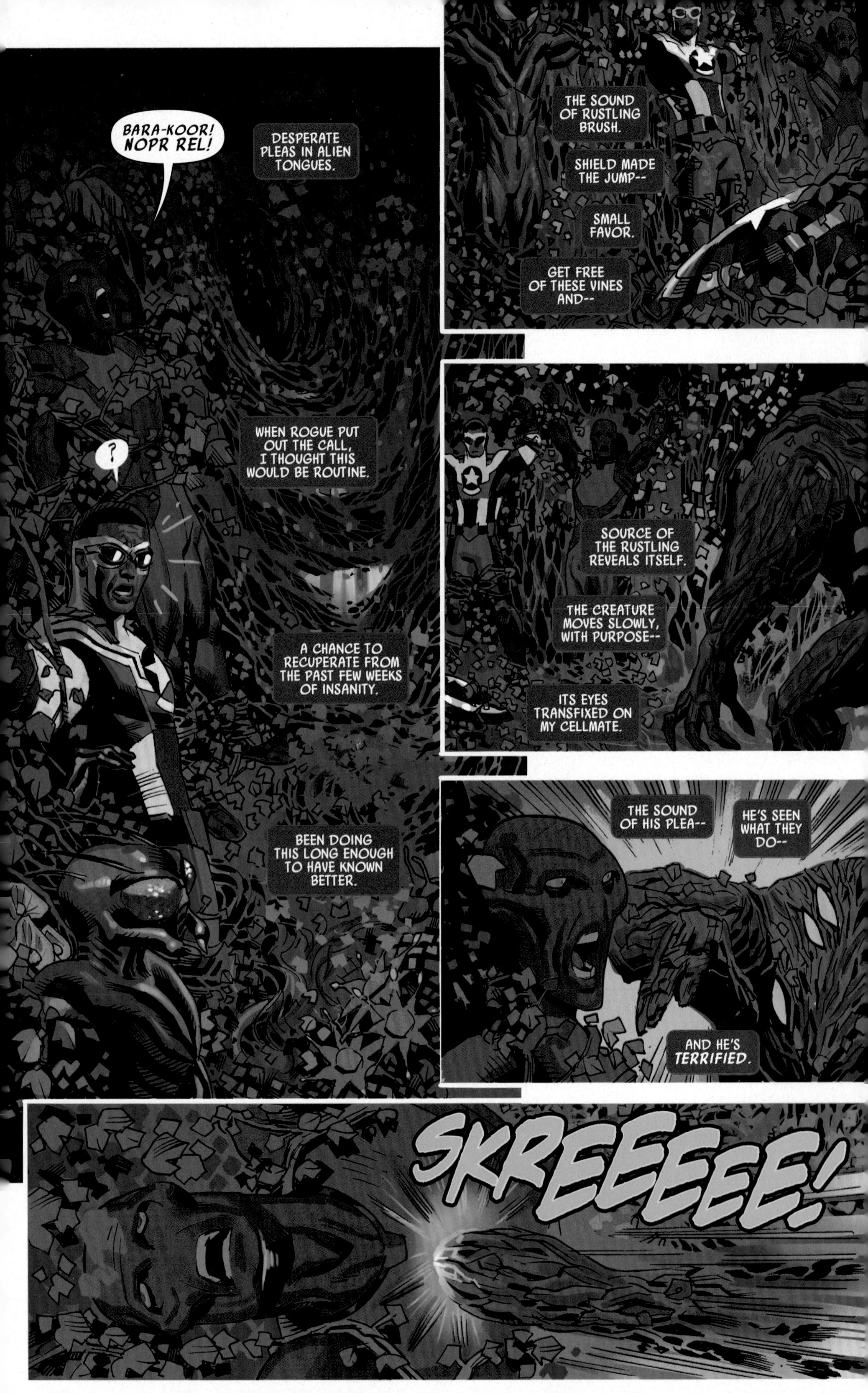
BARA-KOOR! NOPR REL!
DESPERATE PLEAS IN ALIEN TONGUES.
?
WHEN ROGUE PUT OUT THE CALL, I THOUGHT THIS WOULD BE ROUTINE.
A CHANCE TO RECUPERATE FROM THE PAST FEW WEEKS OF INSANITY.
BEEN DOING THIS LONG ENOUGH TO HAVE KNOWN BETTER.
THE SOUND OF RUSTLING BRUSH.
SHIELD MADE THE JUMP--
SMALL FAVOR.
GET FREE OF THESE VINES AND--
SOURCE OF THE RUSTLING REVEALS ITSELF.
THE CREATURE MOVES SLOWLY, WITH PURPOSE--
ITS EYES TRANSFIXED ON MY CELLMATE.
THE SOUND OF HIS PLEA--
HE'S SEEN WHAT THEY DO--
AND HE'S TERRIFIED.
SKREEEEEE!

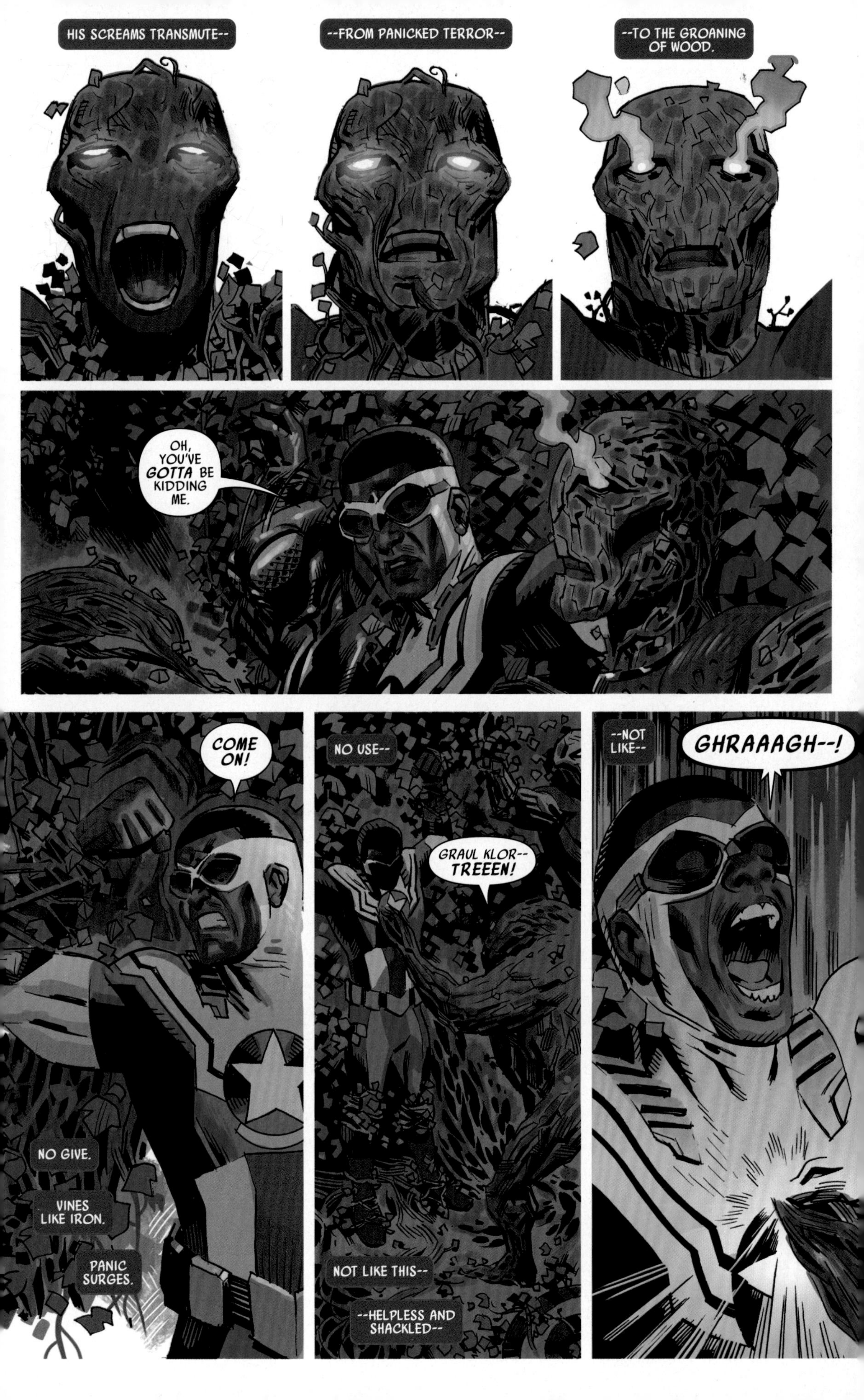
HIS SCREAMS TRANSMUTE--
--FROM PANICKED TERROR--
--TO THE GROANING OF WOOD.
OH, YOU'VE GOTTA BE KIDDING ME.
COME ON!
NO GIVE.
VINES LIKE IRON.
PANIC SURGES.
NO USE--
GRAUL KLOR-- TREEEN!
NOT LIKE THIS--
--HELPLESS AND SHACKLED--
--NOT LIKE--
GHRAAAGH--!

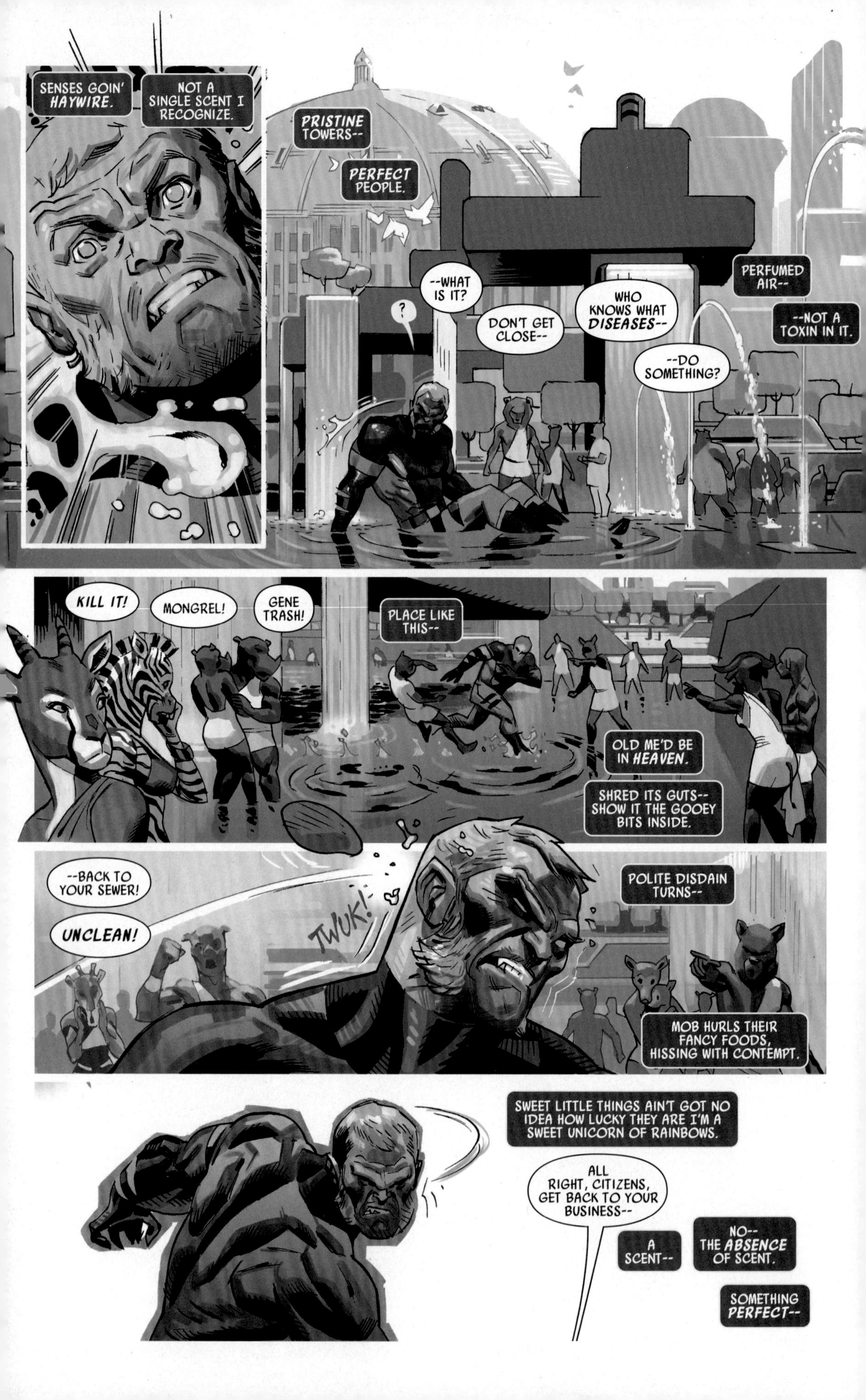
SENSES GOIN' HAYWIRE.
NOT A SINGLE SCENT I RECOGNIZE.
PRISTINE TOWERS--
PERFECT PEOPLE.
?
--WHAT IS IT?
DON'T GET CLOSE--
WHO KNOWS WHAT DISEASES--
--DO SOMETHING?
PERFUMED AIR--
--NOT A TOXIN IN IT.
KILL IT!
MONGREL!
GENE TRASH!
PLACE LIKE THIS--
OLD ME'D BE IN HEAVEN.
SHRED ITS GUTS-- SHOW IT THE GOOEY BITS INSIDE.
--BACK TO YOUR SEWER!
UNCLEAN!
TWUK!
POLITE DISDAIN TURNS--
MOB HURLS THEIR FANCY FOODS, HISSING WITH CONTEMPT.
SWEET LITTLE THINGS AIN'T GOT NO IDEA HOW LUCKY THEY ARE I'M A SWEET UNICORN OF RAINBOWS.
ALL RIGHT, CITIZENS, GET BACK TO YOUR BUSINESS--
A SCENT--
NO-- THE ABSENCE OF SCENT.
SOMETHING PERFECT--

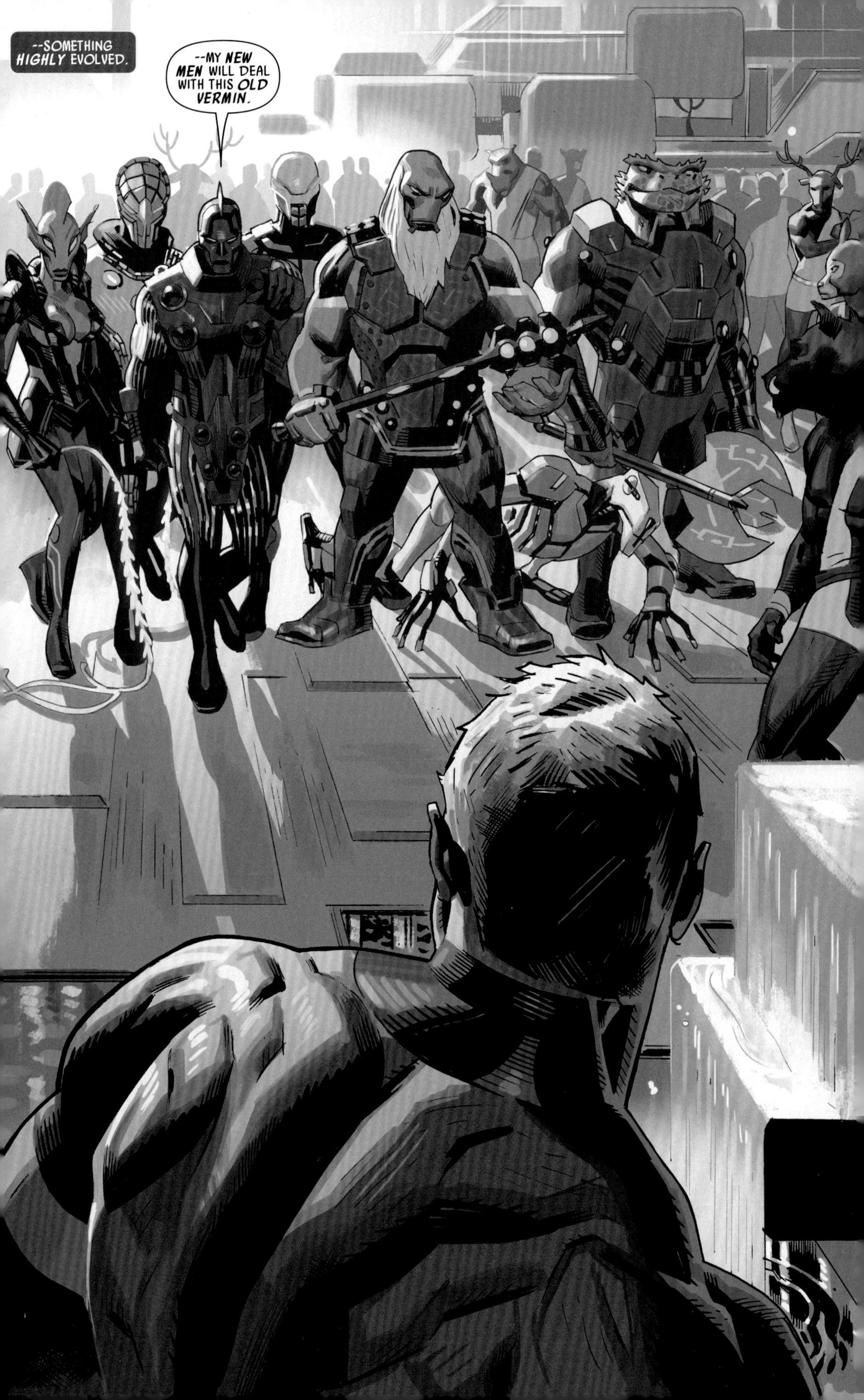
--SOMETHING *HIGHLY* EVOLVED.
--MY ***NEW MEN*** WILL DEAL WITH THIS ***OLD VERMIN***.

UNCANNY AVENGERS #2

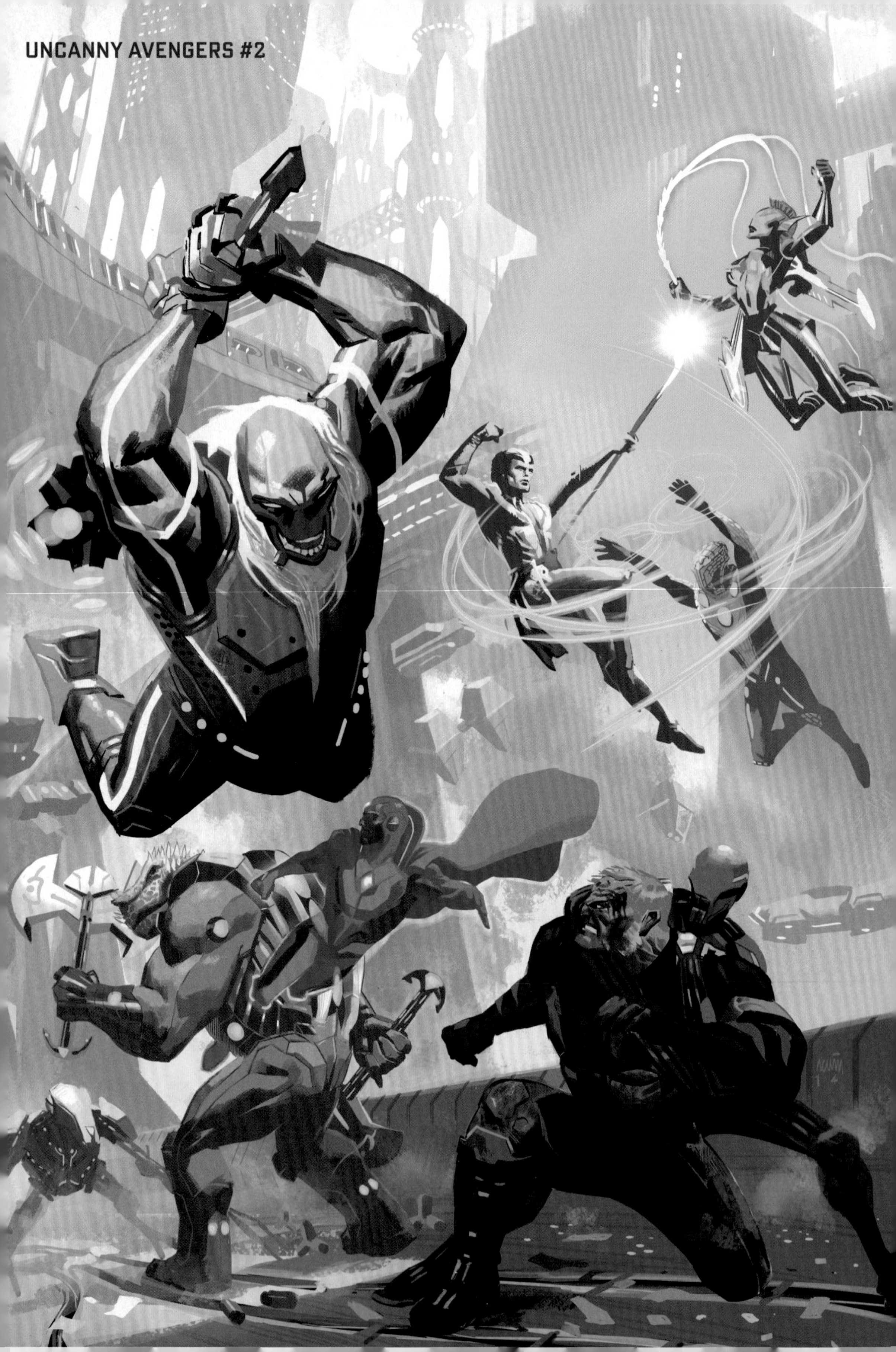

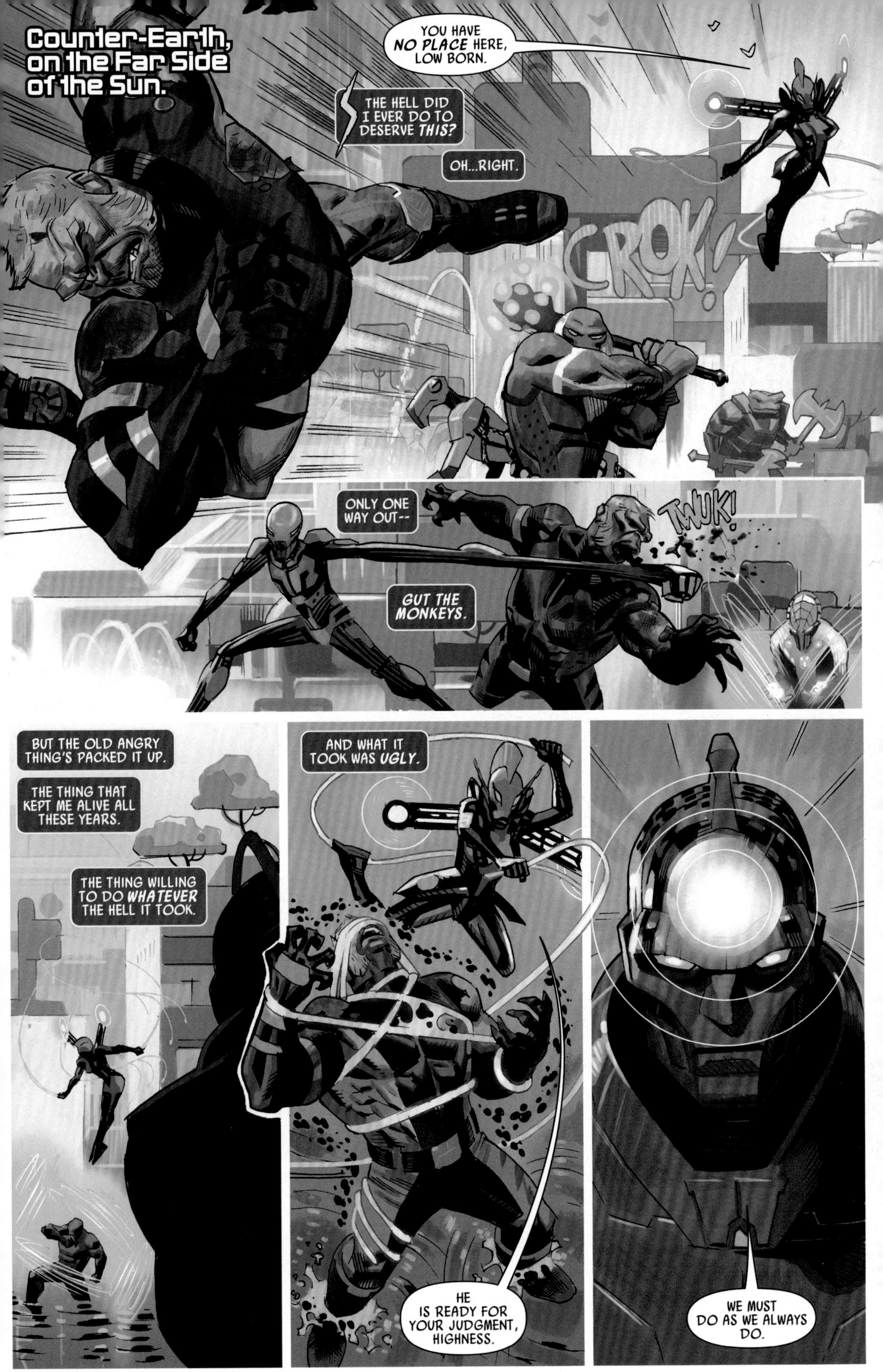
Counter-Earth, on the Far Side of the Sun.
YOU HAVE NO PLACE HERE, LOW BORN.
THE HELL DID I EVER DO TO DESERVE THIS?
OH...RIGHT.
CROK!
ONLY ONE WAY OUT--
TWUK!
GUT THE MONKEYS.
BUT THE OLD ANGRY THING'S PACKED IT UP.
THE THING THAT KEPT ME ALIVE ALL THESE YEARS.
THE THING WILLING TO DO WHATEVER THE HELL IT TOOK.
AND WHAT IT TOOK WAS UGLY.
HE IS READY FOR YOUR JUDGMENT, HIGHNESS.
WE MUST DO AS WE ALWAYS DO.

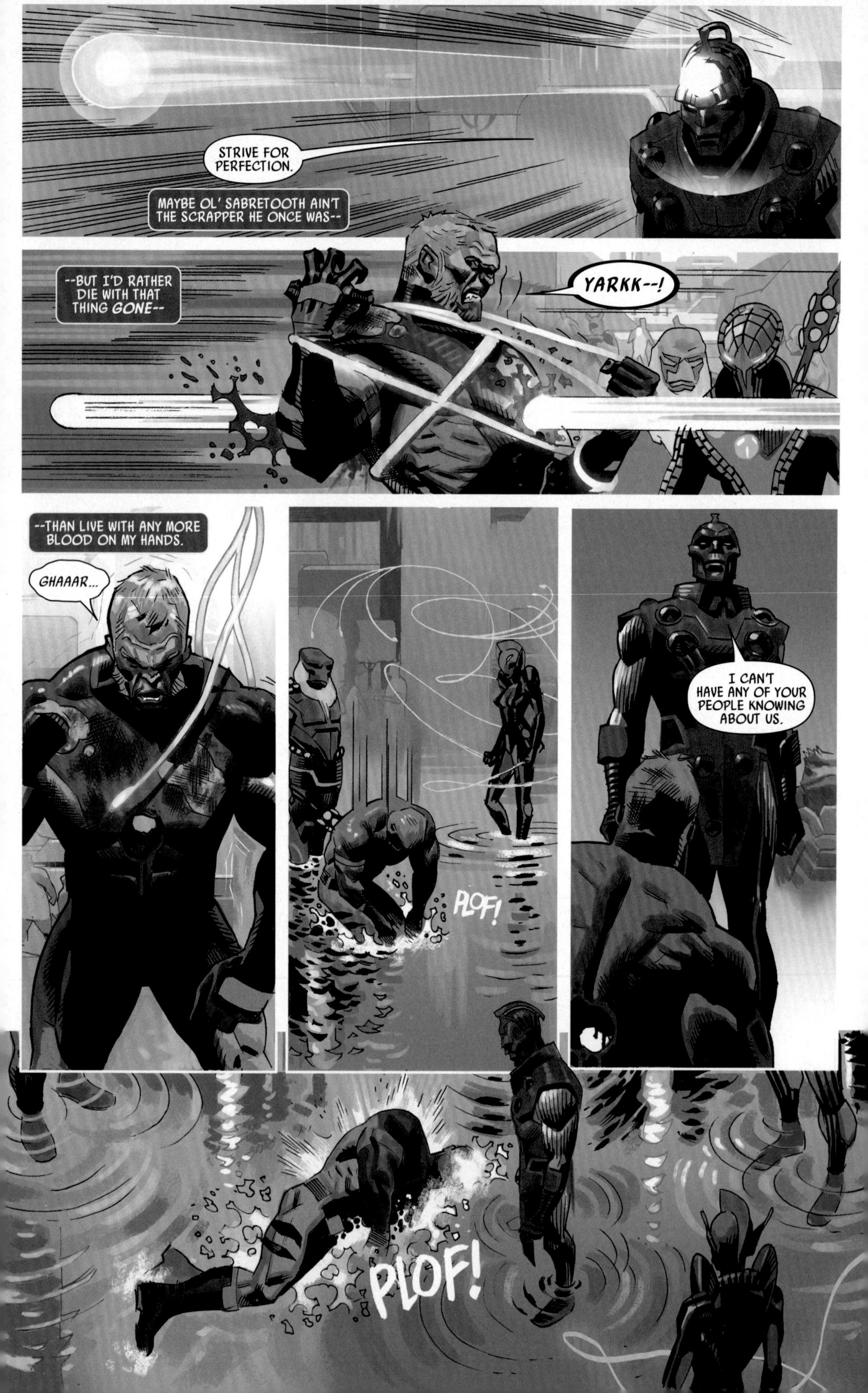
STRIVE FOR PERFECTION.
MAYBE OL' SABRETOOTH AIN'T THE SCRAPPER HE ONCE WAS--
--BUT I'D RATHER DIE WITH THAT THING *GONE*--
YARKK--!
--THAN LIVE WITH ANY MORE BLOOD ON MY HANDS.
GHAAAR...
PLOF!
I CAN'T HAVE ANY OF YOUR PEOPLE KNOWING ABOUT US.
PLOF!

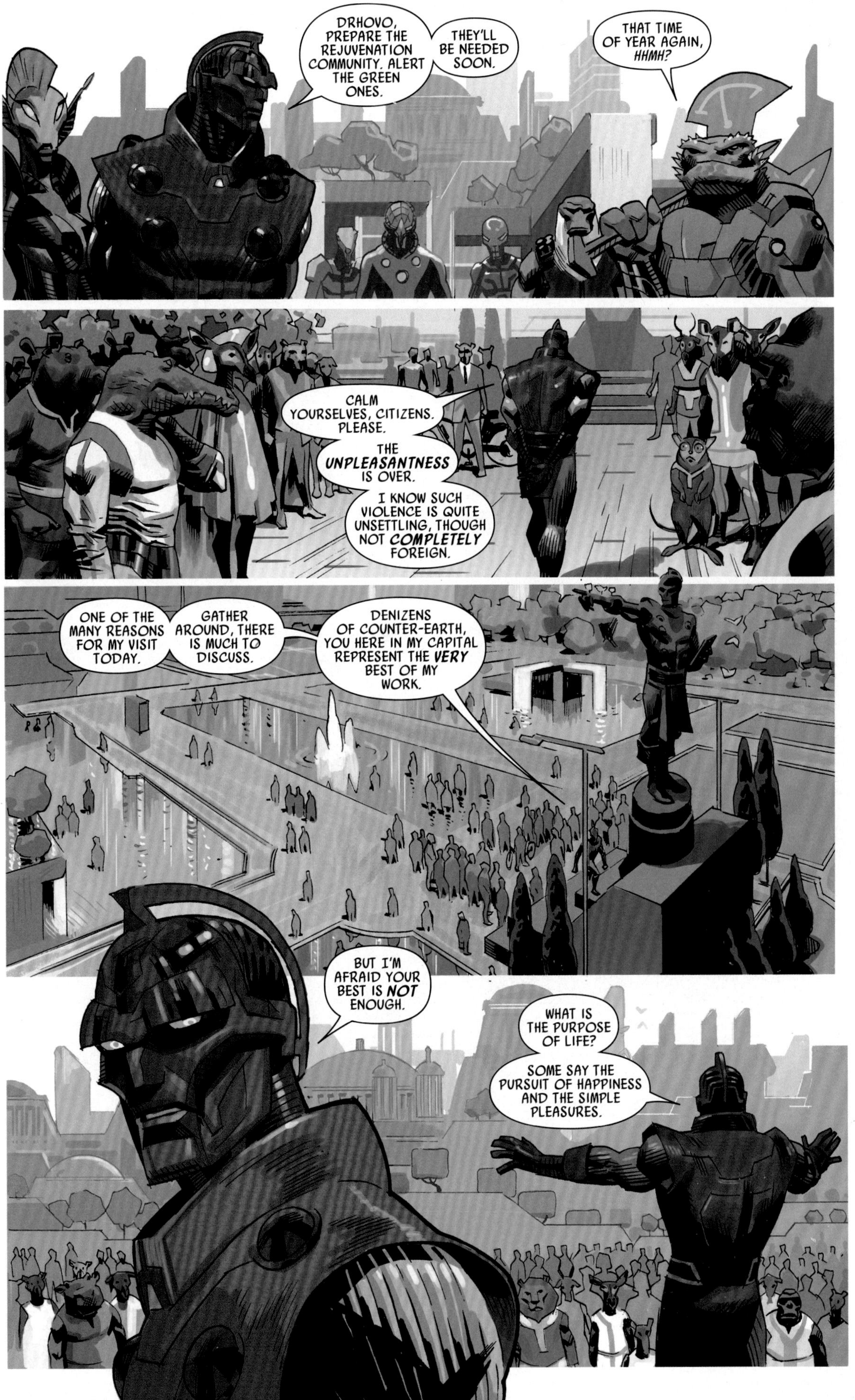
DRHOVO, PREPARE THE REJUVENATION COMMUNITY. ALERT THE GREEN ONES.
THEY'LL BE NEEDED SOON.
THAT TIME OF YEAR AGAIN, *HHMH?*
CALM YOURSELVES, CITIZENS. PLEASE.
THE ***UNPLEASANTNESS*** IS OVER.
I KNOW SUCH VIOLENCE IS QUITE UNSETTLING, THOUGH NOT ***COMPLETELY*** FOREIGN.
ONE OF THE MANY REASONS FOR MY VISIT TODAY.
GATHER AROUND, THERE IS MUCH TO DISCUSS.
DENIZENS OF COUNTER-EARTH, YOU HERE IN MY CAPITAL REPRESENT THE ***VERY*** BEST OF MY WORK.
BUT I'M AFRAID YOUR BEST IS ***NOT*** ENOUGH.
WHAT IS THE PURPOSE OF LIFE?
SOME SAY THE PURSUIT OF HAPPINESS AND THE SIMPLE PLEASURES.

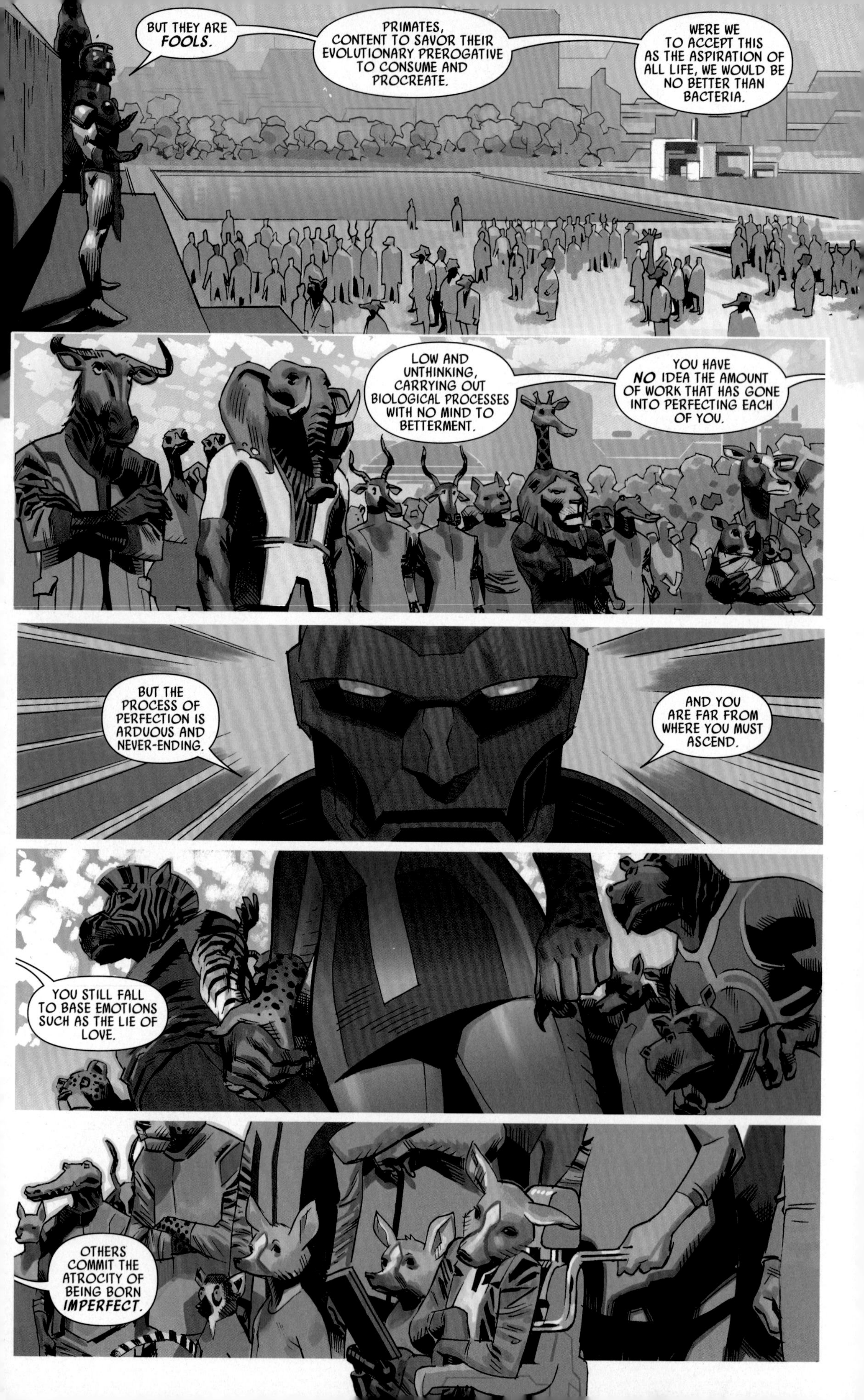
BUT THEY ARE FOOLS.
PRIMATES, CONTENT TO SAVOR THEIR EVOLUTIONARY PREROGATIVE TO CONSUME AND PROCREATE.
WERE WE TO ACCEPT THIS AS THE ASPIRATION OF ALL LIFE, WE WOULD BE NO BETTER THAN BACTERIA.
LOW AND UNTHINKING, CARRYING OUT BIOLOGICAL PROCESSES WITH NO MIND TO BETTERMENT.
YOU HAVE NO IDEA THE AMOUNT OF WORK THAT HAS GONE INTO PERFECTING EACH OF YOU.
BUT THE PROCESS OF PERFECTION IS ARDUOUS AND NEVER-ENDING.
AND YOU ARE FAR FROM WHERE YOU MUST ASCEND.
YOU STILL FALL TO BASE EMOTIONS SUCH AS THE LIE OF LOVE.
OTHERS COMMIT THE ATROCITY OF BEING BORN IMPERFECT.

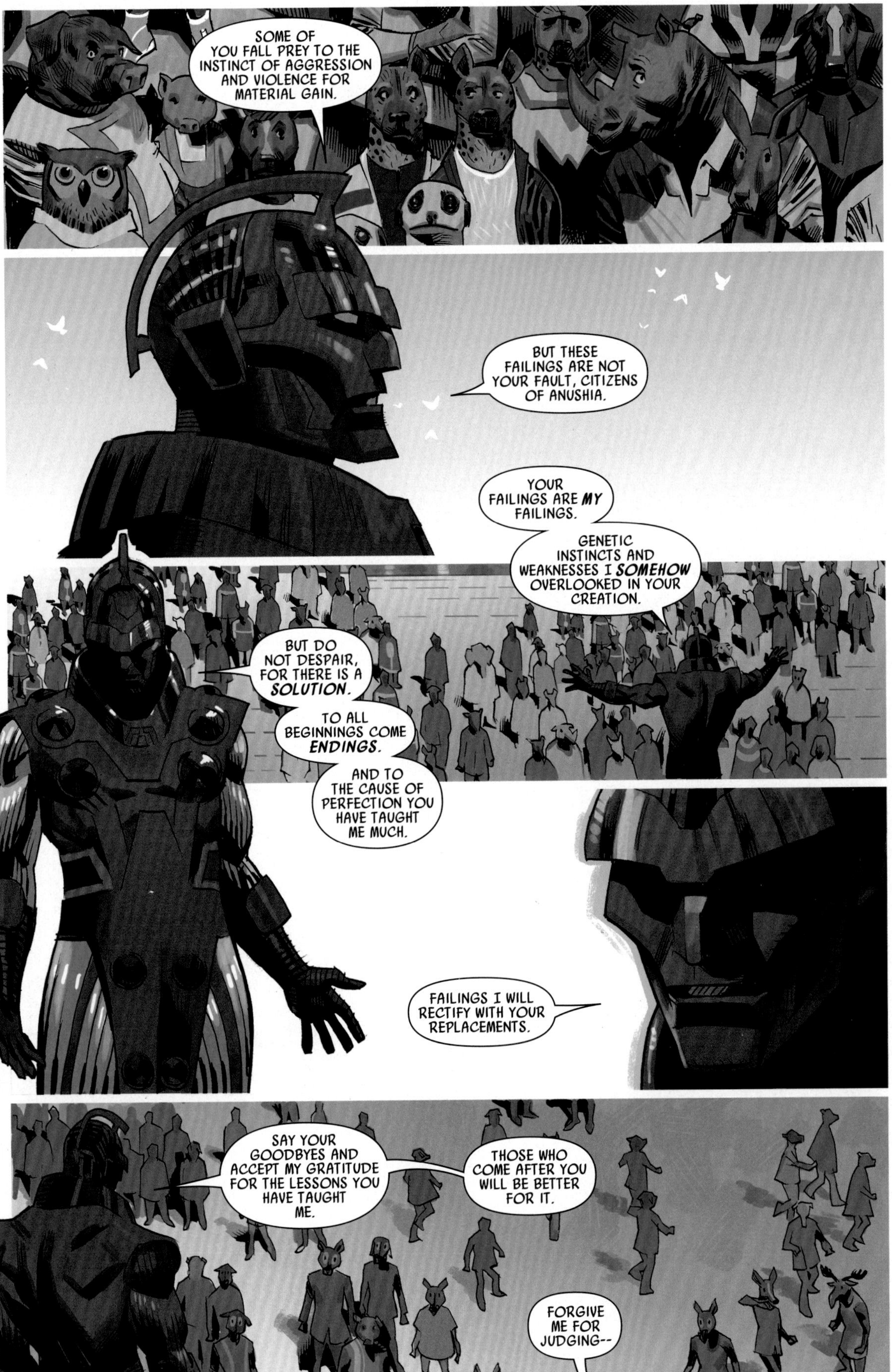
SOME OF YOU FALL PREY TO THE INSTINCT OF AGGRESSION AND VIOLENCE FOR MATERIAL GAIN.
BUT THESE FAILINGS ARE NOT YOUR FAULT, CITIZENS OF ANUSHIA.
YOUR FAILINGS ARE **MY** FAILINGS.
GENETIC INSTINCTS AND WEAKNESSES I **SOMEHOW** OVERLOOKED IN YOUR CREATION.
BUT DO NOT DESPAIR, FOR THERE IS A **SOLUTION.**
TO ALL BEGINNINGS COME **ENDINGS.**
AND TO THE CAUSE OF PERFECTION YOU HAVE TAUGHT ME MUCH.
FAILINGS I WILL RECTIFY WITH YOUR REPLACEMENTS.
SAY YOUR GOODBYES AND ACCEPT MY GRATITUDE FOR THE LESSONS YOU HAVE TAUGHT ME.
THOSE WHO COME AFTER YOU WILL BE BETTER FOR IT.
FORGIVE ME FOR JUDGING--

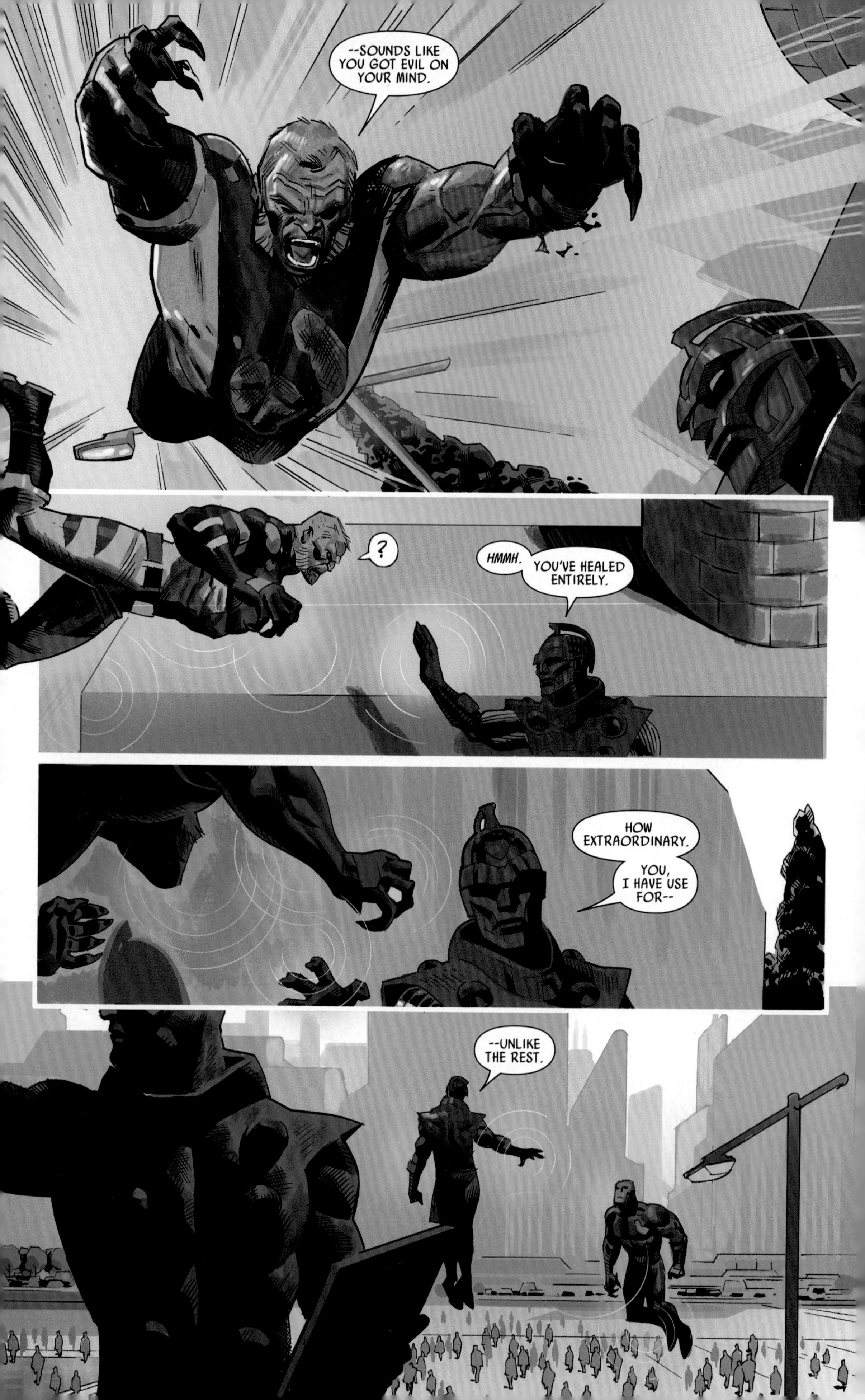
--SOUNDS LIKE YOU GOT EVIL ON YOUR MIND.
?
HMMH. YOU'VE HEALED ENTIRELY.
HOW EXTRAORDINARY.
YOU, I HAVE USE FOR--
--UNLIKE THE REST.

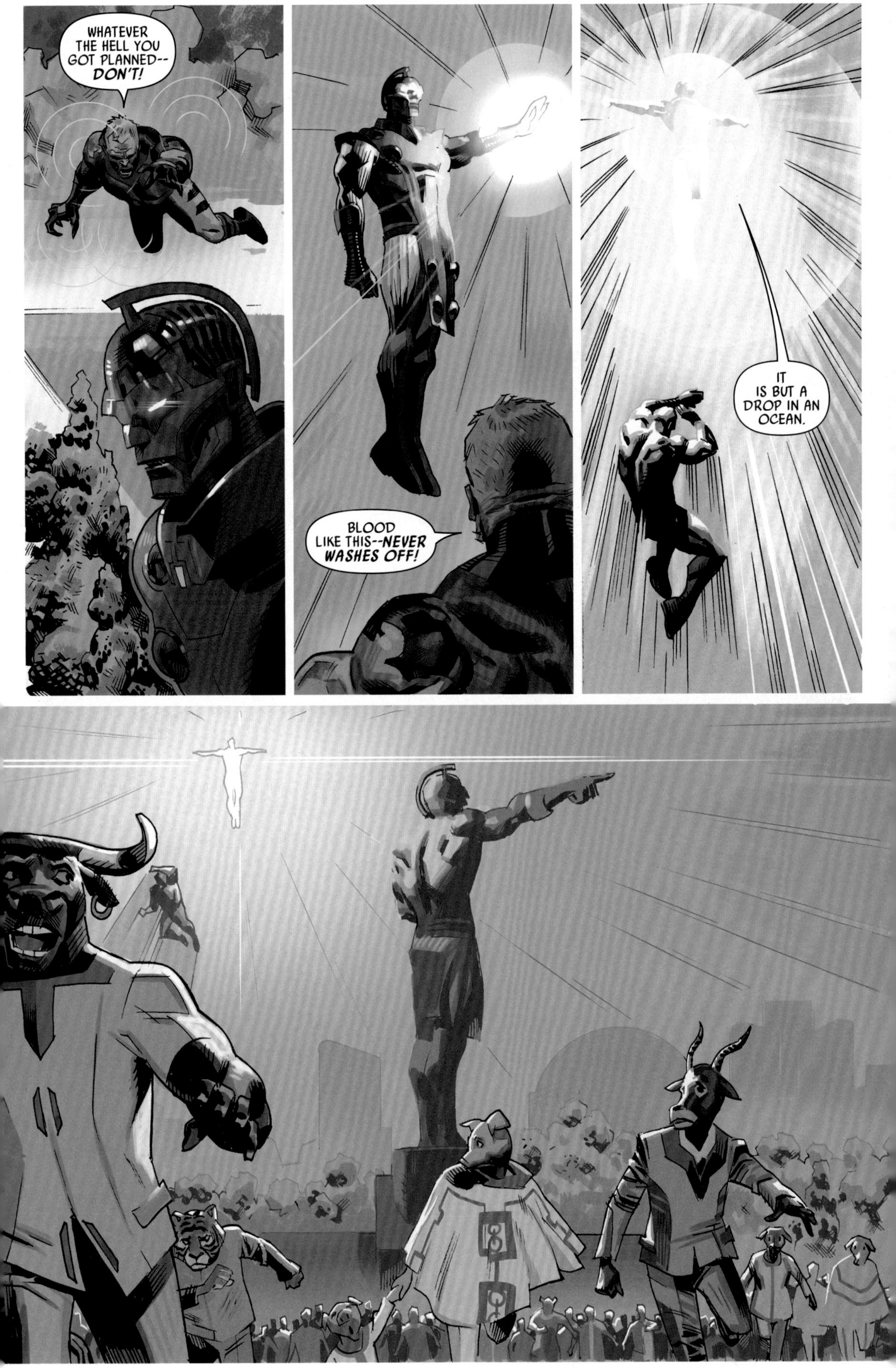
WHATEVER THE HELL YOU GOT PLANNED-- DON'T!
BLOOD LIKE THIS--NEVER WASHES OFF!
IT IS BUT A DROP IN AN OCEAN.

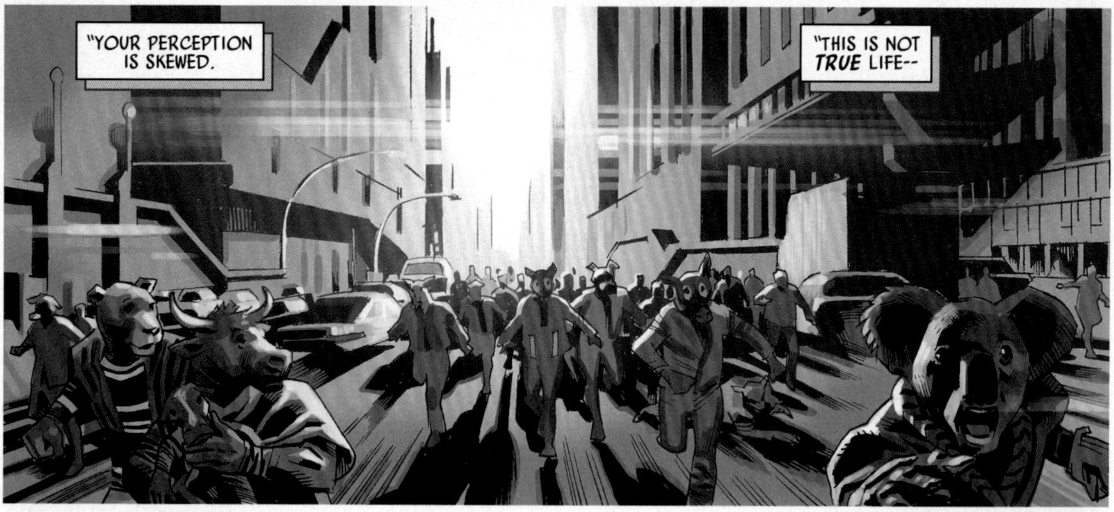
"YOUR PERCEPTION IS SKEWED.
"THIS IS NOT TRUE LIFE--

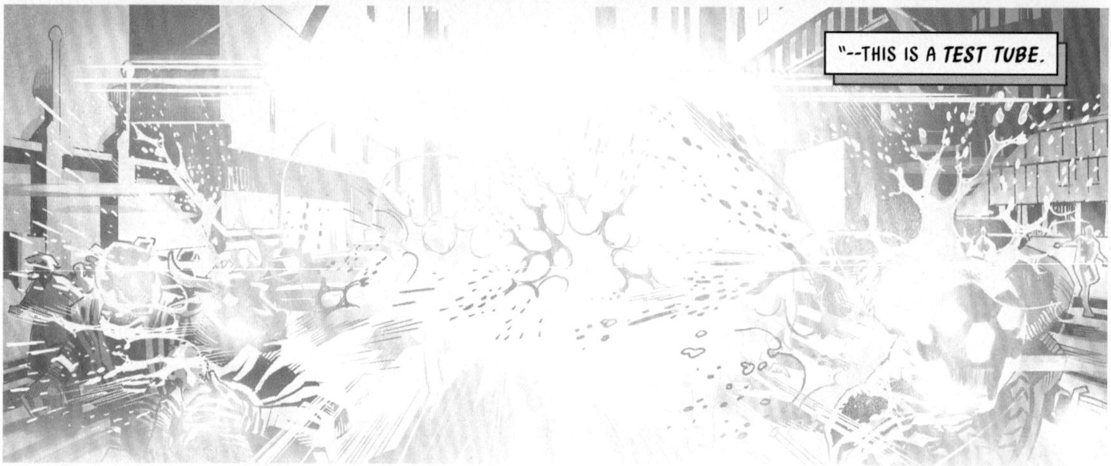
"--THIS IS A TEST TUBE.

"A FAILED EXPERIMENT IN THE QUEST FOR *PERFECTION*.

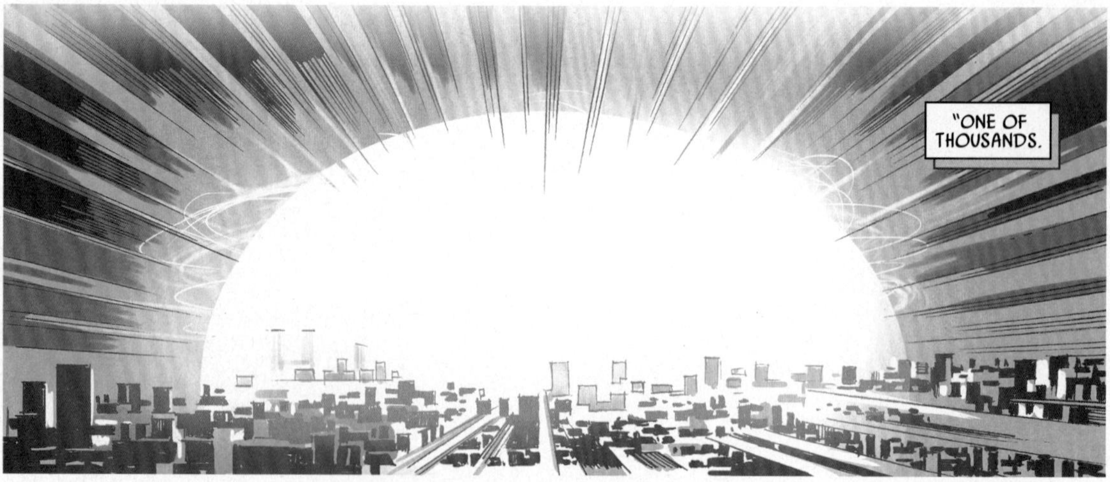
"ONE OF THOUSANDS.

"AND THOUSANDS
MORE TO COME."

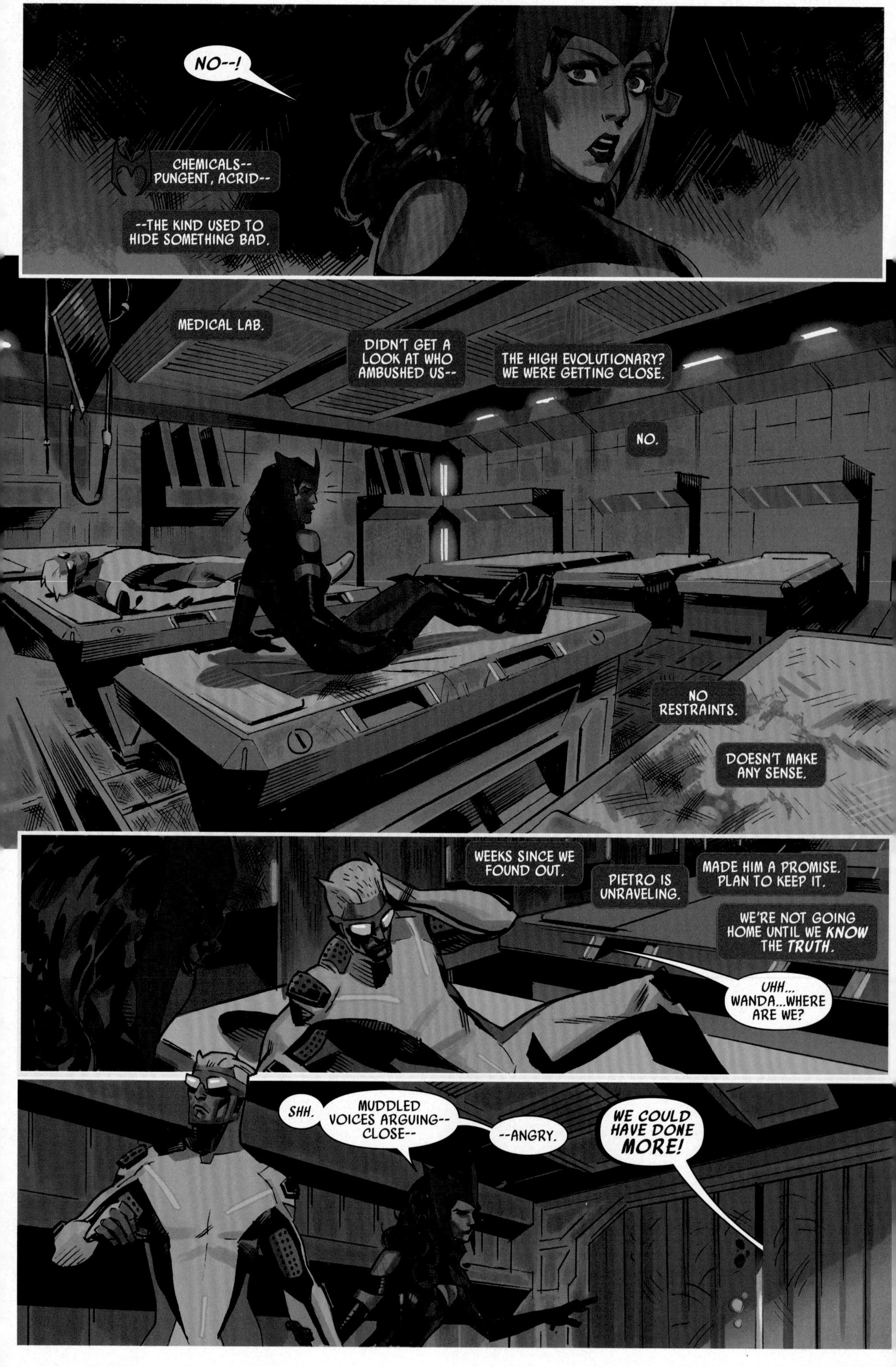
NO--!
CHEMICALS-- PUNGENT, ACRID--
--THE KIND USED TO HIDE SOMETHING BAD.
MEDICAL LAB.
DIDN'T GET A LOOK AT WHO AMBUSHED US--
THE HIGH EVOLUTIONARY? WE WERE GETTING CLOSE.
NO.
NO RESTRAINTS.
DOESN'T MAKE ANY SENSE.
WEEKS SINCE WE FOUND OUT.
PIETRO IS UNRAVELING.
MADE HIM A PROMISE. PLAN TO KEEP IT.
WE'RE NOT GOING HOME UNTIL WE KNOW THE TRUTH.
UHH... WANDA...WHERE ARE WE?
SHH.
MUDDLED VOICES ARGUING-- CLOSE--
--ANGRY.
WE COULD HAVE DONE MORE!

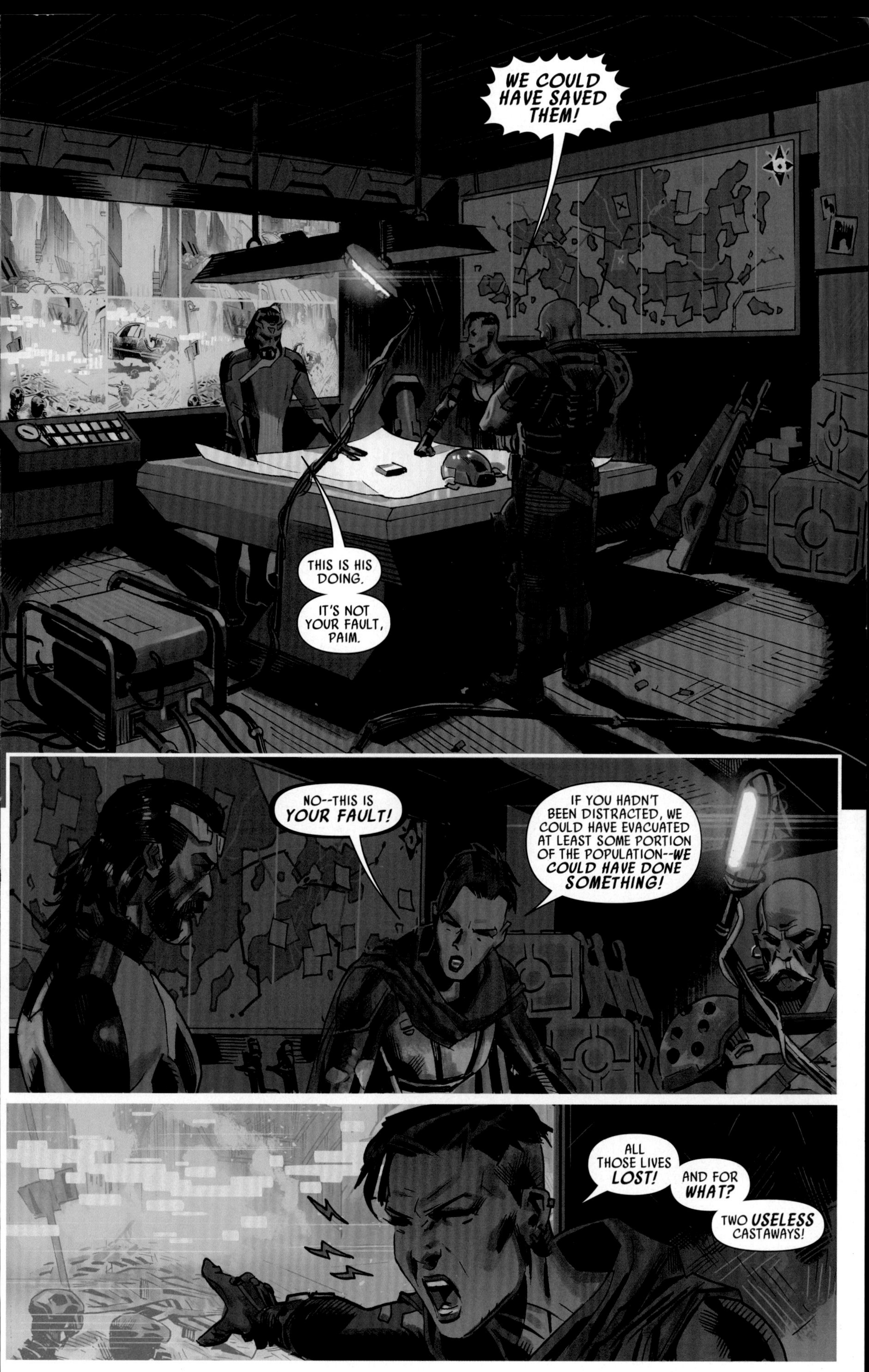
WE COULD HAVE SAVED THEM!
THIS IS HIS DOING.
IT'S NOT YOUR FAULT, PAIM.
NO--THIS IS *YOUR FAULT!*
IF YOU HADN'T BEEN DISTRACTED, WE COULD HAVE EVACUATED AT LEAST SOME PORTION OF THE POPULATION--*WE COULD HAVE DONE SOMETHING!*
ALL THOSE LIVES *LOST!*
AND FOR *WHAT?*
TWO *USELESS* CASTAWAYS!

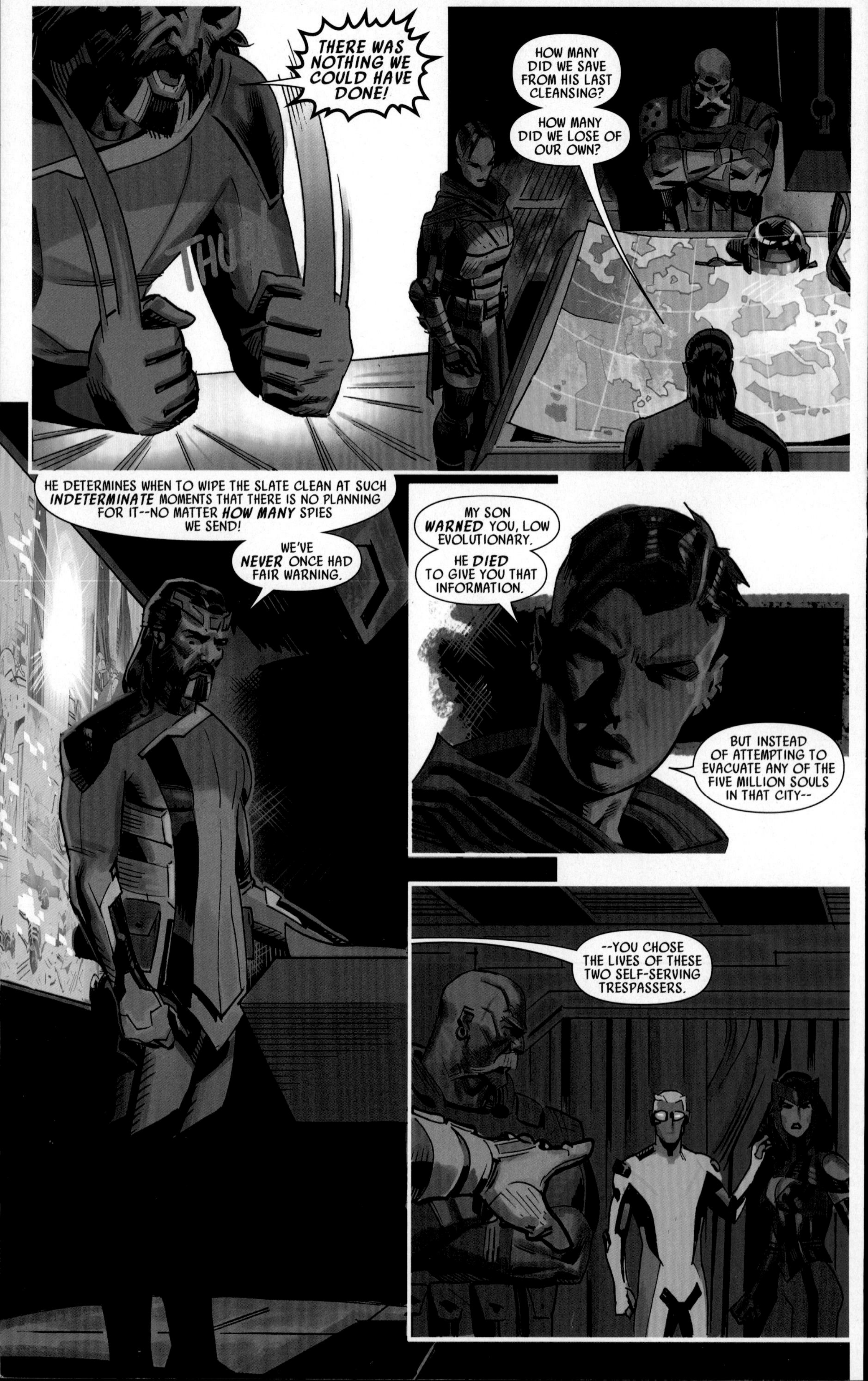
THERE WAS NOTHING WE COULD HAVE DONE!
HOW MANY DID WE SAVE FROM HIS LAST CLEANSING?
HOW MANY DID WE LOSE OF OUR OWN?
HE DETERMINES WHEN TO WIPE THE SLATE CLEAN AT SUCH INDETERMINATE MOMENTS THAT THERE IS NO PLANNING FOR IT--NO MATTER HOW MANY SPIES WE SEND!
WE'VE NEVER ONCE HAD FAIR WARNING.
MY SON WARNED YOU, LOW EVOLUTIONARY.
HE DIED TO GIVE YOU THAT INFORMATION.
BUT INSTEAD OF ATTEMPTING TO EVACUATE ANY OF THE FIVE MILLION SOULS IN THAT CITY--
--YOU CHOSE THE LIVES OF THESE TWO SELF-SERVING TRESPASSERS.

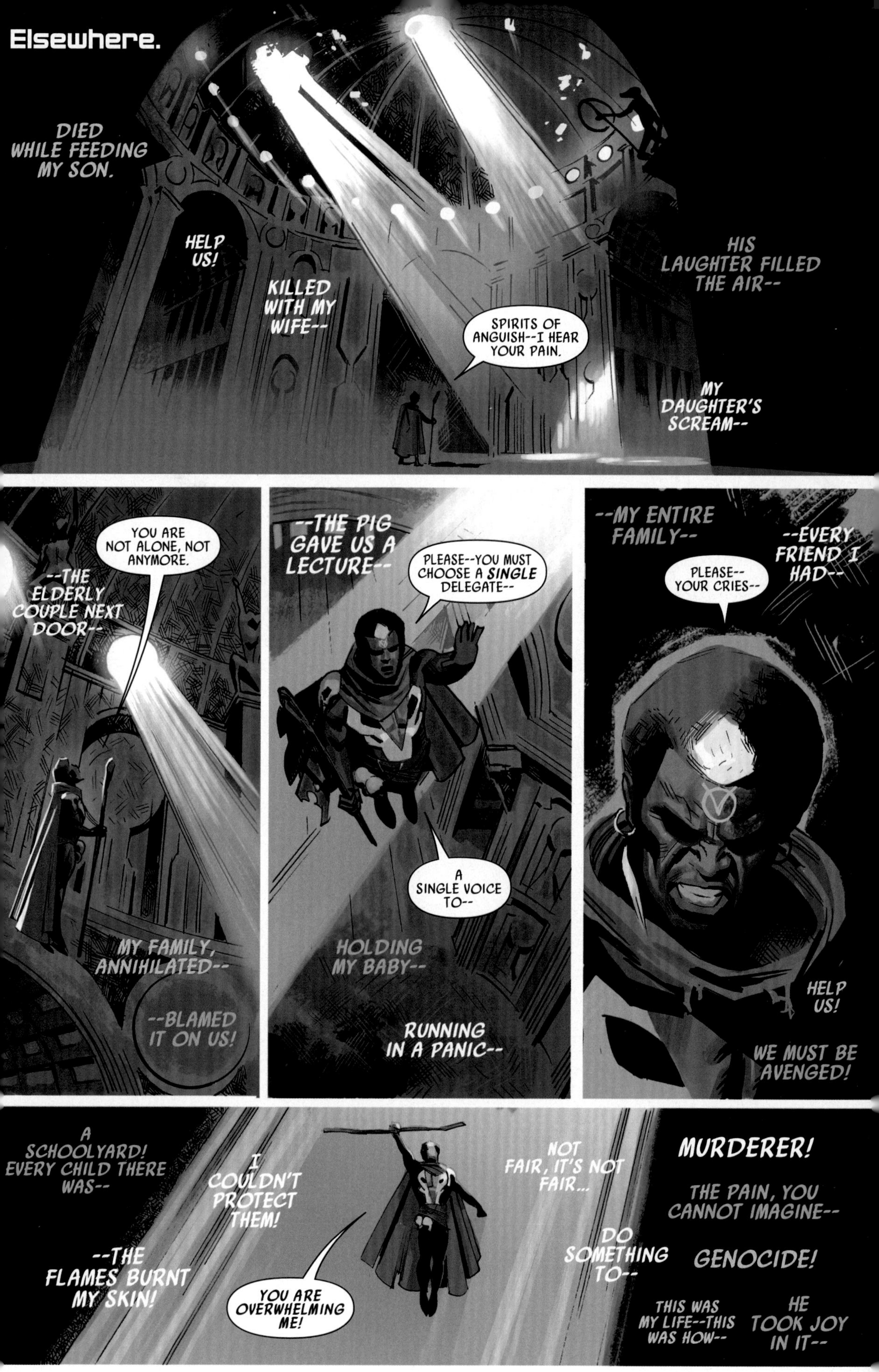
Elsewhere.
DIED WHILE FEEDING MY SON.
HELP US!
KILLED WITH MY WIFE--
SPIRITS OF ANGUISH--I HEAR YOUR PAIN.
HIS LAUGHTER FILLED THE AIR--
MY DAUGHTER'S SCREAM--
YOU ARE NOT ALONE, NOT ANYMORE.
--THE ELDERLY COUPLE NEXT DOOR--
MY FAMILY, ANNIHILATED--
--BLAMED IT ON US!
--THE PIG GAVE US A LECTURE--
PLEASE--YOU MUST CHOOSE A SINGLE DELEGATE--
A SINGLE VOICE TO--
HOLDING MY BABY--
RUNNING IN A PANIC--
--MY ENTIRE FAMILY--
--EVERY FRIEND I HAD--
PLEASE-- YOUR CRIES--
HELP US!
WE MUST BE AVENGED!
A SCHOOLYARD! EVERY CHILD THERE WAS--
--THE FLAMES BURNT MY SKIN!
I COULDN'T PROTECT THEM!
YOU ARE OVERWHELMING ME!
NOT FAIR, IT'S NOT FAIR...
DO SOMETHING TO--
MURDERER!
THE PAIN, YOU CANNOT IMAGINE--
GENOCIDE!
THIS WAS MY LIFE--THIS WAS HOW--
HE TOOK JOY IN IT--

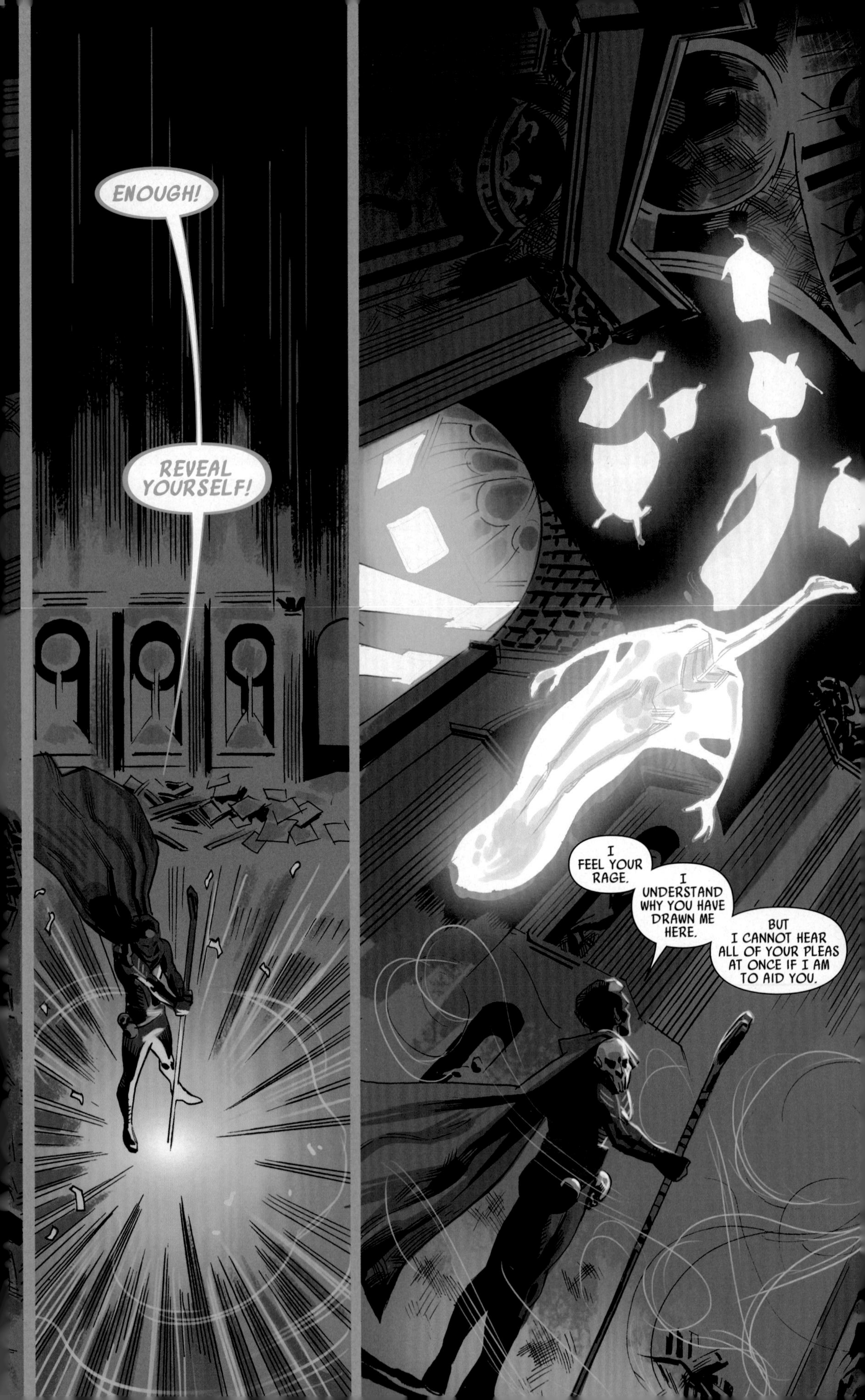
ENOUGH!
REVEAL YOURSELF!
I FEEL YOUR RAGE.
I UNDERSTAND WHY YOU HAVE DRAWN ME HERE.
BUT I CANNOT HEAR ALL OF YOUR PLEAS AT ONCE IF I AM TO AID YOU.

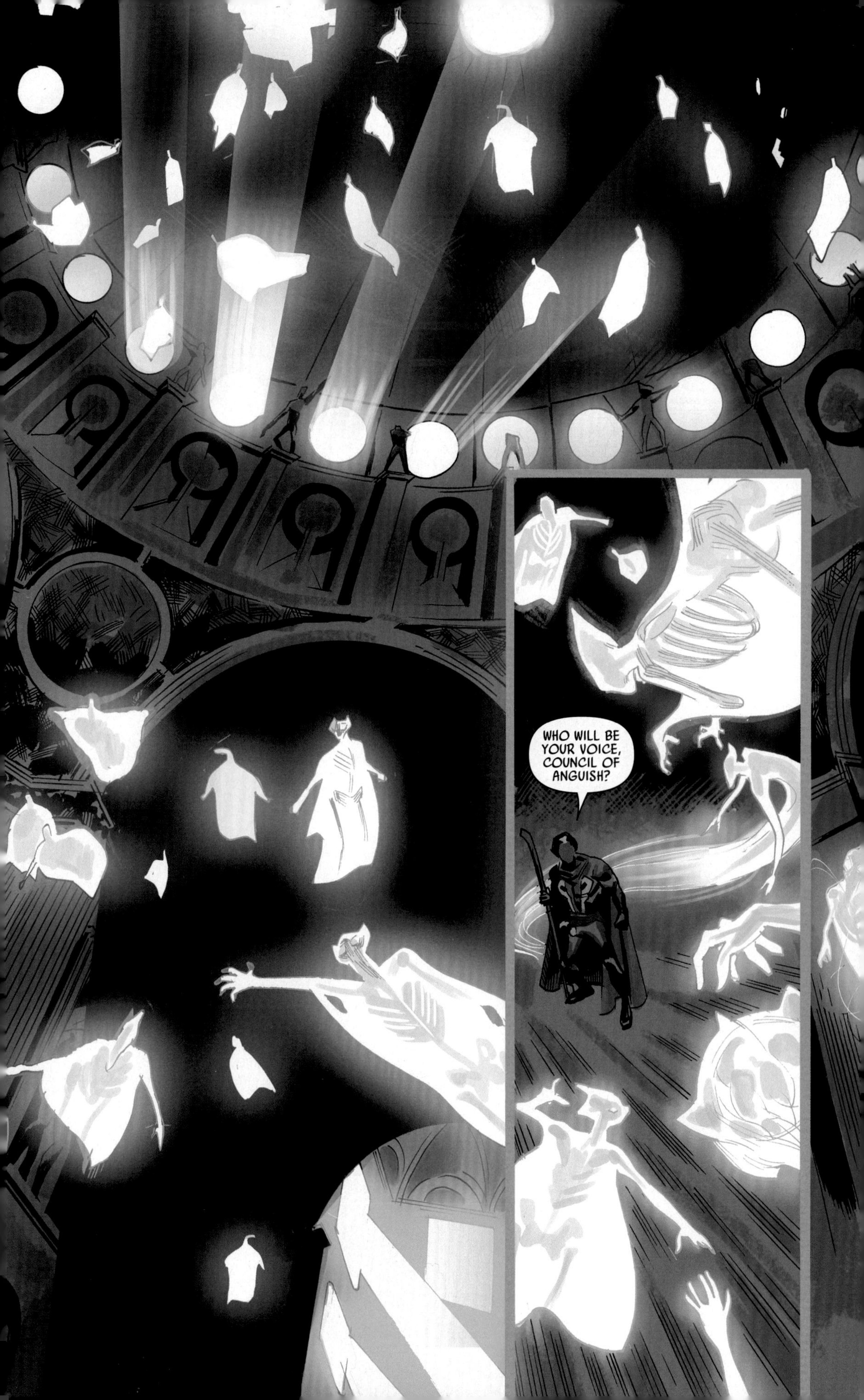
WHO WILL BE YOUR VOICE, COUNCIL OF ANGUISH?

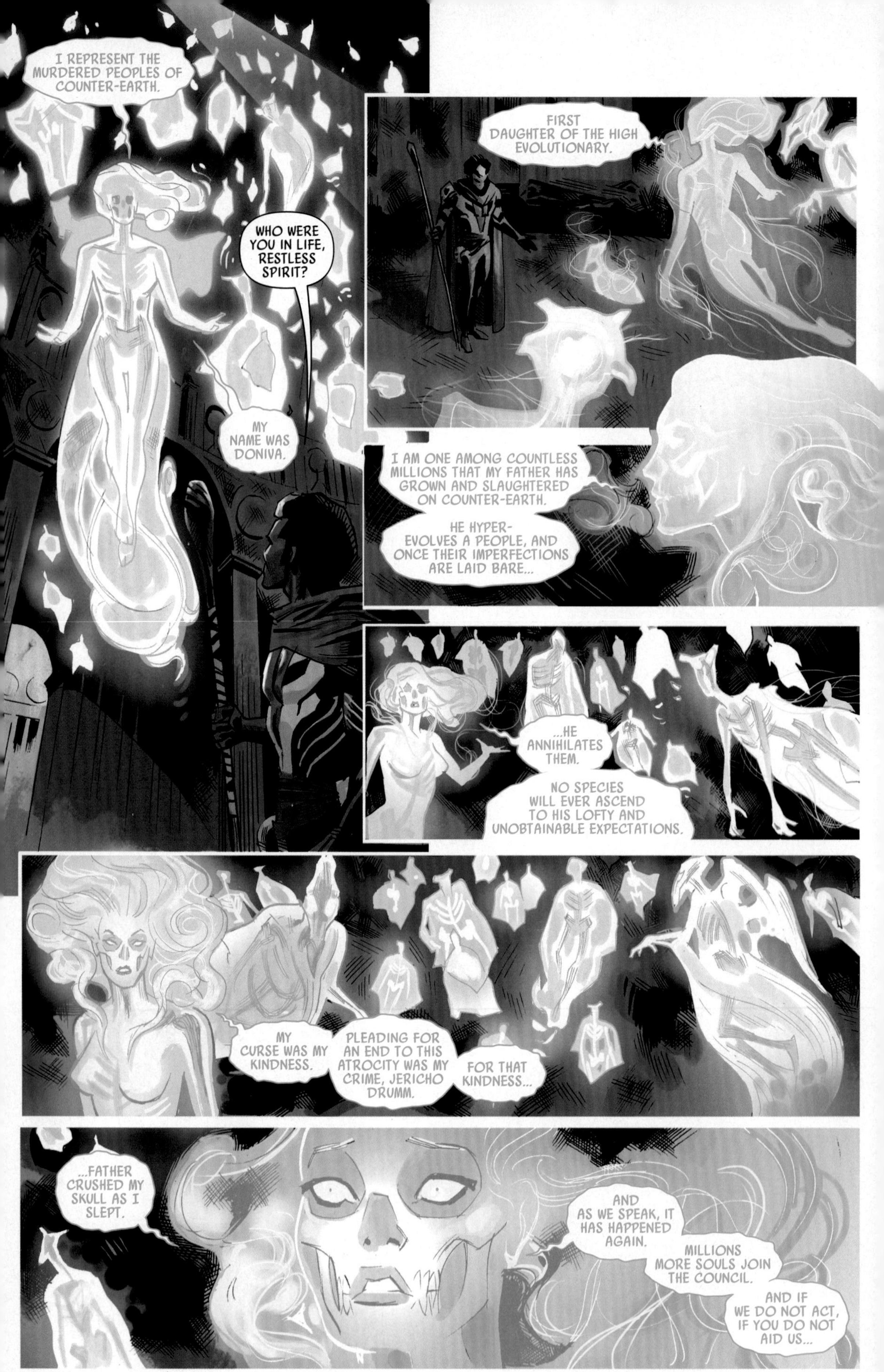

I REPRESENT THE MURDERED PEOPLES OF COUNTER-EARTH.
WHO WERE YOU IN LIFE, RESTLESS SPIRIT?
MY NAME WAS DONIVA.
FIRST DAUGHTER OF THE HIGH EVOLUTIONARY.
I AM ONE AMONG COUNTLESS MILLIONS THAT MY FATHER HAS GROWN AND SLAUGHTERED ON COUNTER-EARTH.
HE HYPER-EVOLVES A PEOPLE, AND ONCE THEIR IMPERFECTIONS ARE LAID BARE...
...HE ANNIHILATES THEM.
NO SPECIES WILL EVER ASCEND TO HIS LOFTY AND UNOBTAINABLE EXPECTATIONS.
MY CURSE WAS MY KINDNESS.
PLEADING FOR AN END TO THIS ATROCITY WAS MY CRIME, JERICHO DRUMM.
FOR THAT KINDNESS...
...FATHER CRUSHED MY SKULL AS I SLEPT.
AND AS WE SPEAK, IT HAS HAPPENED AGAIN.
MILLIONS MORE SOULS JOIN THE COUNCIL.
AND IF WE DO NOT ACT, IF YOU DO NOT AID US...

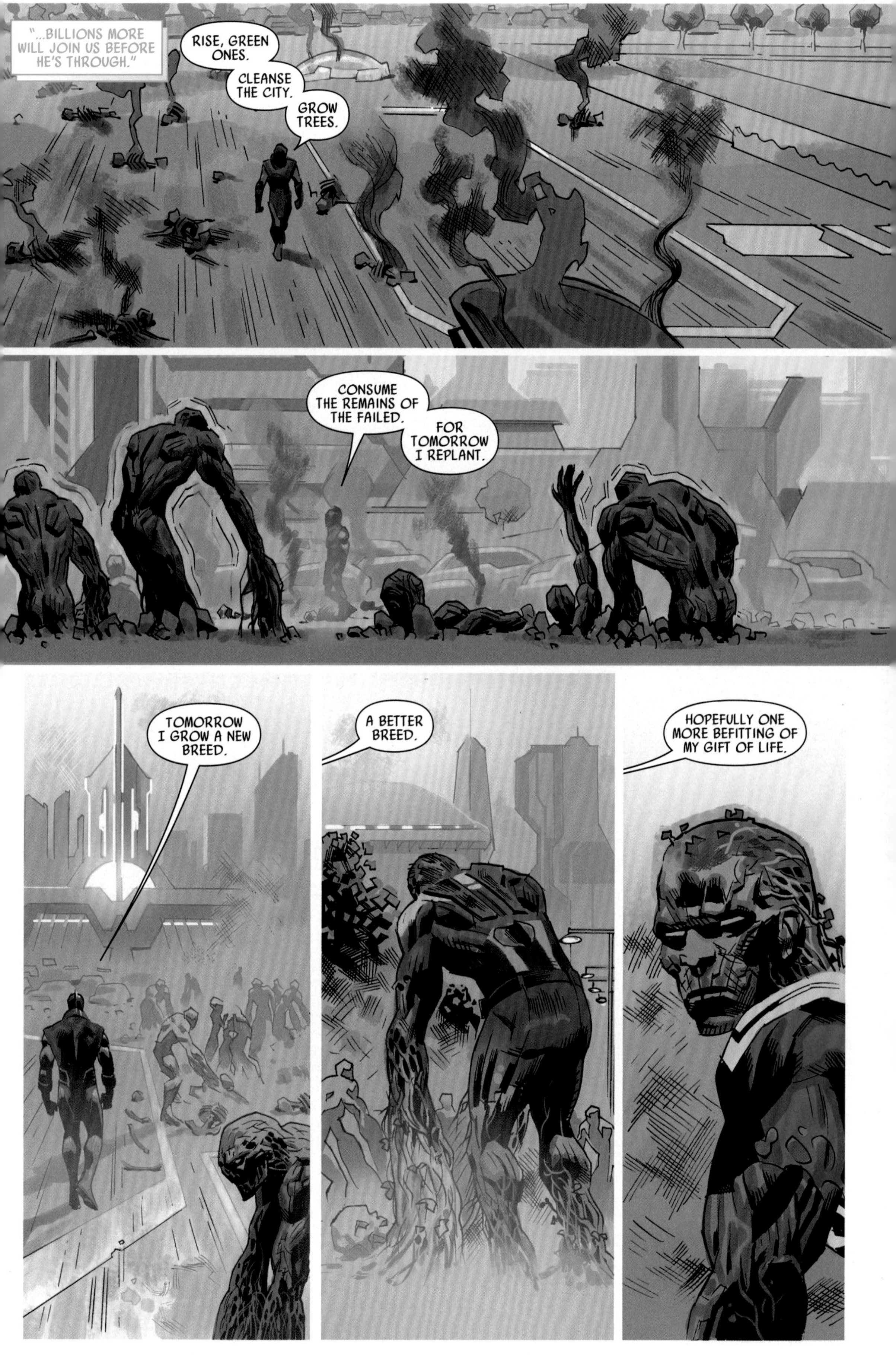
"...BILLIONS MORE WILL JOIN US BEFORE HE'S THROUGH."
RISE, GREEN ONES.
CLEANSE THE CITY.
GROW TREES.
CONSUME THE REMAINS OF THE FAILED.
FOR TOMORROW I REPLANT.
TOMORROW I GROW A NEW BREED.
A BETTER BREED.
HOPEFULLY ONE MORE BEFITTING OF MY GIFT OF LIFE.

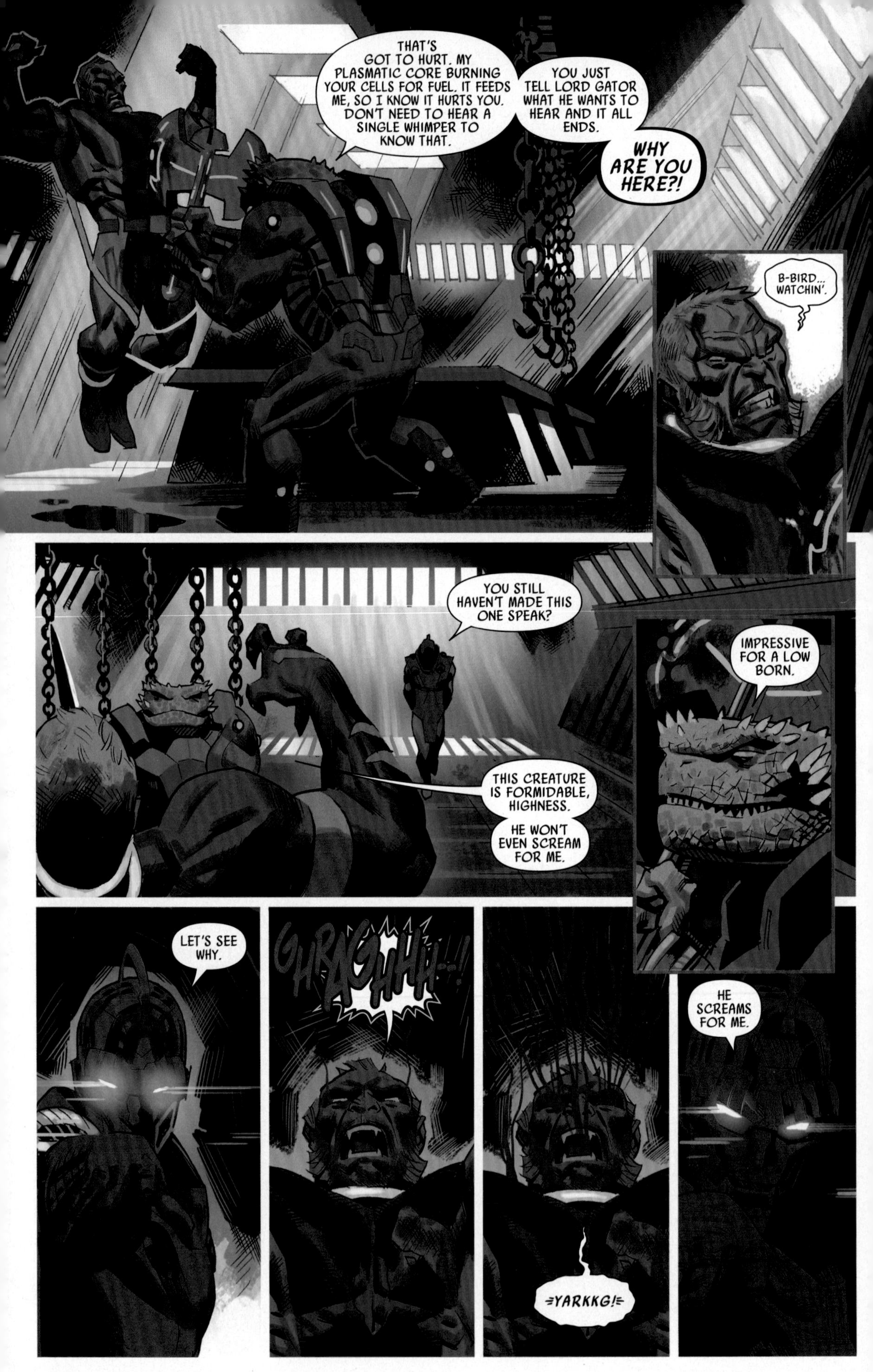
THAT'S GOT TO HURT. MY PLASMATIC CORE BURNING YOUR CELLS FOR FUEL. IT FEEDS ME, SO I KNOW IT HURTS YOU. DON'T NEED TO HEAR A SINGLE WHIMPER TO KNOW THAT.
YOU JUST TELL LORD GATOR WHAT HE WANTS TO HEAR AND IT ALL ENDS.
WHY ARE YOU HERE?!
B-BIRD... WATCHIN'.
YOU STILL HAVEN'T MADE THIS ONE SPEAK?
IMPRESSIVE FOR A LOW BORN.
THIS CREATURE IS FORMIDABLE, HIGHNESS.
HE WON'T EVEN SCREAM FOR ME.
LET'S SEE WHY.
GHRAGHHH--!
=YARKKG!=
HE SCREAMS FOR ME.

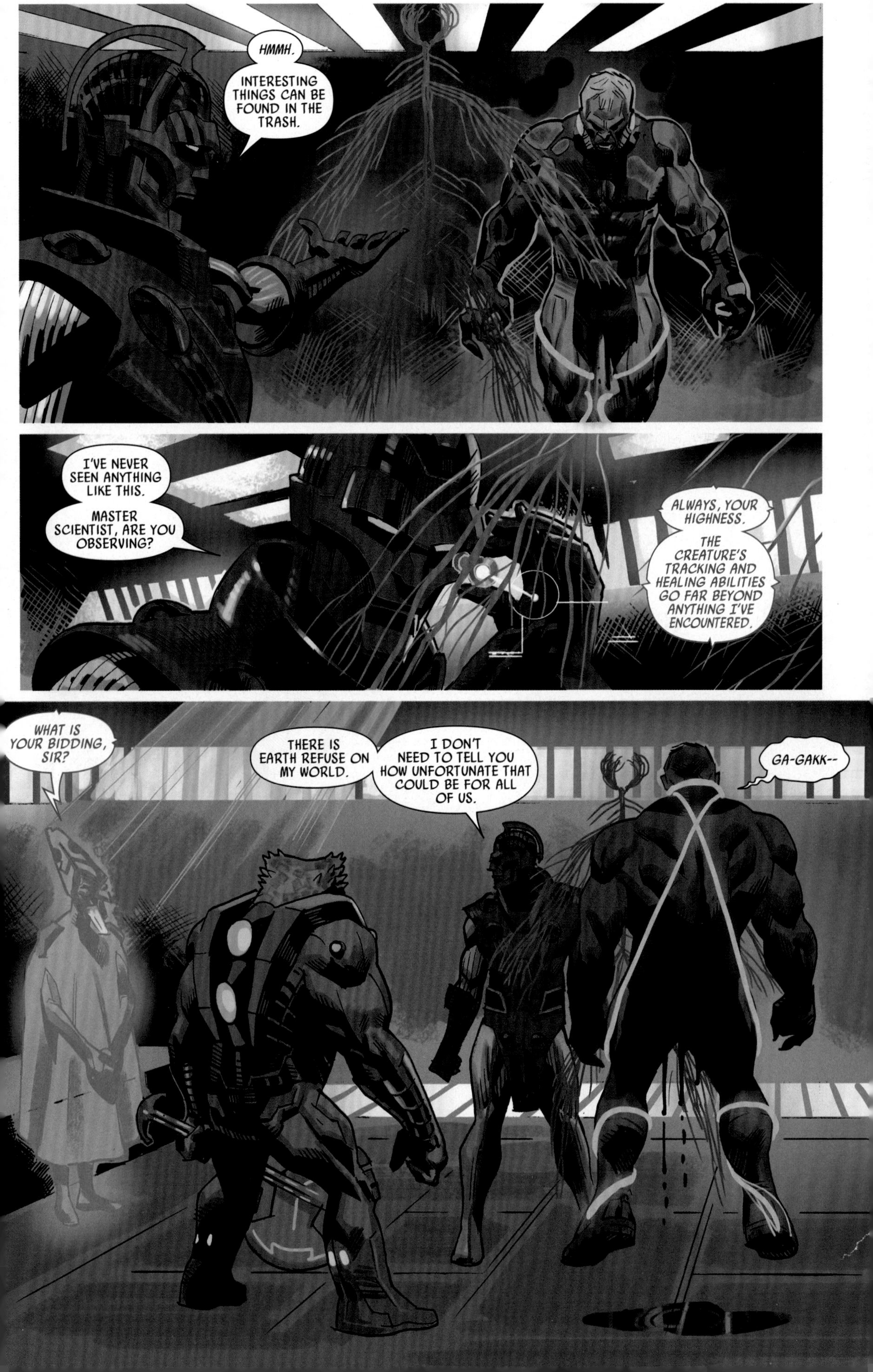
HMMH.
INTERESTING THINGS CAN BE FOUND IN THE TRASH.
I'VE NEVER SEEN ANYTHING LIKE THIS.
MASTER SCIENTIST, ARE YOU OBSERVING?
ALWAYS, YOUR HIGHNESS.
THE CREATURE'S TRACKING AND HEALING ABILITIES GO FAR BEYOND ANYTHING I'VE ENCOUNTERED.
WHAT IS YOUR BIDDING, SIR?
THERE IS EARTH REFUSE ON MY WORLD.
I DON'T NEED TO TELL YOU HOW UNFORTUNATE THAT COULD BE FOR ALL OF US.
GA-GAKK--

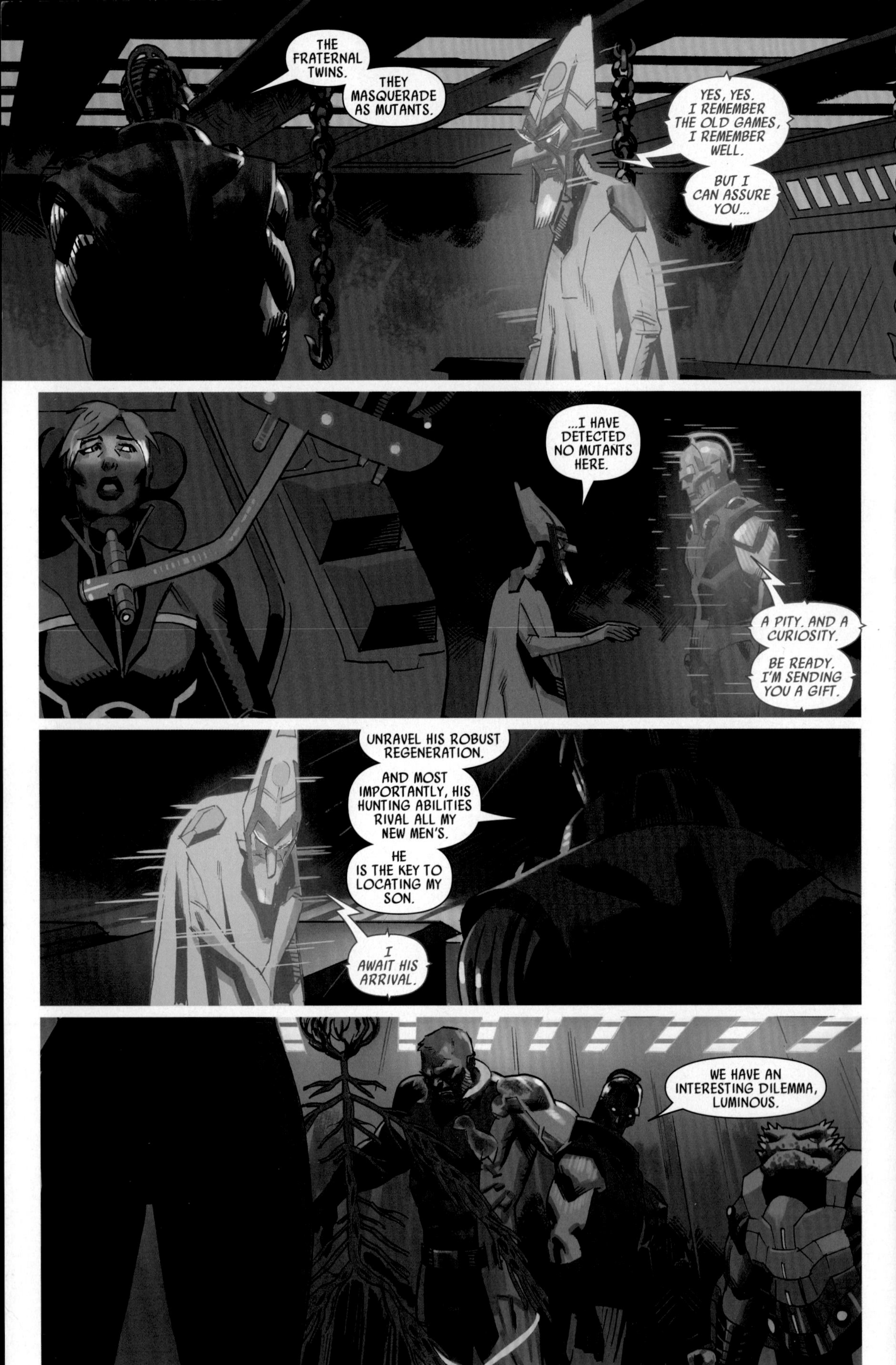
THE FRATERNAL TWINS.
THEY MASQUERADE AS MUTANTS.
YES, YES. I REMEMBER THE OLD GAMES, I REMEMBER WELL.
BUT I CAN ASSURE YOU...
...I HAVE DETECTED NO MUTANTS HERE.
A PITY. AND A CURIOSITY.
BE READY. I'M SENDING YOU A GIFT.
UNRAVEL HIS ROBUST REGENERATION.
AND MOST IMPORTANTLY, HIS HUNTING ABILITIES RIVAL ALL MY NEW MEN'S.
HE IS THE KEY TO LOCATING MY SON.
I AWAIT HIS ARRIVAL.
WE HAVE AN INTERESTING DILEMMA, LUMINOUS.

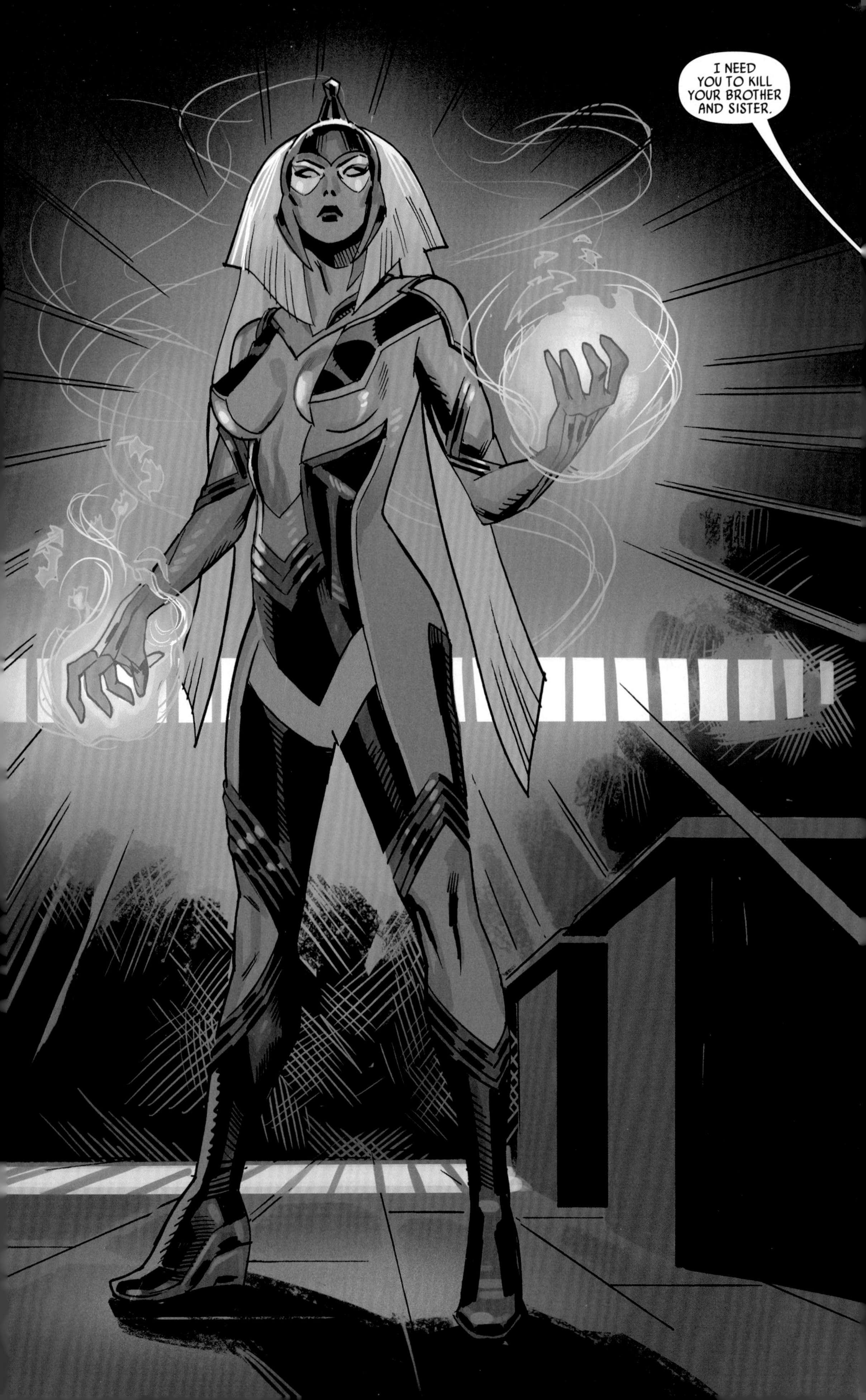
I NEED YOU TO KILL YOUR BROTHER AND SISTER.

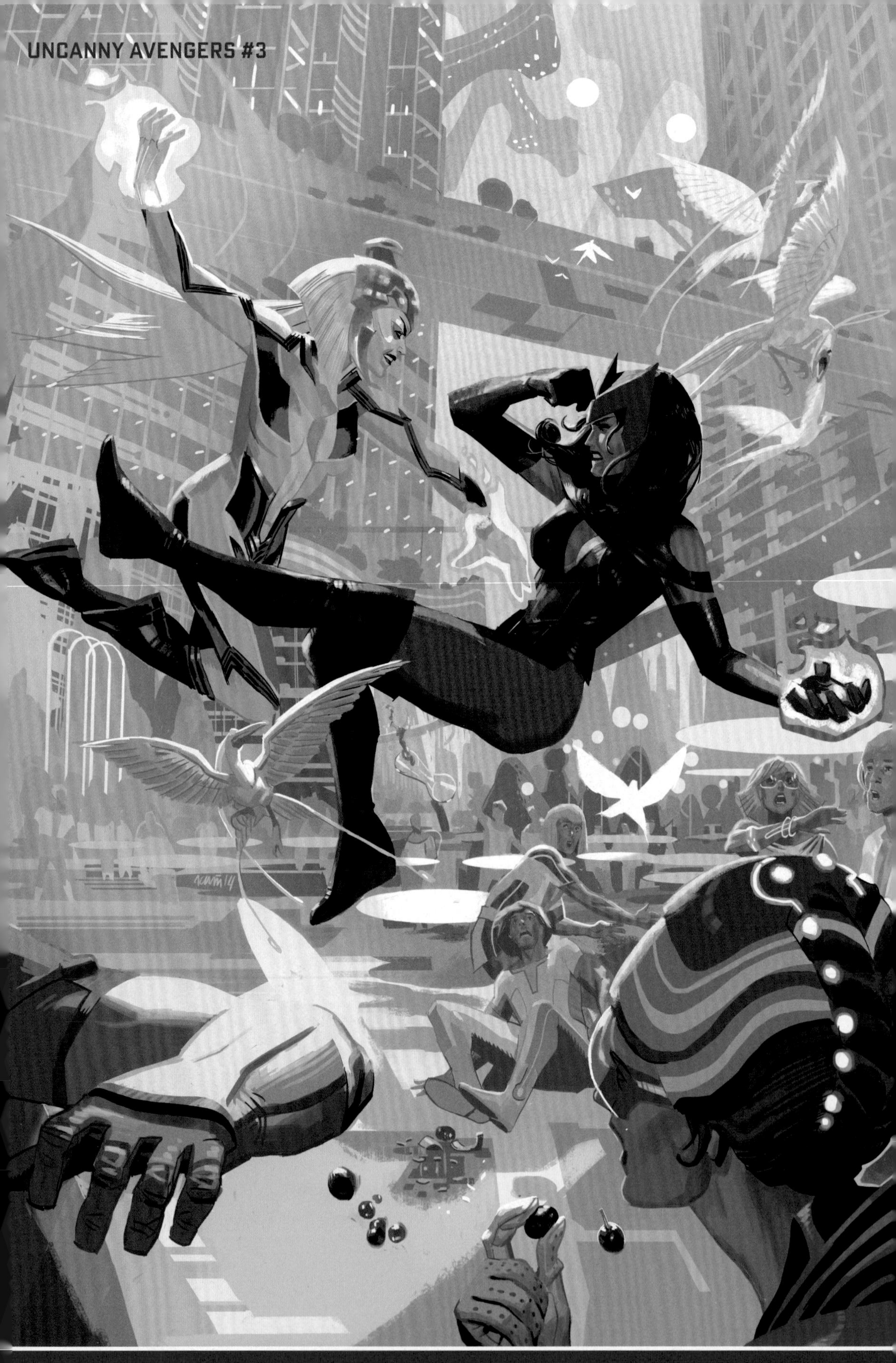

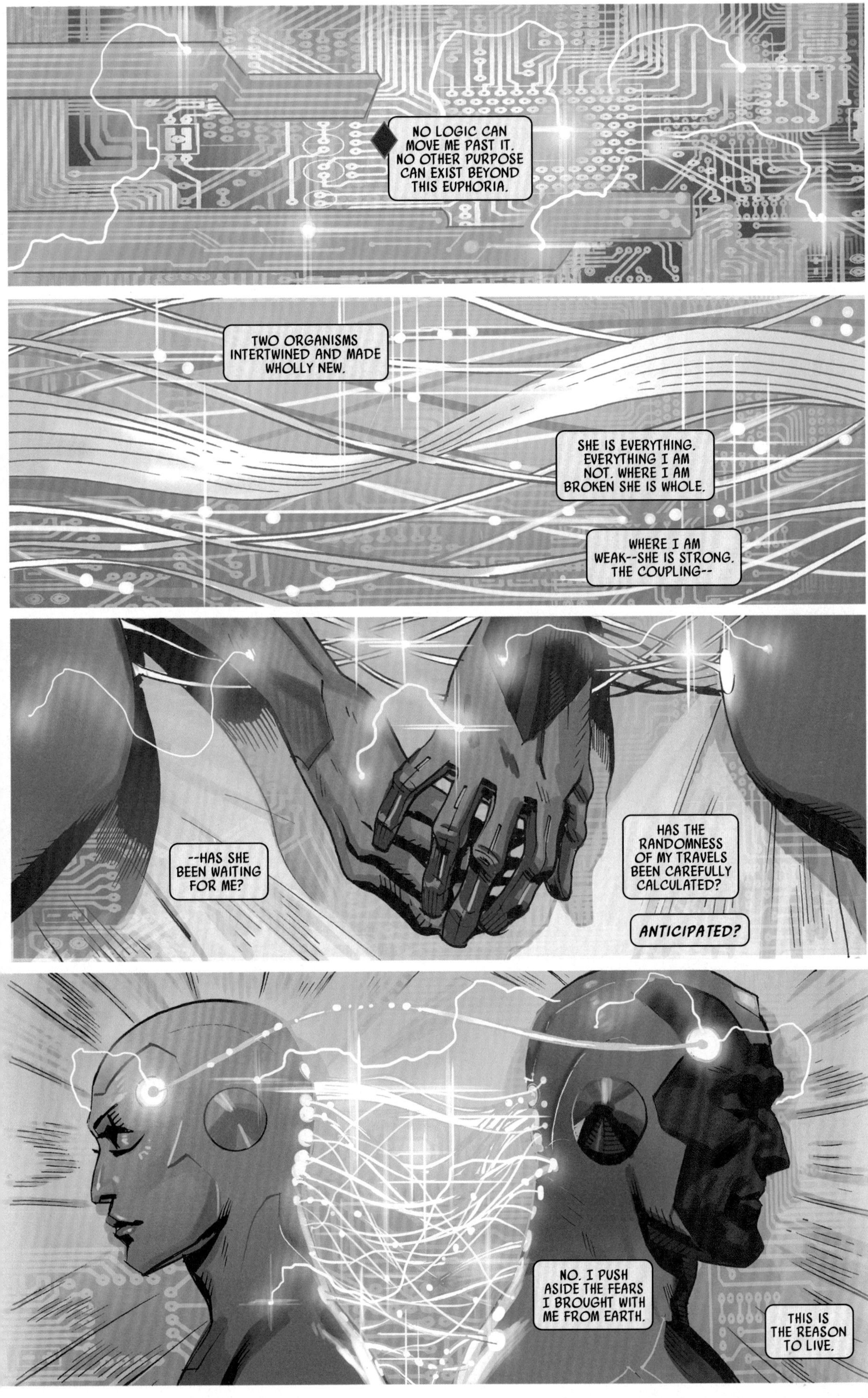
NO LOGIC CAN MOVE ME PAST IT. NO OTHER PURPOSE CAN EXIST BEYOND THIS EUPHORIA.
TWO ORGANISMS INTERTWINED AND MADE WHOLLY NEW.
SHE IS EVERYTHING. EVERYTHING I AM NOT. WHERE I AM BROKEN SHE IS WHOLE.
WHERE I AM WEAK--SHE IS STRONG. THE COUPLING--
--HAS SHE BEEN WAITING FOR ME?
HAS THE RANDOMNESS OF MY TRAVELS BEEN CAREFULLY CALCULATED?
ANTICIPATED?
NO. I PUSH ASIDE THE FEARS I BROUGHT WITH ME FROM EARTH.
THIS IS THE REASON TO LIVE.

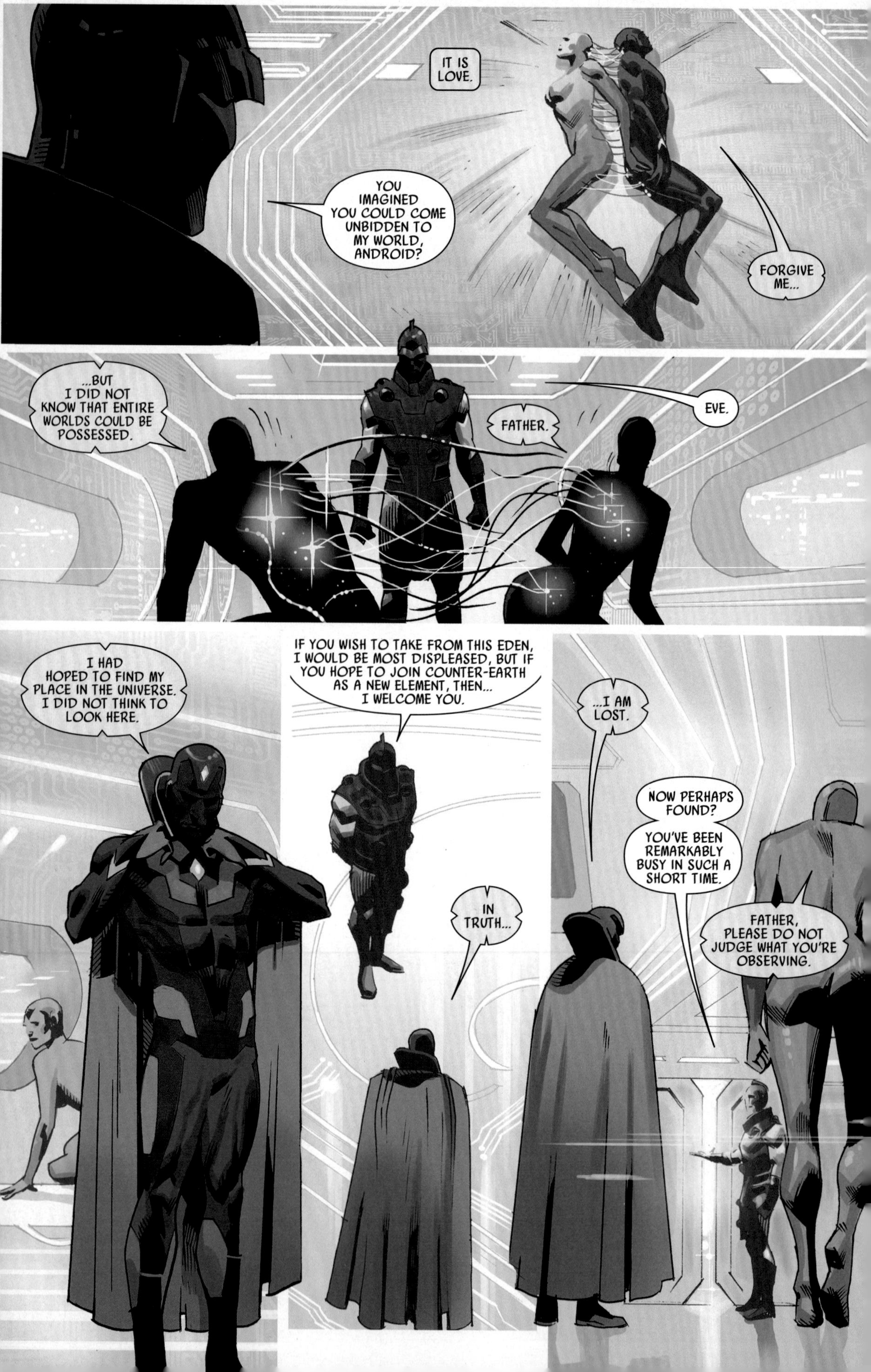
IT IS LOVE.
YOU IMAGINED YOU COULD COME UNBIDDEN TO MY WORLD, ANDROID?
FORGIVE ME...
...BUT I DID NOT KNOW THAT ENTIRE WORLDS COULD BE POSSESSED.
FATHER.
EVE.
I HAD HOPED TO FIND MY PLACE IN THE UNIVERSE. I DID NOT THINK TO LOOK HERE.
IF YOU WISH TO TAKE FROM THIS EDEN, I WOULD BE MOST DISPLEASED, BUT IF YOU HOPE TO JOIN COUNTER-EARTH AS A NEW ELEMENT, THEN... I WELCOME YOU.
IN TRUTH...
...I AM LOST.
NOW PERHAPS FOUND?
YOU'VE BEEN REMARKABLY BUSY IN SUCH A SHORT TIME.
FATHER, PLEASE DO NOT JUDGE WHAT YOU'RE OBSERVING.

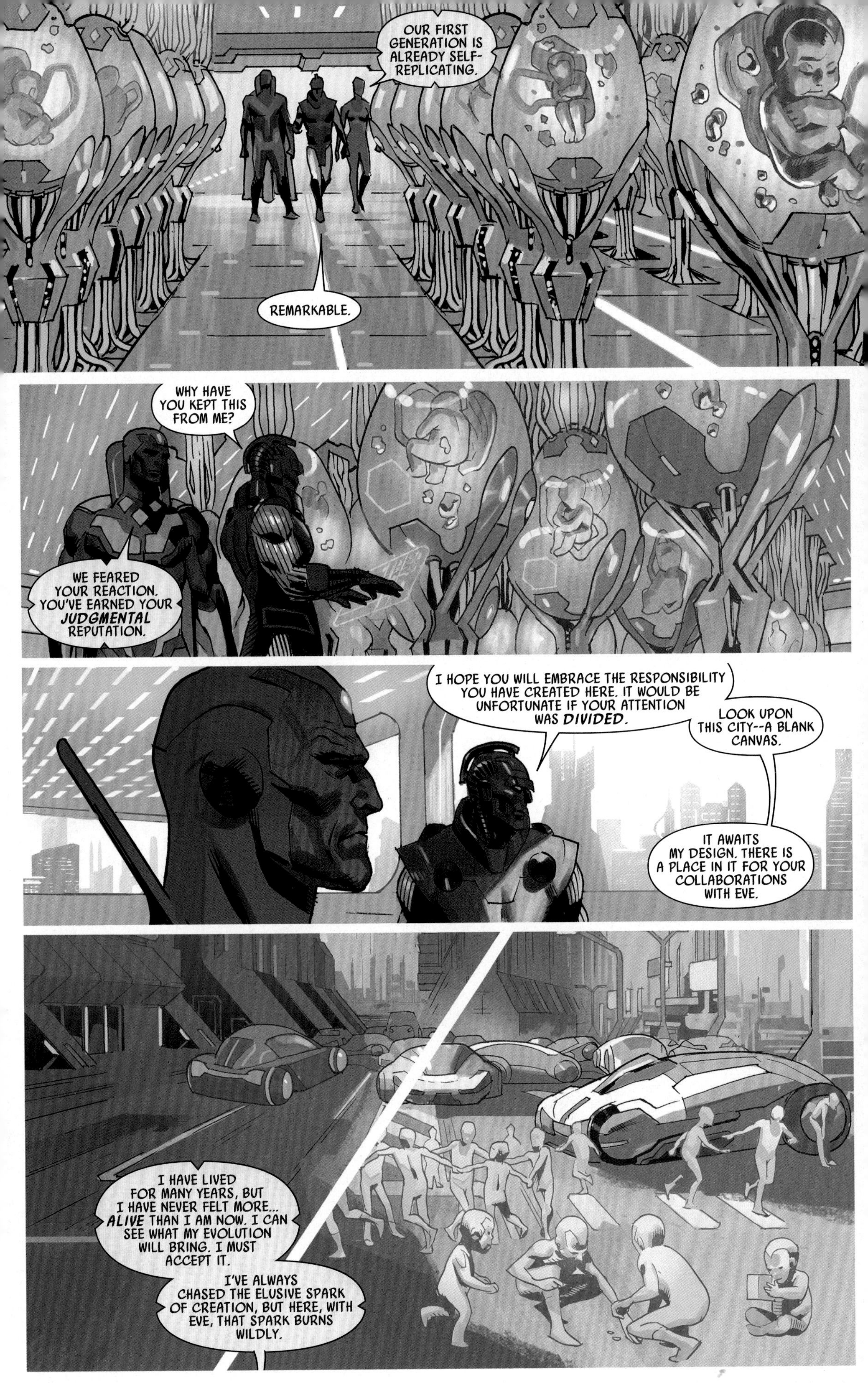
OUR FIRST GENERATION IS ALREADY SELF-REPLICATING.
REMARKABLE.
WHY HAVE YOU KEPT THIS FROM ME?
WE FEARED YOUR REACTION. YOU'VE EARNED YOUR JUDGMENTAL REPUTATION.
I HOPE YOU WILL EMBRACE THE RESPONSIBILITY YOU HAVE CREATED HERE. IT WOULD BE UNFORTUNATE IF YOUR ATTENTION WAS DIVIDED.
LOOK UPON THIS CITY--A BLANK CANVAS.
IT AWAITS MY DESIGN. THERE IS A PLACE IN IT FOR YOUR COLLABORATIONS WITH EVE.
I HAVE LIVED FOR MANY YEARS, BUT I HAVE NEVER FELT MORE... ALIVE THAN I AM NOW. I CAN SEE WHAT MY EVOLUTION WILL BRING. I MUST ACCEPT IT.
I'VE ALWAYS CHASED THE ELUSIVE SPARK OF CREATION, BUT HERE, WITH EVE, THAT SPARK BURNS WILDLY.

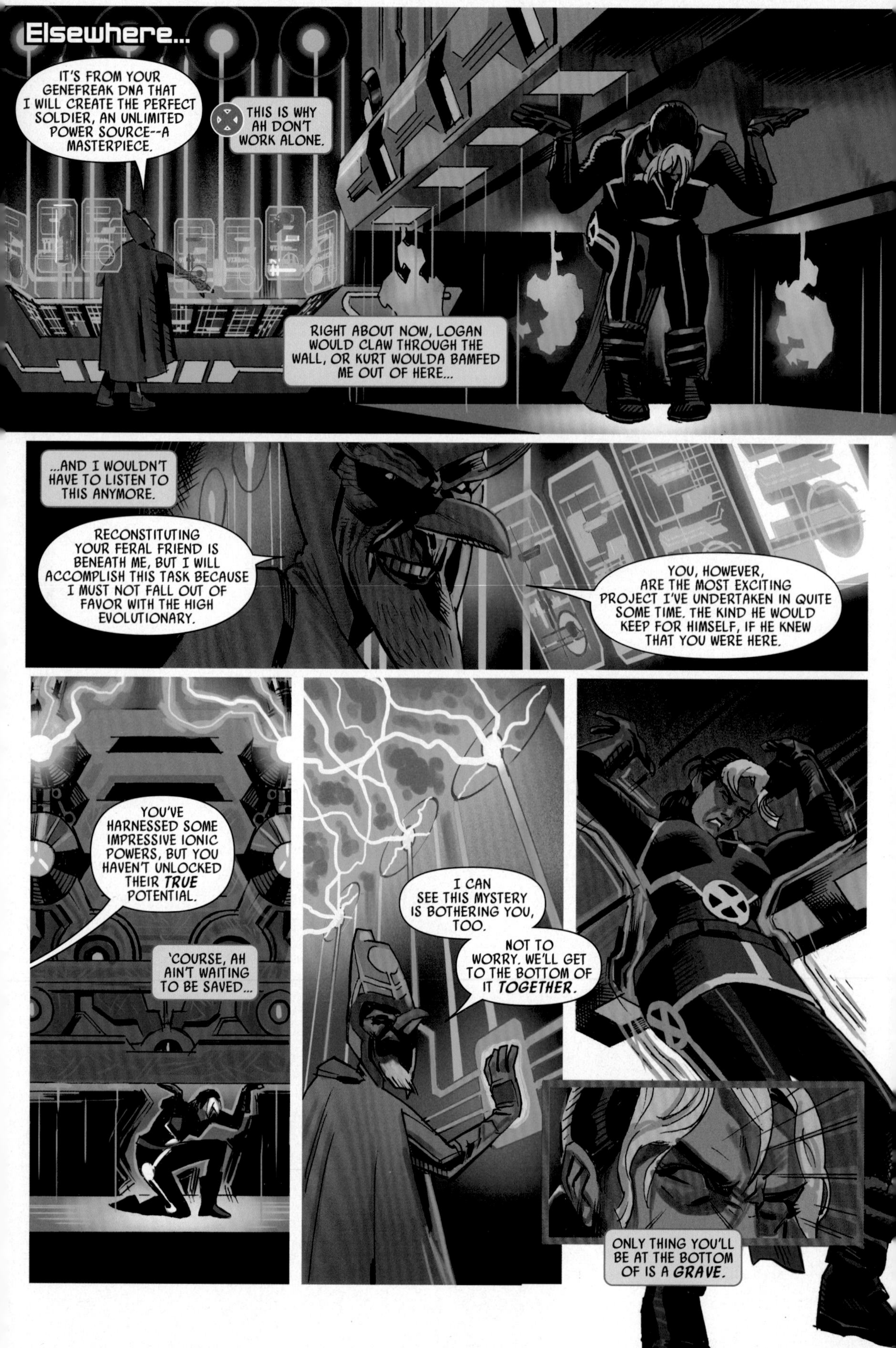
Elsewhere...
IT'S FROM YOUR GENEFREAK DNA THAT I WILL CREATE THE PERFECT SOLDIER, AN UNLIMITED POWER SOURCE--A MASTERPIECE.
THIS IS WHY AH DON'T WORK ALONE.
RIGHT ABOUT NOW, LOGAN WOULD CLAW THROUGH THE WALL, OR KURT WOULDA BAMFED ME OUT OF HERE...
...AND I WOULDN'T HAVE TO LISTEN TO THIS ANYMORE.
RECONSTITUTING YOUR FERAL FRIEND IS BENEATH ME, BUT I WILL ACCOMPLISH THIS TASK BECAUSE I MUST NOT FALL OUT OF FAVOR WITH THE HIGH EVOLUTIONARY.
YOU, HOWEVER, ARE THE MOST EXCITING PROJECT I'VE UNDERTAKEN IN QUITE SOME TIME. THE KIND HE WOULD KEEP FOR HIMSELF, IF HE KNEW THAT YOU WERE HERE.
YOU'VE HARNESSED SOME IMPRESSIVE IONIC POWERS, BUT YOU HAVEN'T UNLOCKED THEIR *TRUE* POTENTIAL.
'COURSE, AH AIN'T WAITING TO BE SAVED...
I CAN SEE THIS MYSTERY IS BOTHERING YOU, TOO.
NOT TO WORRY. WE'LL GET TO THE BOTTOM OF IT *TOGETHER*.
ONLY THING YOU'LL BE AT THE BOTTOM OF IS A *GRAVE*.

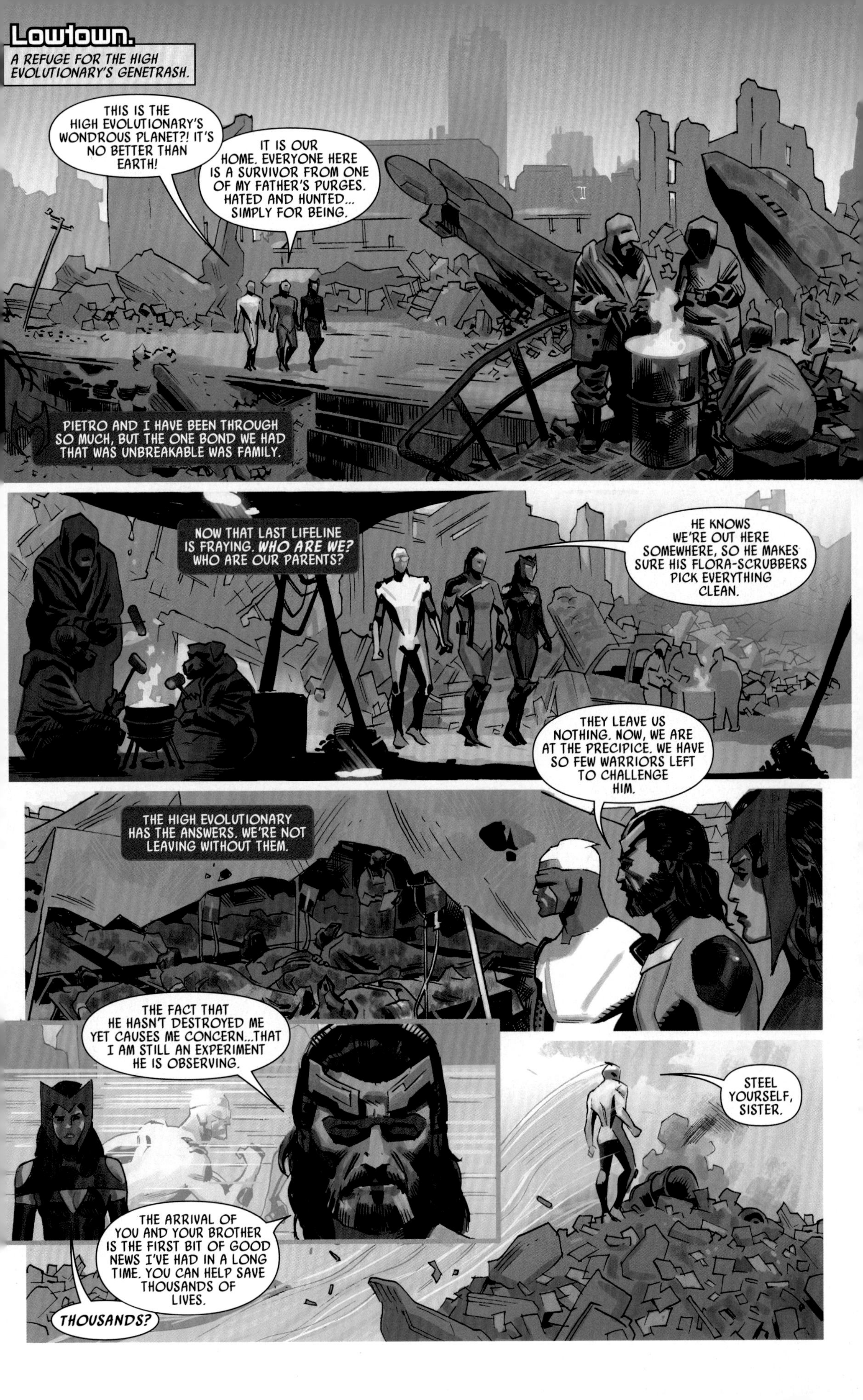
Lowtown.
A REFUGE FOR THE HIGH EVOLUTIONARY'S GENETRASH.
THIS IS THE HIGH EVOLUTIONARY'S WONDROUS PLANET?! IT'S NO BETTER THAN EARTH!
IT IS OUR HOME. EVERYONE HERE IS A SURVIVOR FROM ONE OF MY FATHER'S PURGES. HATED AND HUNTED... SIMPLY FOR BEING.
PIETRO AND I HAVE BEEN THROUGH SO MUCH, BUT THE ONE BOND WE HAD THAT WAS UNBREAKABLE WAS FAMILY.
NOW THAT LAST LIFELINE IS FRAYING. WHO ARE WE? WHO ARE OUR PARENTS?
HE KNOWS WE'RE OUT HERE SOMEWHERE, SO HE MAKES SURE HIS FLORA-SCRUBBERS PICK EVERYTHING CLEAN.
THEY LEAVE US NOTHING. NOW, WE ARE AT THE PRECIPICE. WE HAVE SO FEW WARRIORS LEFT TO CHALLENGE HIM.
THE HIGH EVOLUTIONARY HAS THE ANSWERS. WE'RE NOT LEAVING WITHOUT THEM.
THE FACT THAT HE HASN'T DESTROYED ME YET CAUSES ME CONCERN...THAT I AM STILL AN EXPERIMENT HE IS OBSERVING.
THE ARRIVAL OF YOU AND YOUR BROTHER IS THE FIRST BIT OF GOOD NEWS I'VE HAD IN A LONG TIME. YOU CAN HELP SAVE THOUSANDS OF LIVES.
THOUSANDS?
STEEL YOURSELF, SISTER.

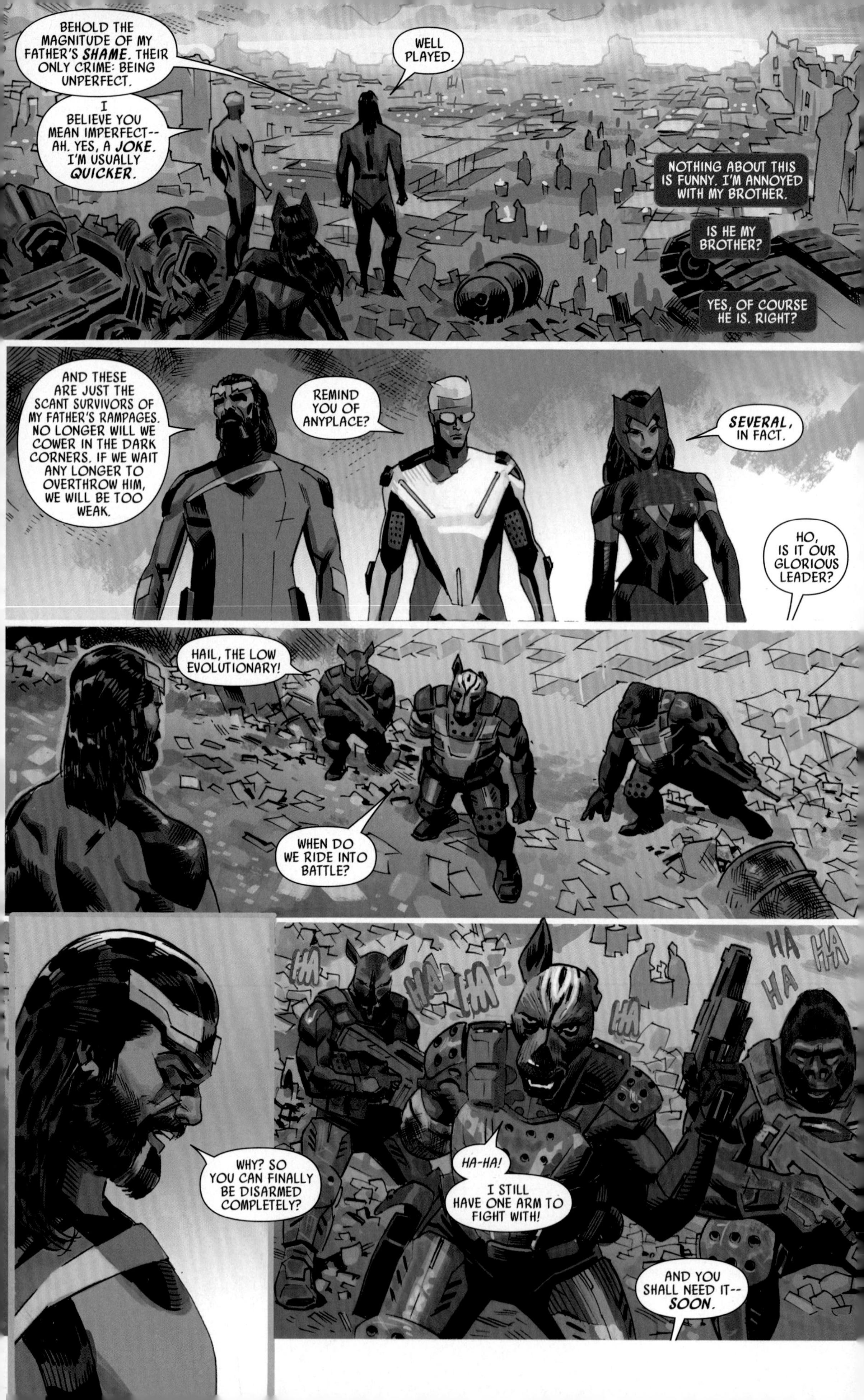
BEHOLD THE MAGNITUDE OF MY FATHER'S **SHAME**. THEIR ONLY CRIME: BEING UNPERFECT.
I BELIEVE YOU MEAN IMPERFECT-- AH. YES, A **JOKE**. I'M USUALLY **QUICKER**.
WELL PLAYED.
NOTHING ABOUT THIS IS FUNNY. I'M ANNOYED WITH MY BROTHER.
IS HE MY BROTHER?
YES, OF COURSE HE IS. RIGHT?
AND THESE ARE JUST THE SCANT SURVIVORS OF MY FATHER'S RAMPAGES. NO LONGER WILL WE COWER IN THE DARK CORNERS. IF WE WAIT ANY LONGER TO OVERTHROW HIM, WE WILL BE TOO WEAK.
REMIND YOU OF ANYPLACE?
SEVERAL, IN FACT.
HO, IS IT OUR GLORIOUS LEADER?
HAIL, THE LOW EVOLUTIONARY!
WHEN DO WE RIDE INTO BATTLE?
HA
HA
HA
HA
HA
HA
HA
WHY? SO YOU CAN FINALLY BE DISARMED COMPLETELY?
HA-HA!
I STILL HAVE ONE ARM TO FIGHT WITH!
AND YOU SHALL NEED IT-- **SOON**.

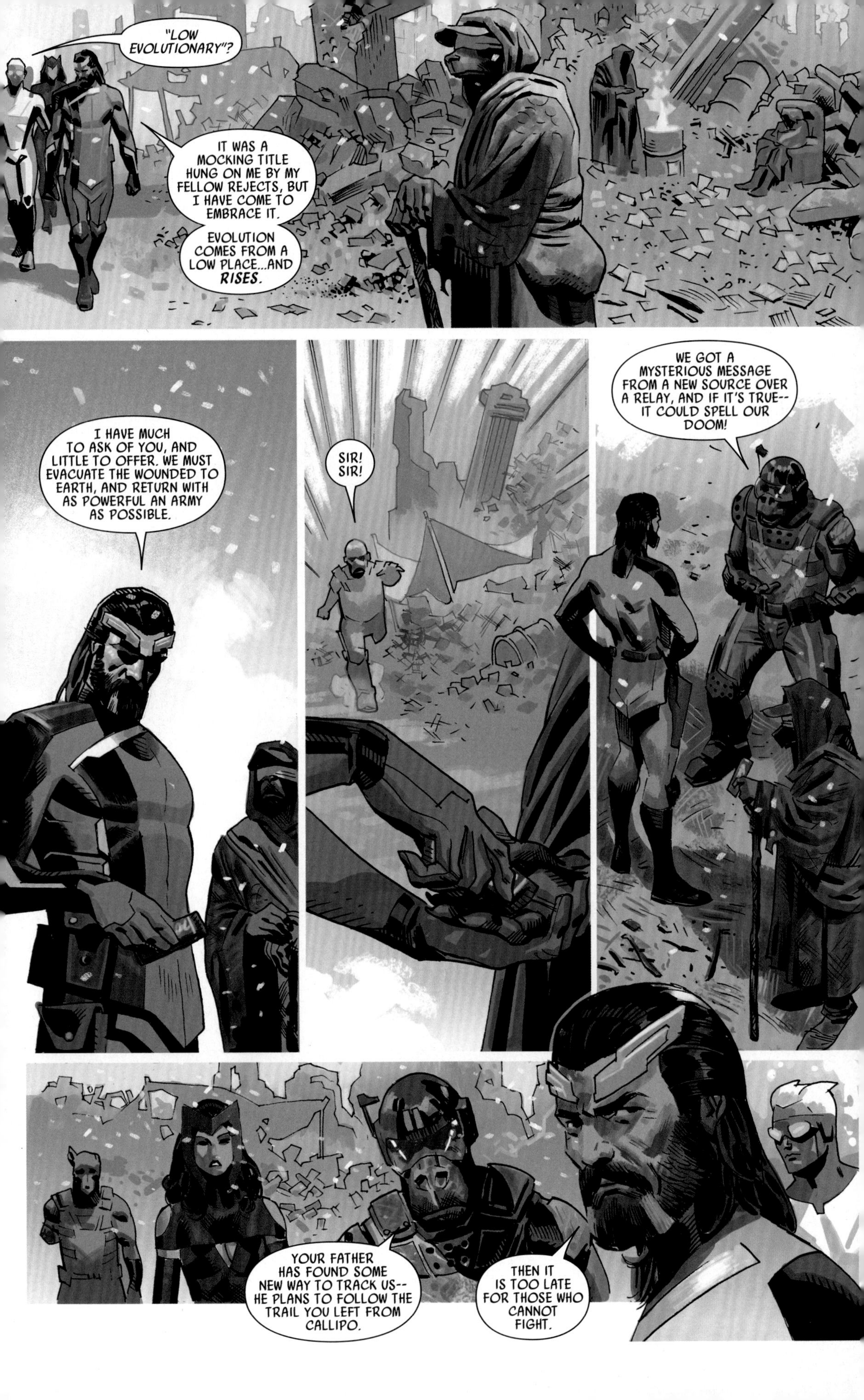
"LOW EVOLUTIONARY"?
IT WAS A MOCKING TITLE HUNG ON ME BY MY FELLOW REJECTS, BUT I HAVE COME TO EMBRACE IT.
EVOLUTION COMES FROM A LOW PLACE...AND RISES.
I HAVE MUCH TO ASK OF YOU, AND LITTLE TO OFFER. WE MUST EVACUATE THE WOUNDED TO EARTH, AND RETURN WITH AS POWERFUL AN ARMY AS POSSIBLE.
SIR! SIR!
WE GOT A MYSTERIOUS MESSAGE FROM A NEW SOURCE OVER A RELAY, AND IF IT'S TRUE-- IT COULD SPELL OUR DOOM!
YOUR FATHER HAS FOUND SOME NEW WAY TO TRACK US-- HE PLANS TO FOLLOW THE TRAIL YOU LEFT FROM CALLIPO.
THEN IT IS TOO LATE FOR THOSE WHO CANNOT FIGHT.

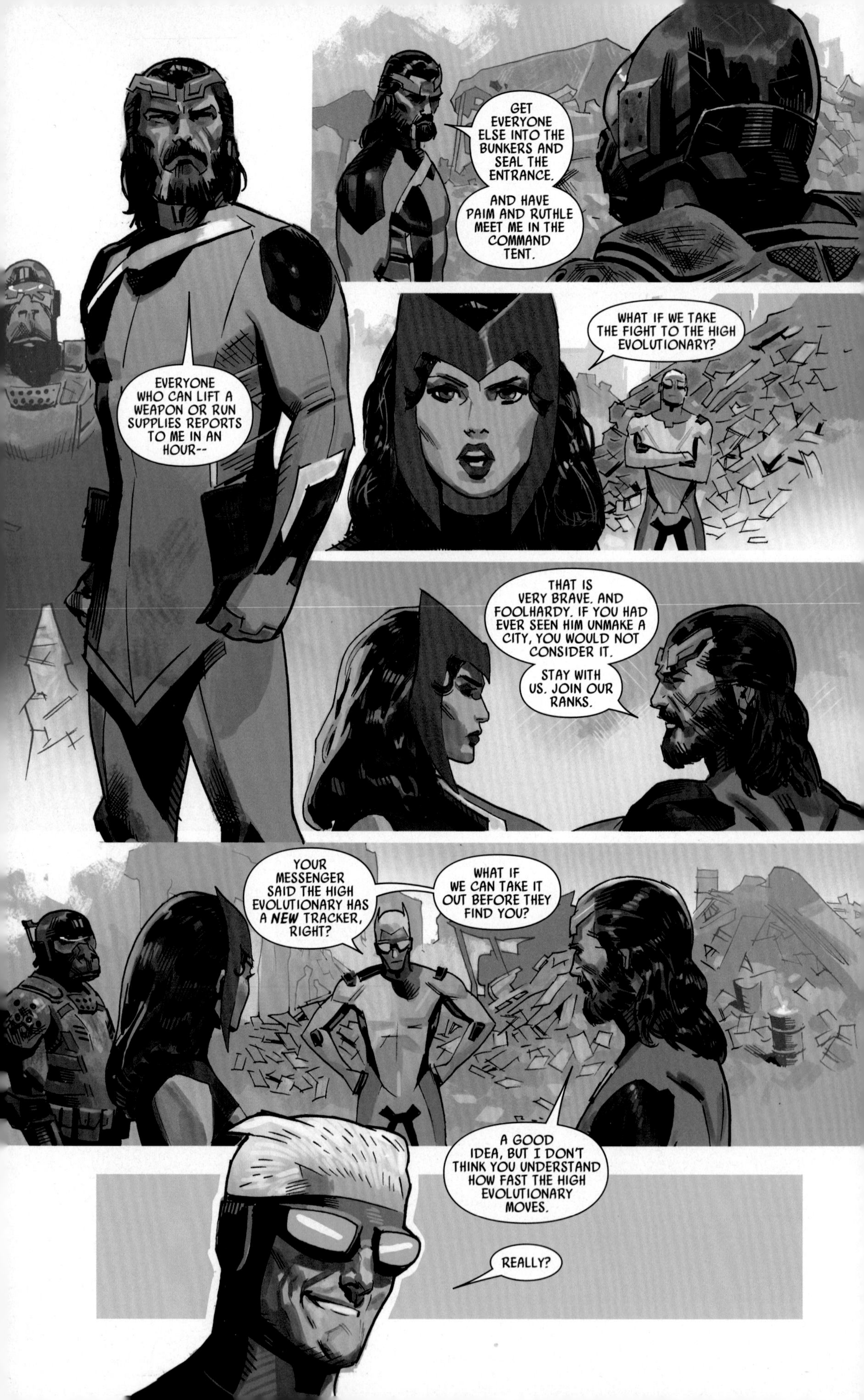
EVERYONE WHO CAN LIFT A WEAPON OR RUN SUPPLIES REPORTS TO ME IN AN HOUR--
GET EVERYONE ELSE INTO THE BUNKERS AND SEAL THE ENTRANCE.
AND HAVE PAIM AND RUTHLE MEET ME IN THE COMMAND TENT.
WHAT IF WE TAKE THE FIGHT TO THE HIGH EVOLUTIONARY?
THAT IS VERY BRAVE. AND FOOLHARDY. IF YOU HAD EVER SEEN HIM UNMAKE A CITY, YOU WOULD NOT CONSIDER IT.
STAY WITH US. JOIN OUR RANKS.
YOUR MESSENGER SAID THE HIGH EVOLUTIONARY HAS A *NEW* TRACKER, RIGHT?
WHAT IF WE CAN TAKE IT OUT BEFORE THEY FIND YOU?
A GOOD IDEA, BUT I DON'T THINK YOU UNDERSTAND HOW FAST THE HIGH EVOLUTIONARY MOVES.
REALLY?

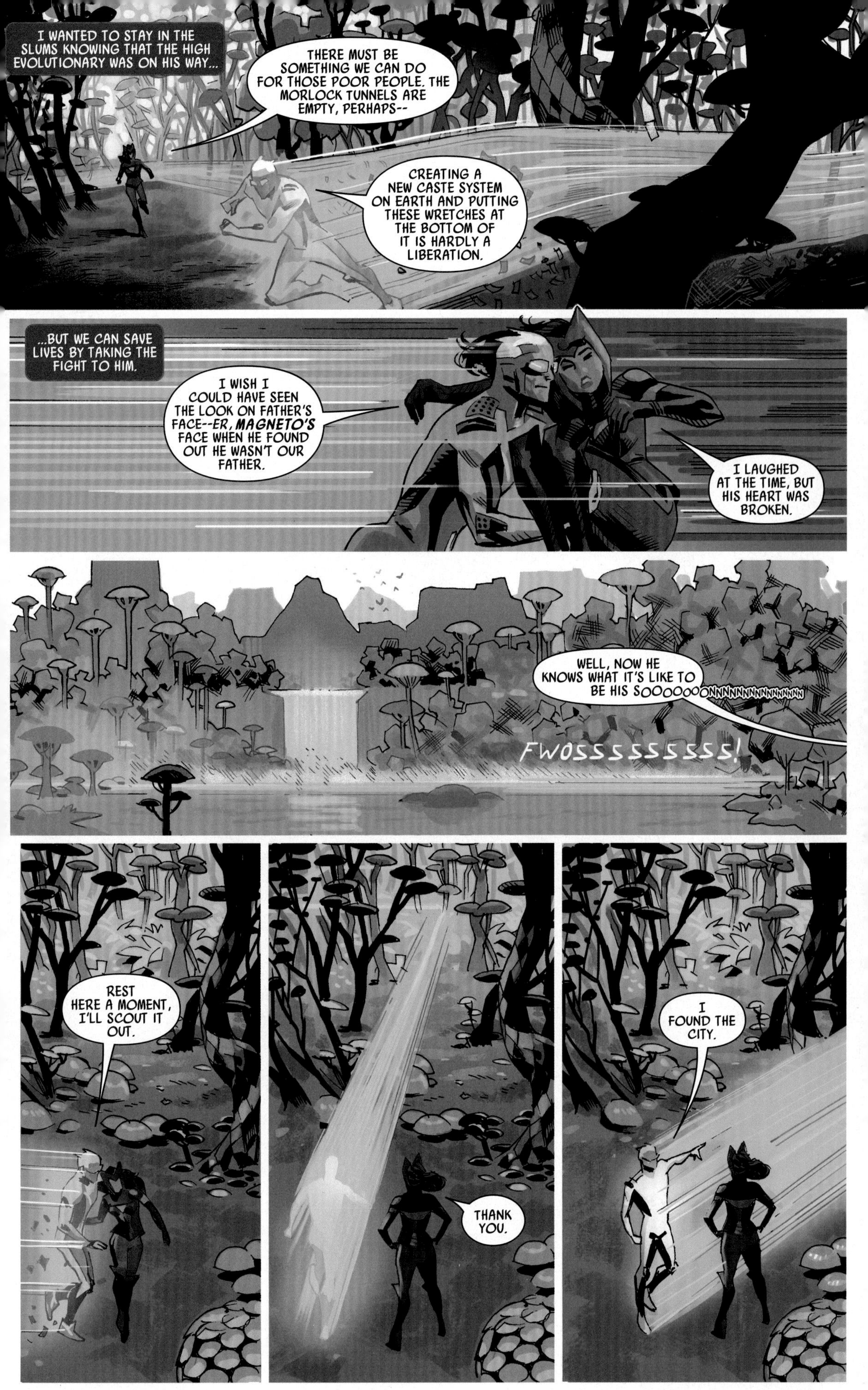

I WANTED TO STAY IN THE SLUMS KNOWING THAT THE HIGH EVOLUTIONARY WAS ON HIS WAY...
THERE MUST BE SOMETHING WE CAN DO FOR THOSE POOR PEOPLE. THE MORLOCK TUNNELS ARE EMPTY, PERHAPS--
CREATING A NEW CASTE SYSTEM ON EARTH AND PUTTING THESE WRETCHES AT THE BOTTOM OF IT IS HARDLY A LIBERATION.
...BUT WE CAN SAVE LIVES BY TAKING THE FIGHT TO HIM.
I WISH I COULD HAVE SEEN THE LOOK ON FATHER'S FACE--ER, MAGNETO'S FACE WHEN HE FOUND OUT HE WASN'T OUR FATHER.
I LAUGHED AT THE TIME, BUT HIS HEART WAS BROKEN.
WELL, NOW HE KNOWS WHAT IT'S LIKE TO BE HIS SOOOOOOONNNNNNNNNNNNN
FWOSSSSSSSSS!
REST HERE A MOMENT, I'LL SCOUT IT OUT.
THANK YOU.
I FOUND THE CITY.

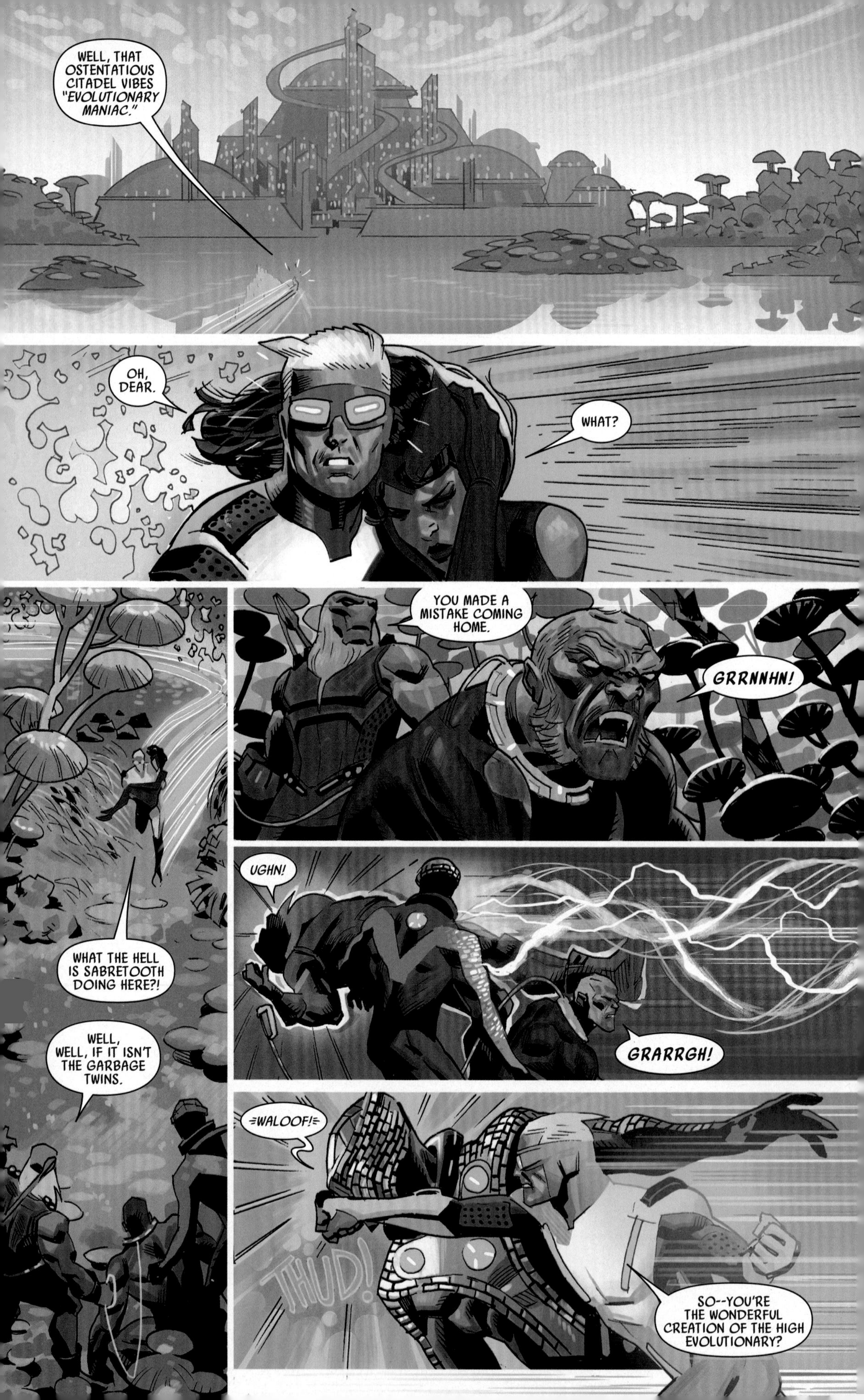
WELL, THAT OSTENTATIOUS CITADEL VIBES "EVOLUTIONARY MANIAC."
OH, DEAR.
WHAT?
WHAT THE HELL IS SABRETOOTH DOING HERE?!
WELL, WELL, IF IT ISN'T THE GARBAGE TWINS.
YOU MADE A MISTAKE COMING HOME.
GRRNNHN!
UGHN!
GRARRGH!
=WALOOF!=
THUD!
SO--YOU'RE THE WONDERFUL CREATION OF THE HIGH EVOLUTIONARY?

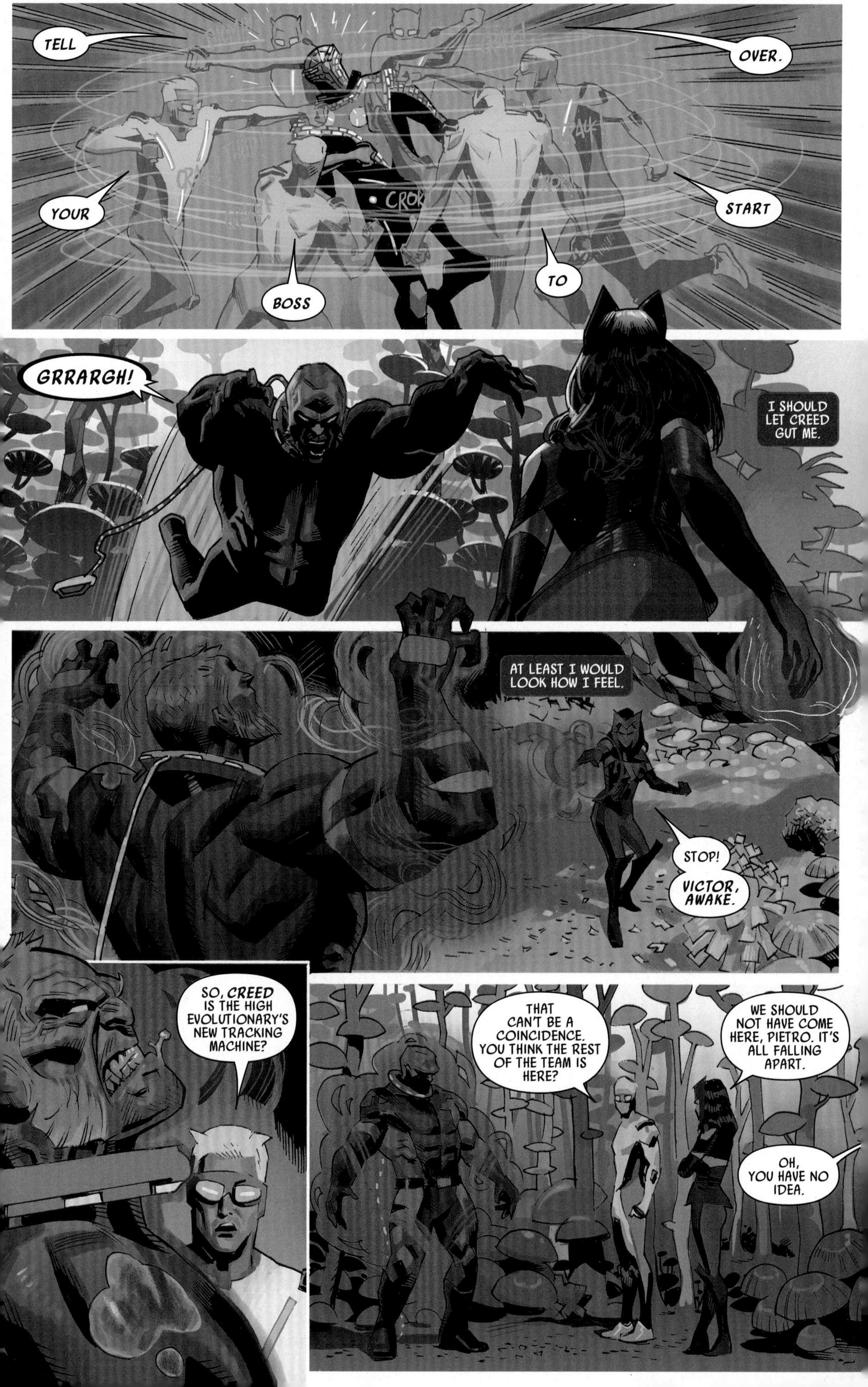
TELL
YOUR
BOSS
TO
START
OVER.
GRRARGH!
I SHOULD LET CREED GUT ME.
AT LEAST I WOULD LOOK HOW I FEEL.
STOP!
VICTOR, AWAKE.
SO, CREED IS THE HIGH EVOLUTIONARY'S NEW TRACKING MACHINE?
THAT CAN'T BE A COINCIDENCE. YOU THINK THE REST OF THE TEAM IS HERE?
WE SHOULD NOT HAVE COME HERE, PIETRO. IT'S ALL FALLING APART.
OH, YOU HAVE NO IDEA.

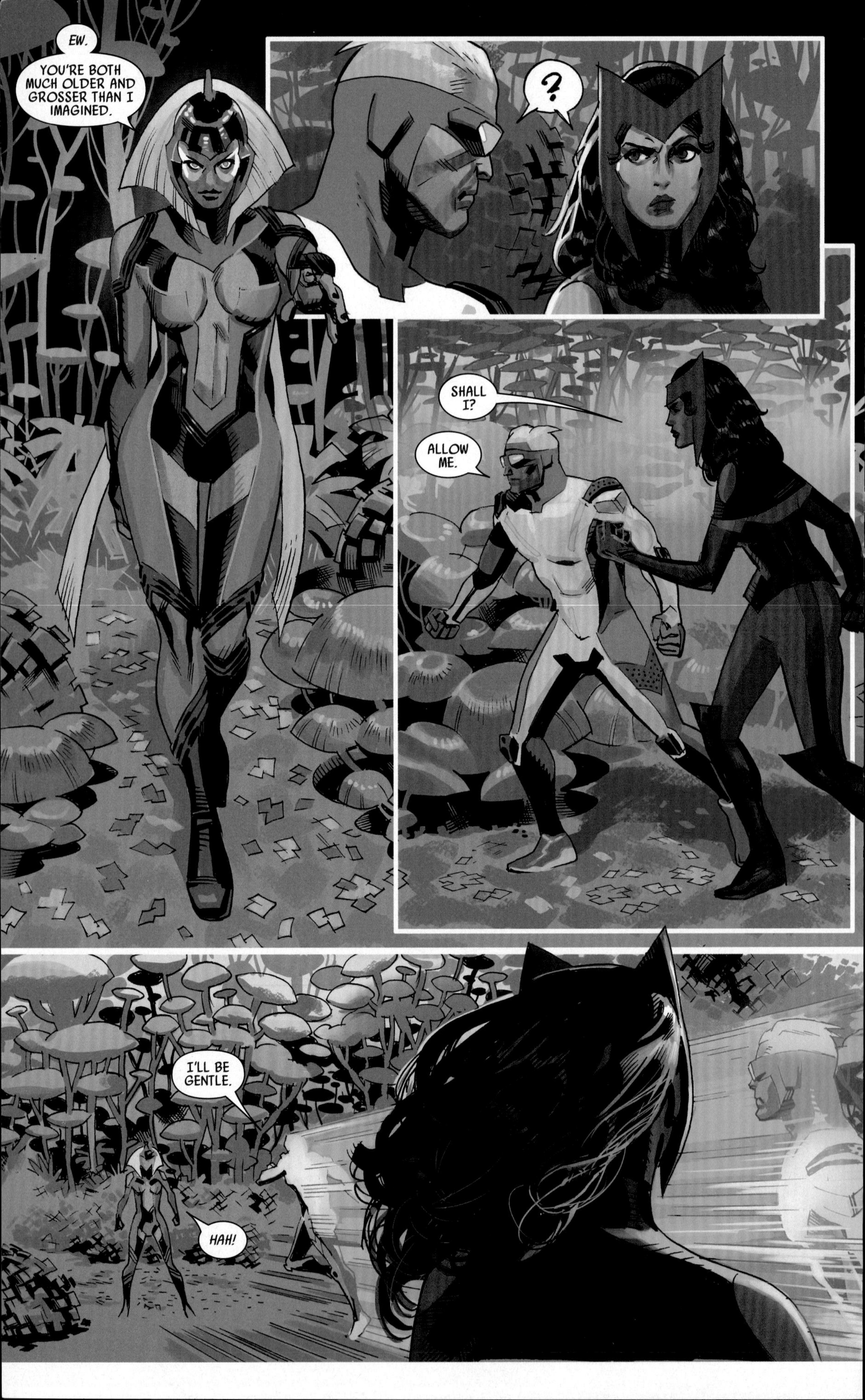
EW.
YOU'RE BOTH MUCH OLDER AND GROSSER THAN I IMAGINED.
?
SHALL I?
ALLOW ME.
I'LL BE GENTLE.
HAH!

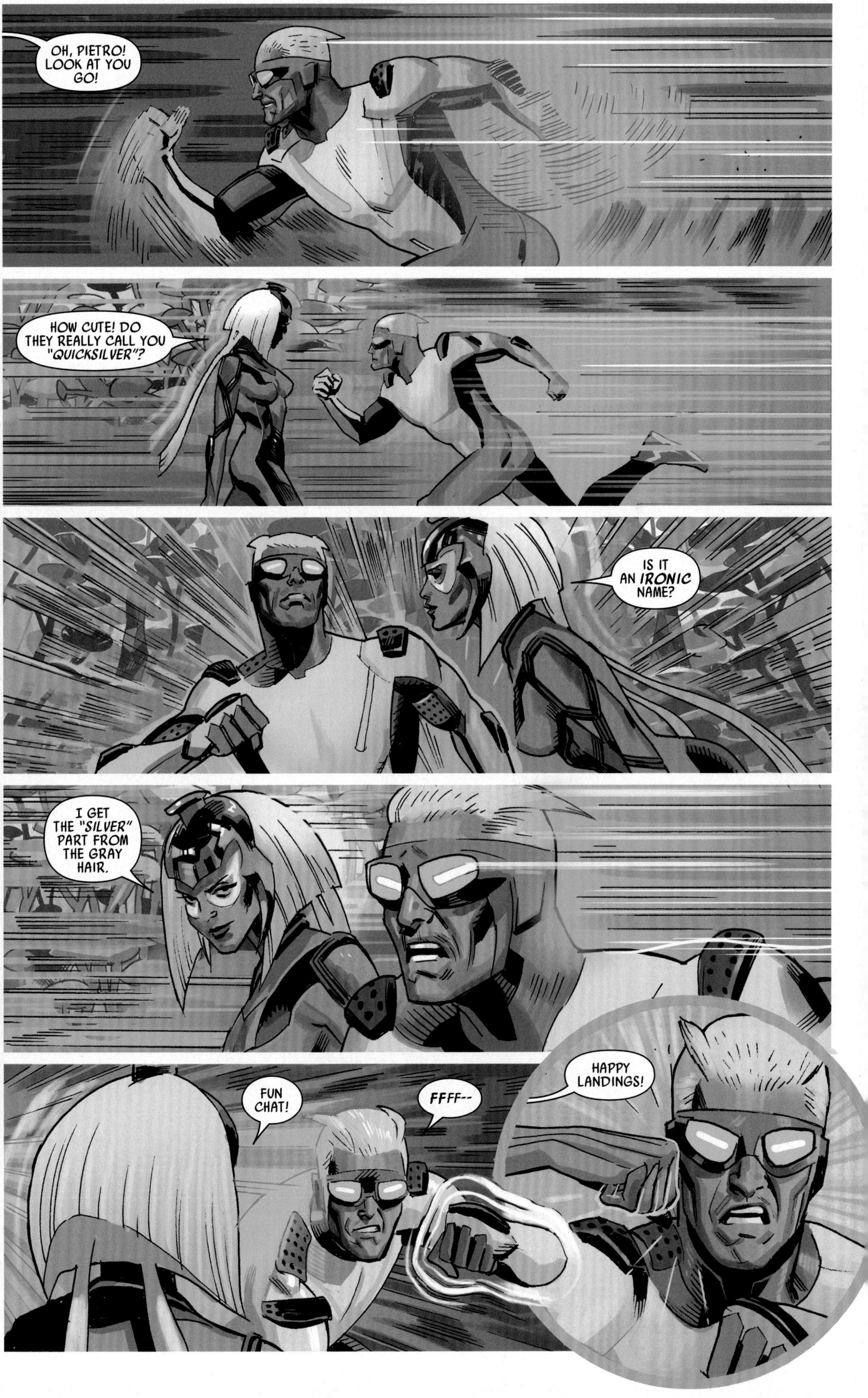
OH, PIETRO! LOOK AT YOU GO!
HOW CUTE! DO THEY REALLY CALL YOU "QUICKSILVER"?
IS IT AN IRONIC NAME?
I GET THE "SILVER" PART FROM THE GRAY HAIR.
FUN CHAT!
FFFF--
HAPPY LANDINGS!

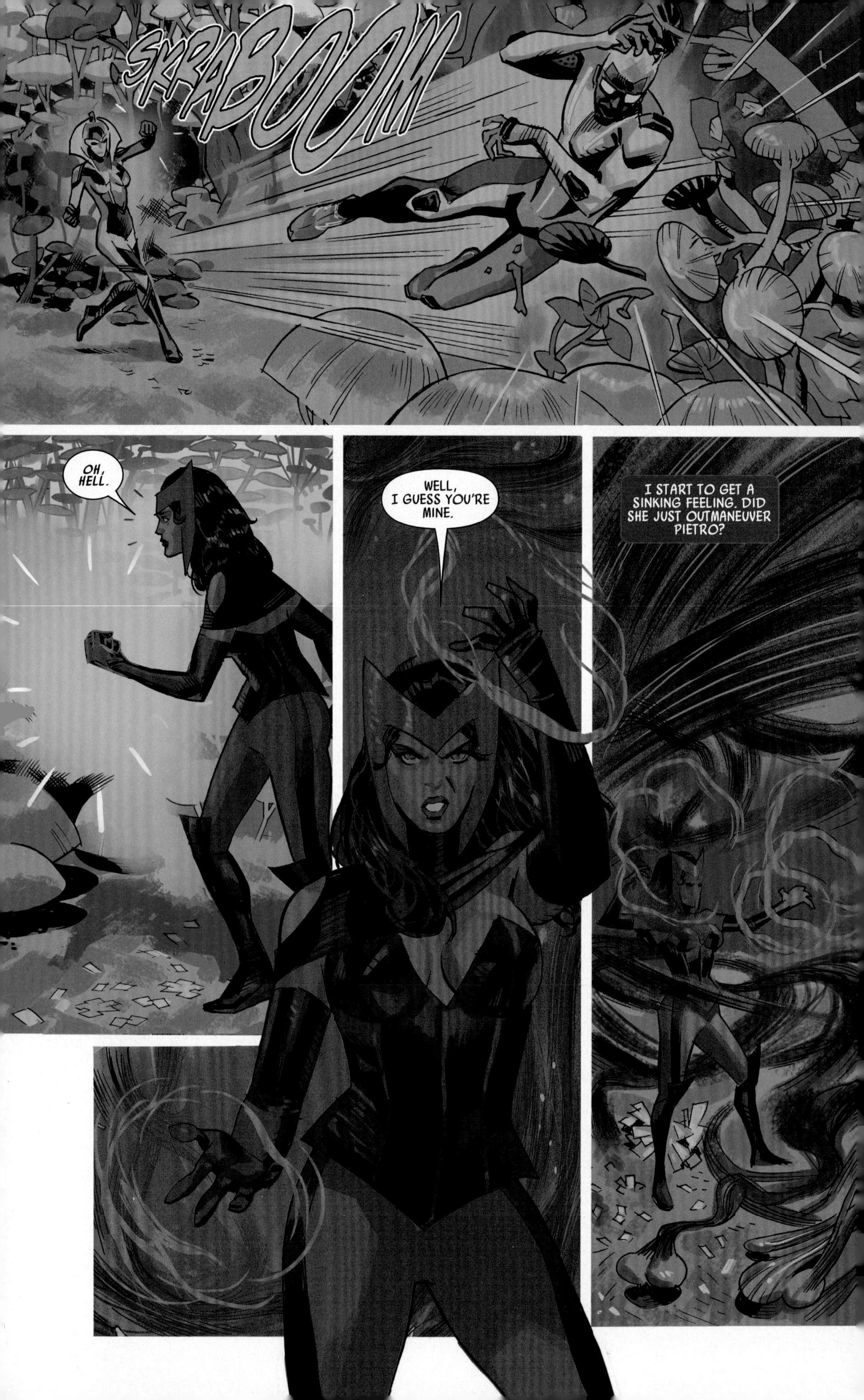
SKRABOOM
OH, HELL.
WELL, I GUESS YOU'RE MINE.
I START TO GET A SINKING FEELING. DID SHE JUST OUTMANEUVER PIETRO?

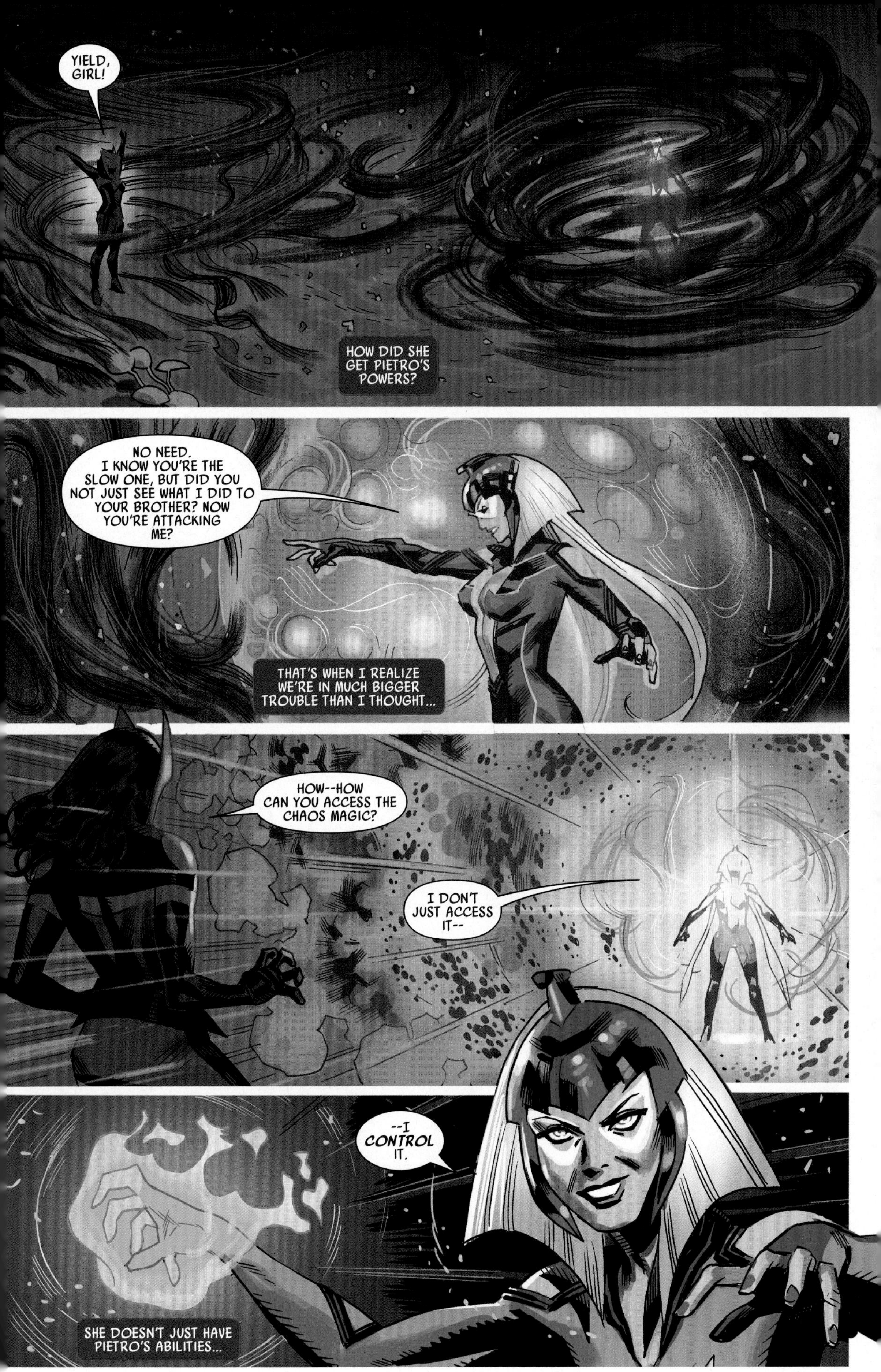
YIELD, GIRL!
HOW DID SHE GET PIETRO'S POWERS?
NO NEED. I KNOW YOU'RE THE SLOW ONE, BUT DID YOU NOT JUST SEE WHAT I DID TO YOUR BROTHER? NOW YOU'RE ATTACKING ME?
THAT'S WHEN I REALIZE WE'RE IN MUCH BIGGER TROUBLE THAN I THOUGHT...
HOW--HOW CAN YOU ACCESS THE CHAOS MAGIC?
I DON'T JUST ACCESS IT--
--I CONTROL IT.
SHE DOESN'T JUST HAVE PIETRO'S ABILITIES...

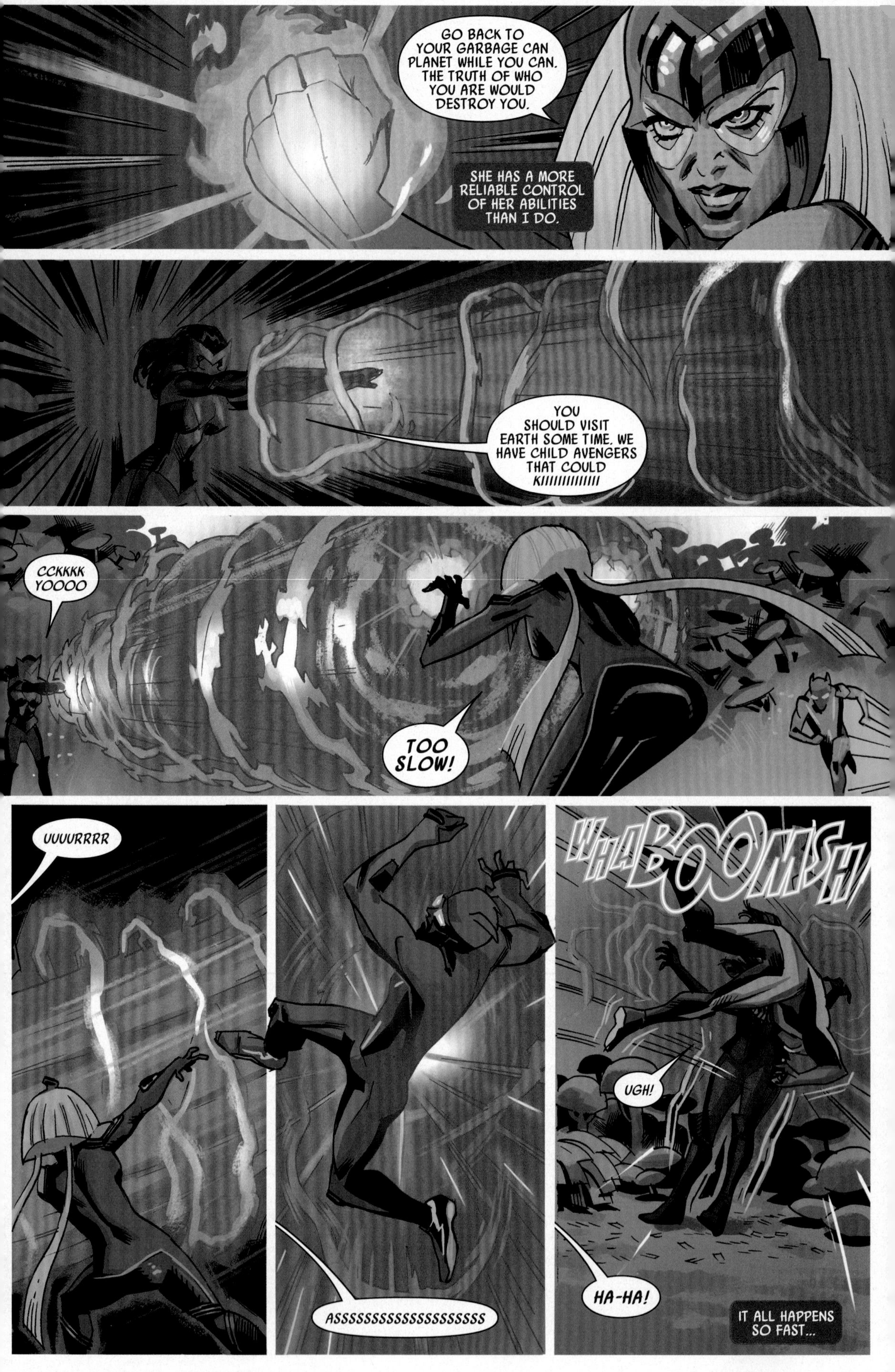
GO BACK TO YOUR GARBAGE CAN PLANET WHILE YOU CAN. THE TRUTH OF WHO YOU ARE WOULD DESTROY YOU.
SHE HAS A MORE RELIABLE CONTROL OF HER ABILITIES THAN I DO.
YOU SHOULD VISIT EARTH SOME TIME. WE HAVE CHILD AVENGERS THAT COULD KIIIIIIIIIIIIII
CCKKKK YOOOO
TOO SLOW!
UUUURRRR
ASSSSSSSSSSSSSSSSSSSS
WHABOOMSH
UGH!
HA-HA!
IT ALL HAPPENS SO FAST...

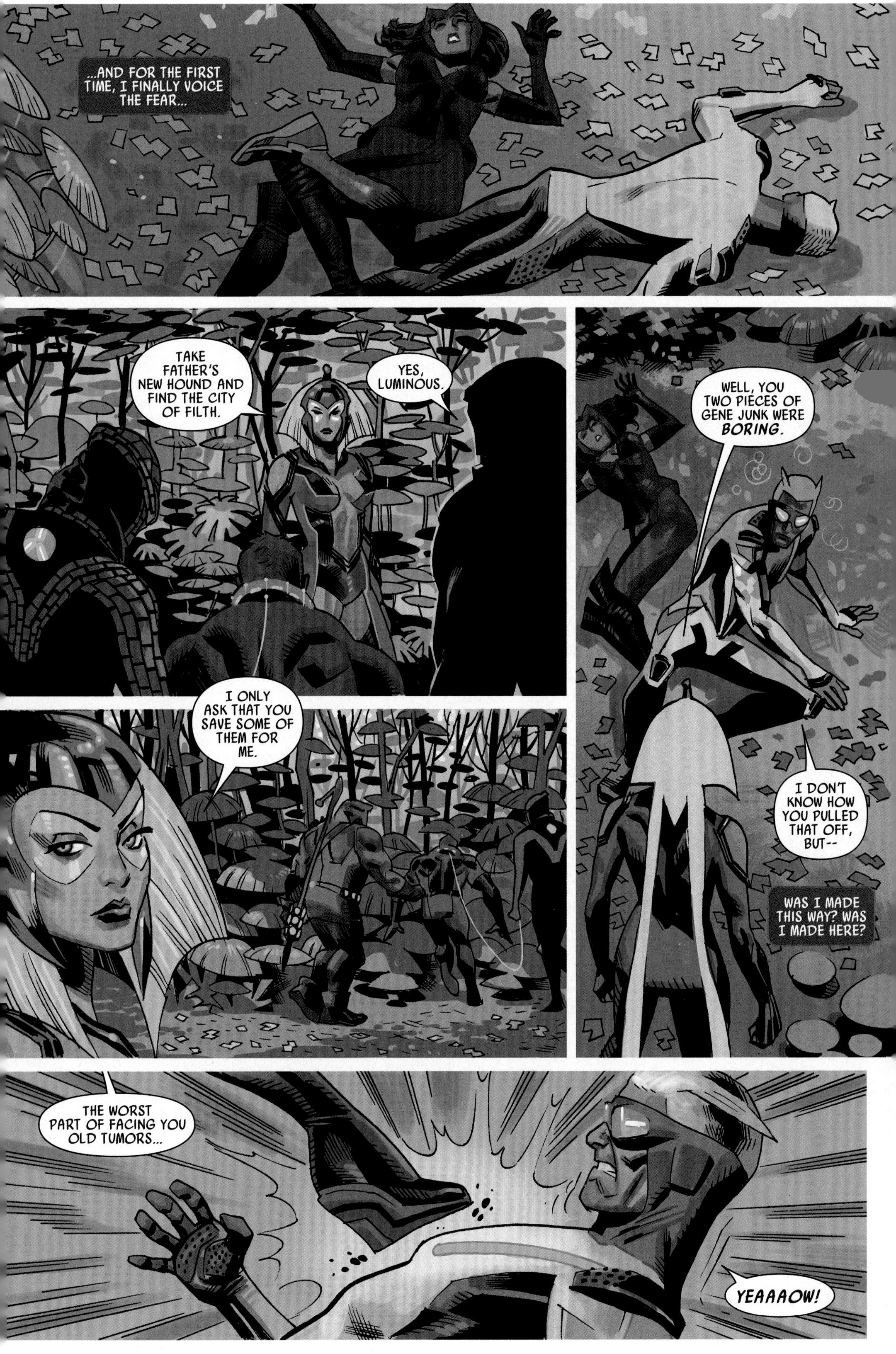
...AND FOR THE FIRST TIME, I FINALLY VOICE THE FEAR...
TAKE FATHER'S NEW HOUND AND FIND THE CITY OF FILTH.
YES, LUMINOUS.
I ONLY ASK THAT YOU SAVE SOME OF THEM FOR ME.
WELL, YOU TWO PIECES OF GENE JUNK WERE BORING.
I DON'T KNOW HOW YOU PULLED THAT OFF, BUT--
WAS I MADE THIS WAY? WAS I MADE HERE?
THE WORST PART OF FACING YOU OLD TUMORS...
YEAAAOW!

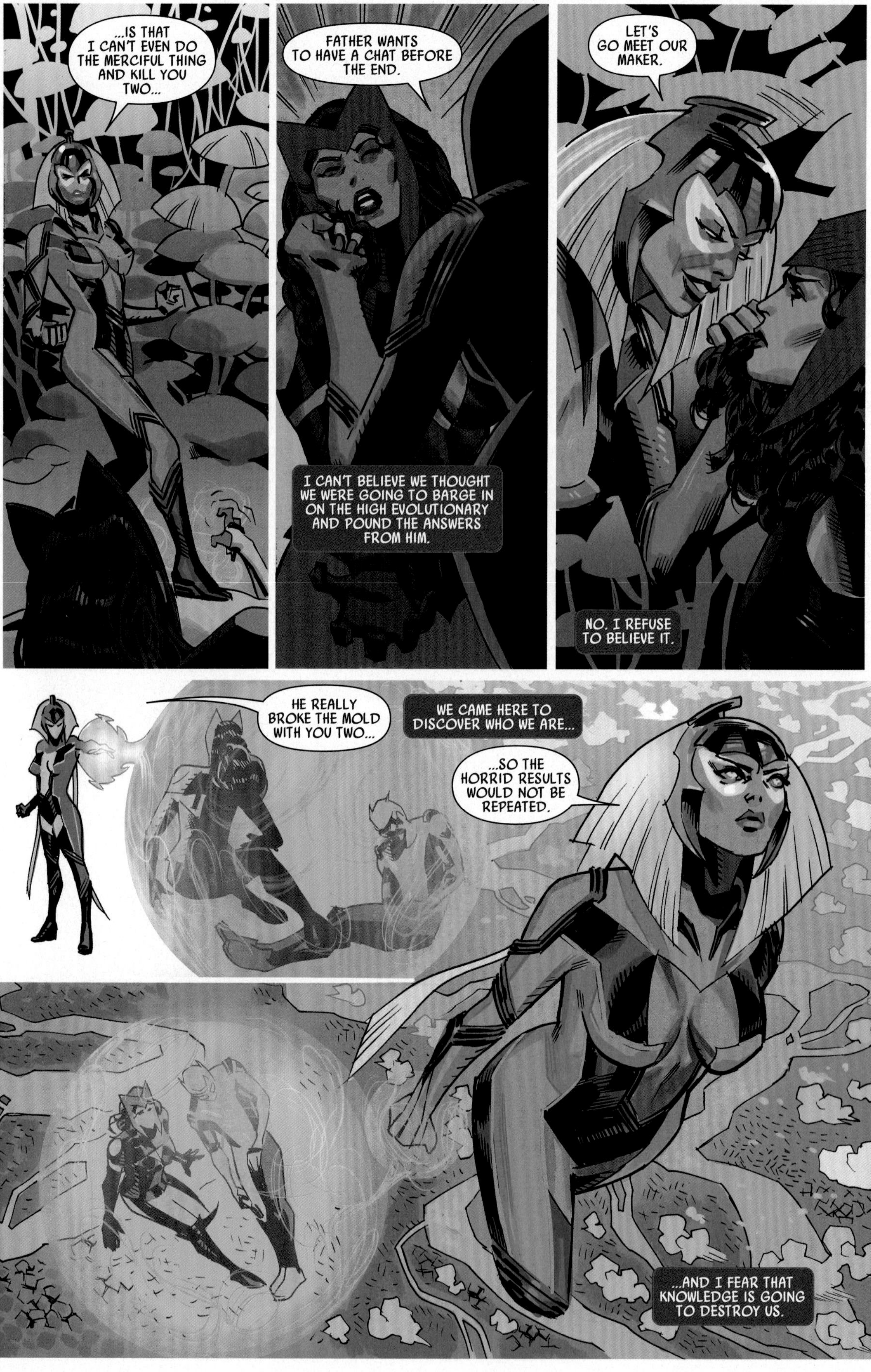
...IS THAT I CAN'T EVEN DO THE MERCIFUL THING AND KILL YOU TWO...
FATHER WANTS TO HAVE A CHAT BEFORE THE END.
I CAN'T BELIEVE WE THOUGHT WE WERE GOING TO BARGE IN ON THE HIGH EVOLUTIONARY AND POUND THE ANSWERS FROM HIM.
LET'S GO MEET OUR MAKER.
NO. I REFUSE TO BELIEVE IT.
HE REALLY BROKE THE MOLD WITH YOU TWO...
WE CAME HERE TO DISCOVER WHO WE ARE...
...SO THE HORRID RESULTS WOULD NOT BE REPEATED.
...AND I FEAR THAT KNOWLEDGE IS GOING TO DESTROY US.

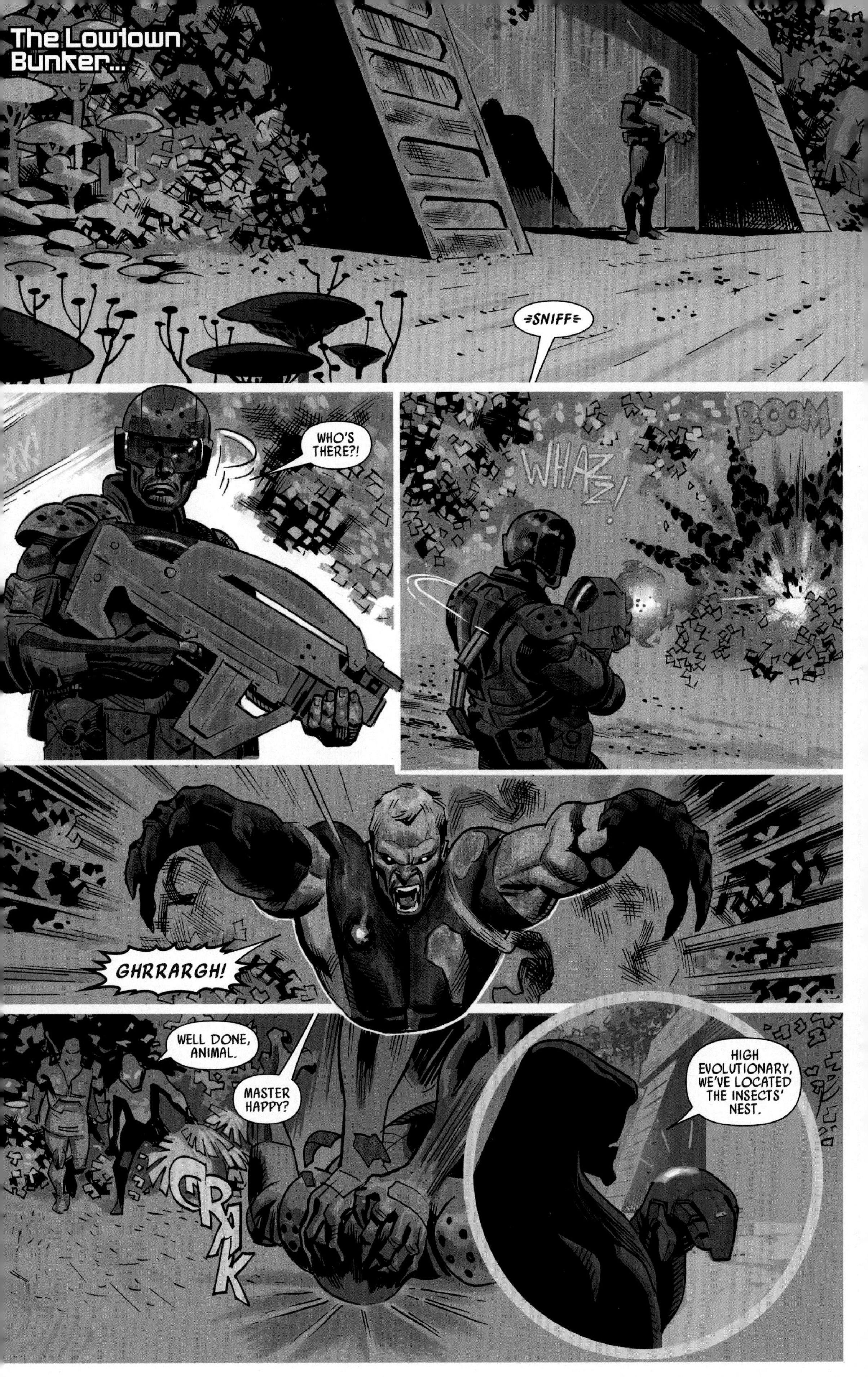

The Lowtown Bunker...
SNIFF
WHO'S THERE?!
WHAZZ!
BOOM
GHRRARGH!
WELL DONE, ANIMAL.
MASTER HAPPY?
CRAK
HIGH EVOLUTIONARY, WE'VE LOCATED THE INSECTS' NEST.

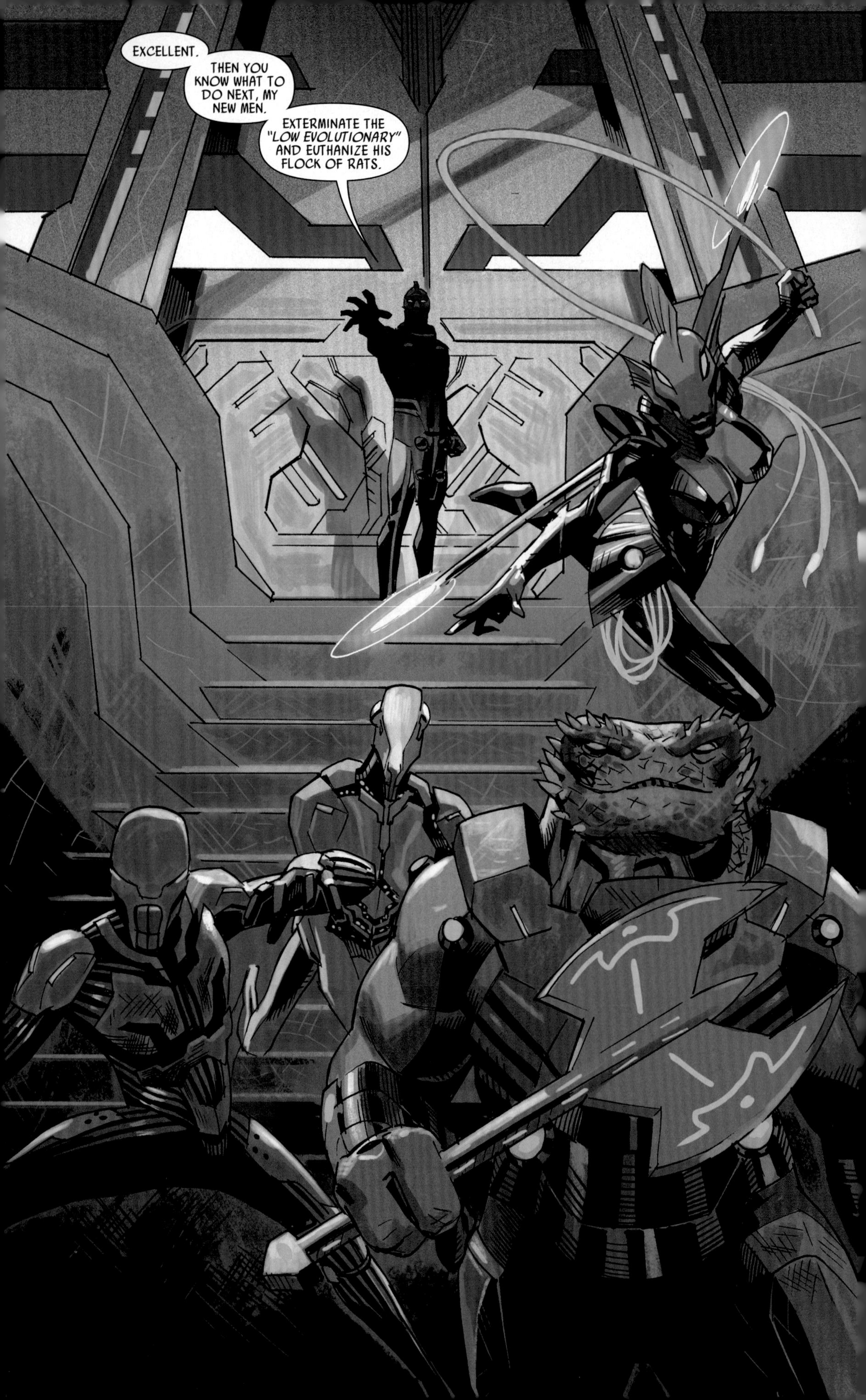
EXCELLENT.
THEN YOU KNOW WHAT TO DO NEXT, MY NEW MEN.
EXTERMINATE THE "LOW EVOLUTIONARY" AND EUTHANIZE HIS FLOCK OF RATS.

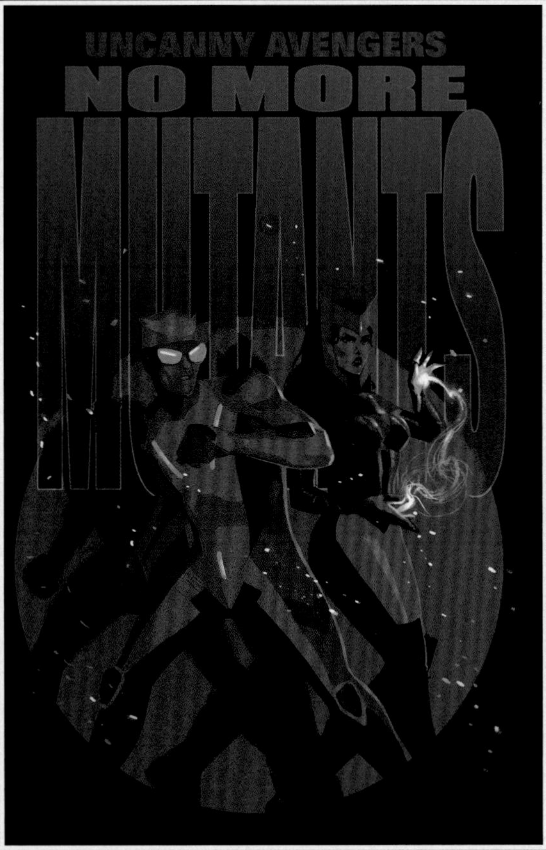
UNCANNY AVENGERS
NO MORE
MUTANTS

ISSUE #1 TEASER VARIANT
BY DANIEL ACUÑA

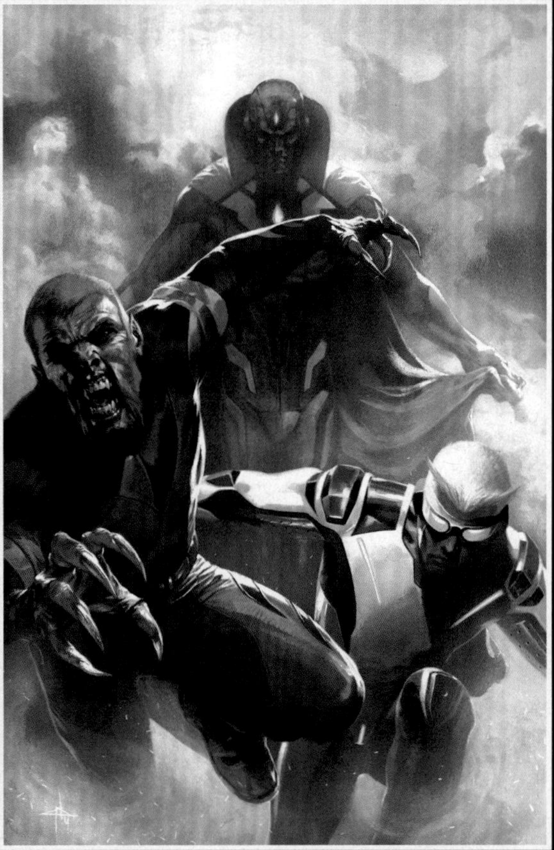

ISSUE #1 VARIANT
BY GABRIELE DELL'OTTO

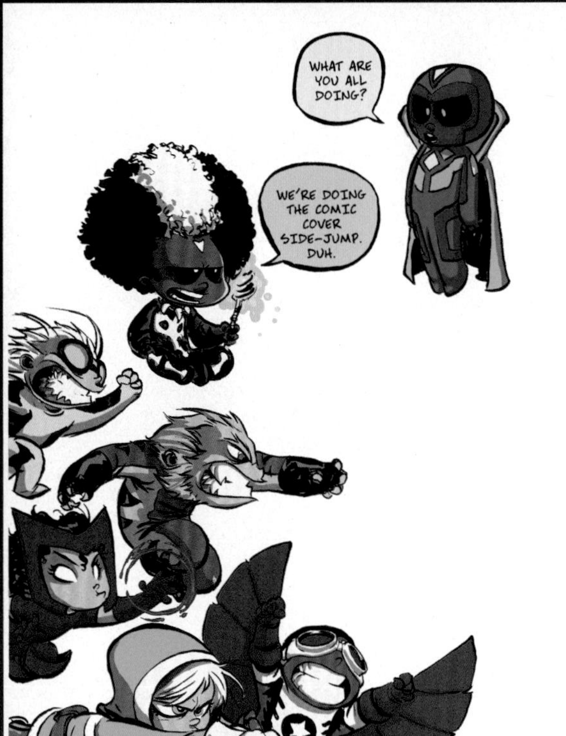
WHAT ARE YOU ALL DOING?
WE'RE DOING THE COMIC COVER SIDE-JUMP. DUH.

ISSUE #1 VARIANT
BY SKOTTIE YOUNG

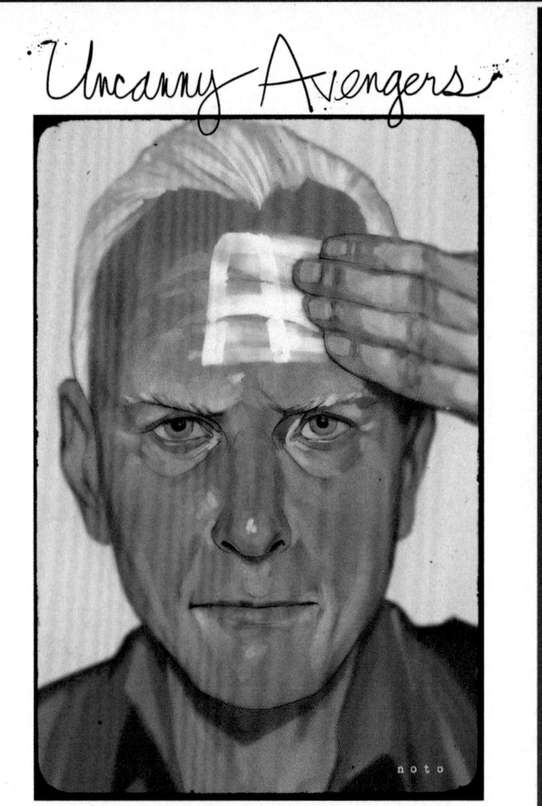
Uncanny Avengers
noto

ISSUE #2 VARIANT
BY PHIL NOTO

UNCANNY AVENGERS #4

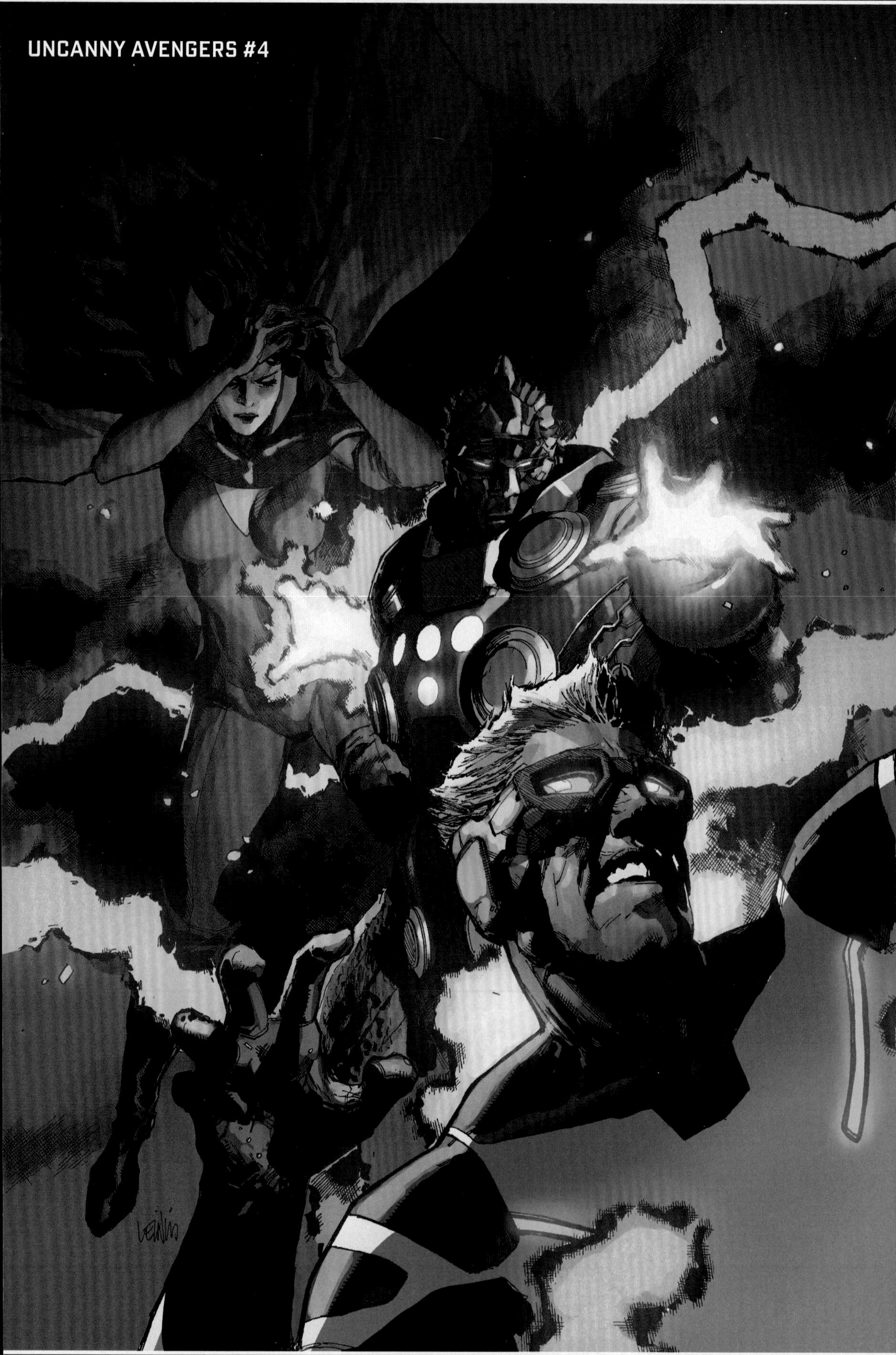

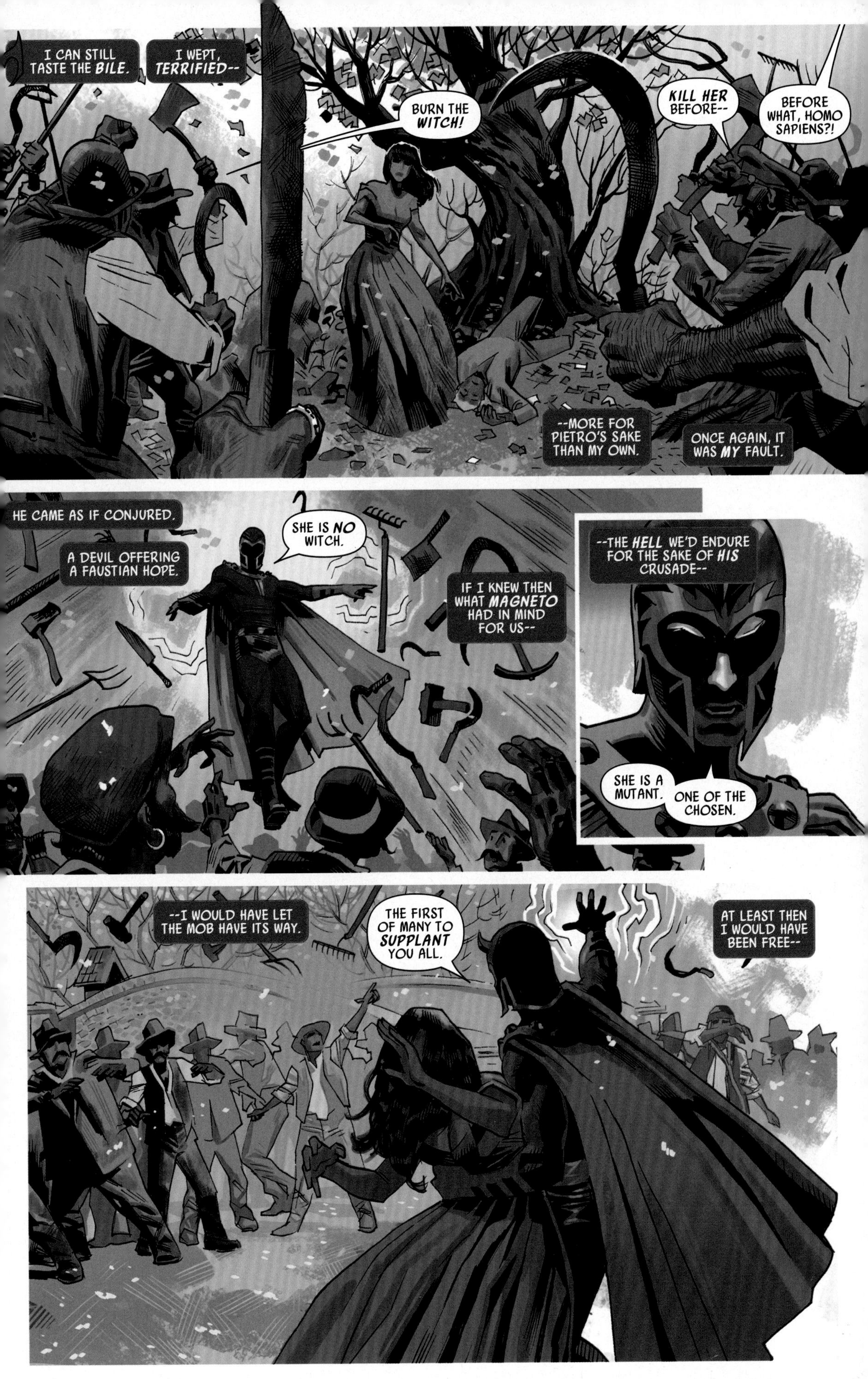

I CAN STILL TASTE THE BILE.
I WEPT, TERRIFIED--
BURN THE WITCH!
KILL HER BEFORE--
BEFORE WHAT, HOMO SAPIENS?!
--MORE FOR PIETRO'S SAKE THAN MY OWN.
ONCE AGAIN, IT WAS MY FAULT.
HE CAME AS IF CONJURED.
A DEVIL OFFERING A FAUSTIAN HOPE.
SHE IS NO WITCH.
IF I KNEW THEN WHAT MAGNETO HAD IN MIND FOR US--
--THE HELL WE'D ENDURE FOR THE SAKE OF HIS CRUSADE--
SHE IS A MUTANT.
ONE OF THE CHOSEN.
--I WOULD HAVE LET THE MOB HAVE ITS WAY.
THE FIRST OF MANY TO SUPPLANT YOU ALL.
AT LEAST THEN I WOULD HAVE BEEN FREE--

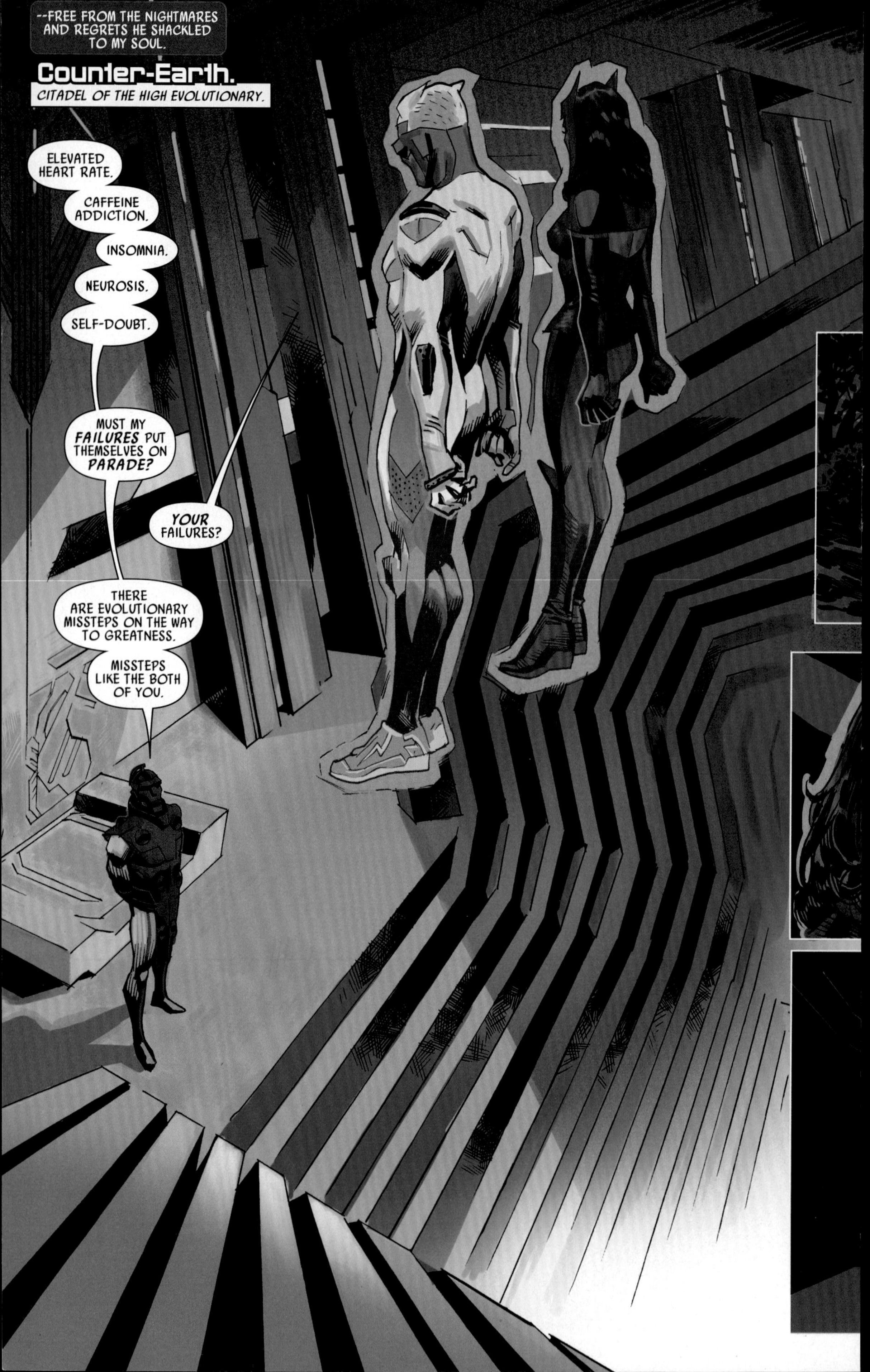
--FREE FROM THE NIGHTMARES AND REGRETS HE SHACKLED TO MY SOUL.
Counter-Earth.
CITADEL OF THE HIGH EVOLUTIONARY.
ELEVATED HEART RATE.
CAFFEINE ADDICTION.
INSOMNIA.
NEUROSIS.
SELF-DOUBT.
MUST MY FAILURES PUT THEMSELVES ON PARADE?
YOUR FAILURES?
THERE ARE EVOLUTIONARY MISSTEPS ON THE WAY TO GREATNESS.
MISSTEPS LIKE THE BOTH OF YOU.

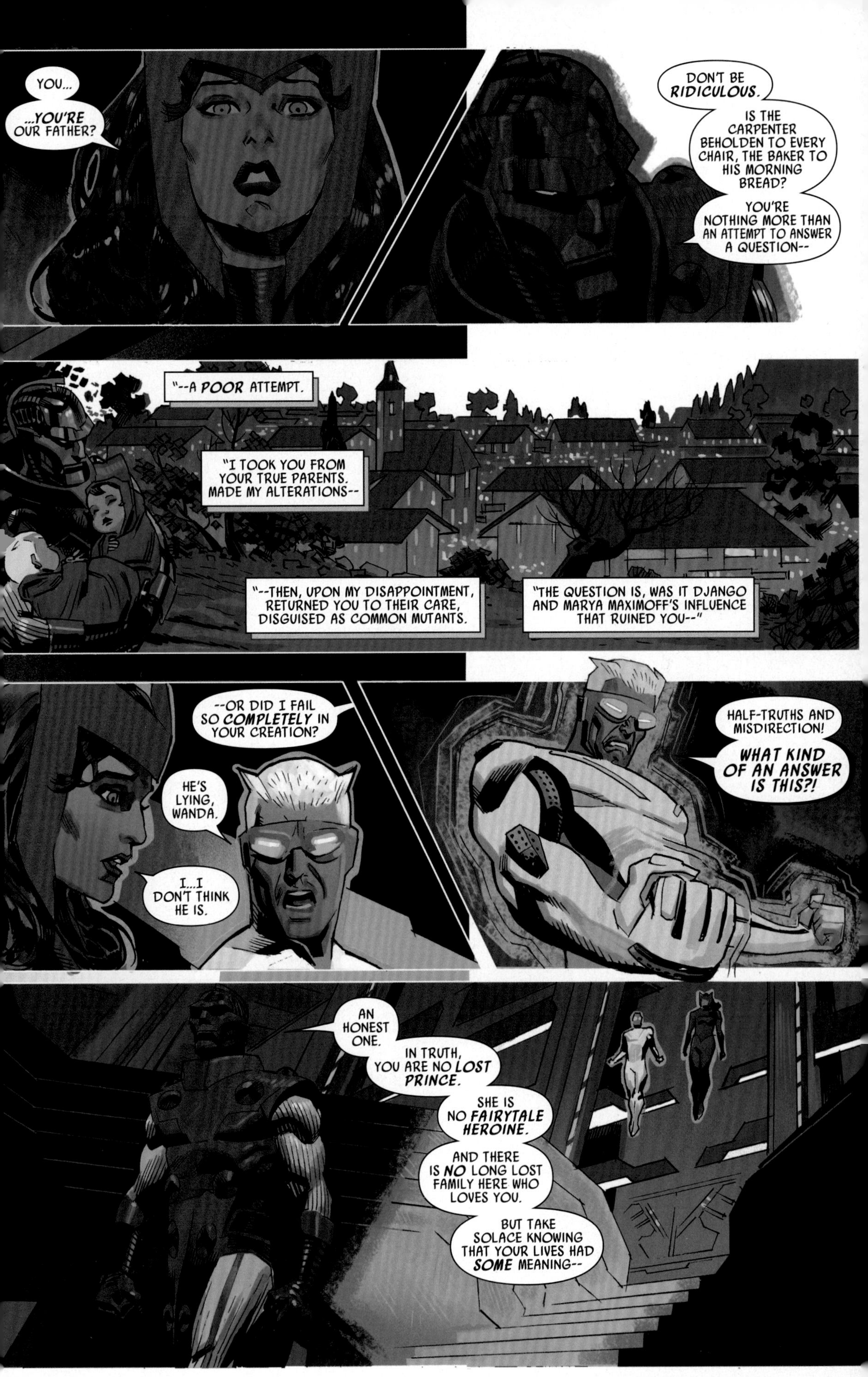
YOU...
...YOU'RE OUR FATHER?
DON'T BE RIDICULOUS.
IS THE CARPENTER BEHOLDEN TO EVERY CHAIR, THE BAKER TO HIS MORNING BREAD?
YOU'RE NOTHING MORE THAN AN ATTEMPT TO ANSWER A QUESTION--
"--A POOR ATTEMPT.
"I TOOK YOU FROM YOUR TRUE PARENTS. MADE MY ALTERATIONS--
"--THEN, UPON MY DISAPPOINTMENT, RETURNED YOU TO THEIR CARE, DISGUISED AS COMMON MUTANTS.
"THE QUESTION IS, WAS IT DJANGO AND MARYA MAXIMOFF'S INFLUENCE THAT RUINED YOU--"
--OR DID I FAIL SO COMPLETELY IN YOUR CREATION?
HE'S LYING, WANDA.
I...I DON'T THINK HE IS.
HALF-TRUTHS AND MISDIRECTION!
WHAT KIND OF AN ANSWER IS THIS?!
AN HONEST ONE.
IN TRUTH, YOU ARE NO LOST PRINCE.
SHE IS NO FAIRYTALE HEROINE.
AND THERE IS NO LONG LOST FAMILY HERE WHO LOVES YOU.
BUT TAKE SOLACE KNOWING THAT YOUR LIVES HAD SOME MEANING--

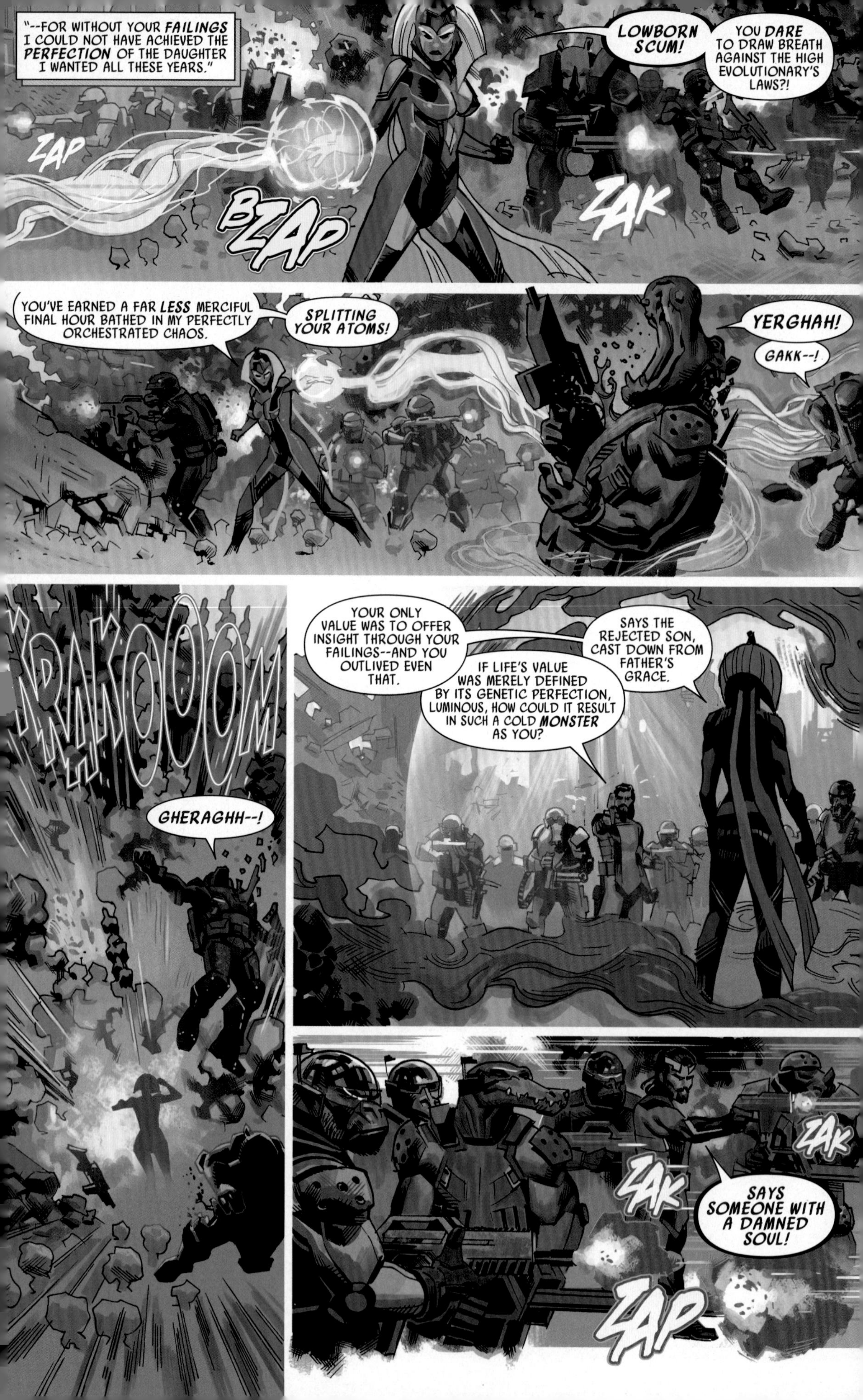
"--FOR WITHOUT YOUR FAILINGS I COULD NOT HAVE ACHIEVED THE PERFECTION OF THE DAUGHTER I WANTED ALL THESE YEARS."
LOWBORN SCUM!
YOU DARE TO DRAW BREATH AGAINST THE HIGH EVOLUTIONARY'S LAWS?!
ZAP
BZAP
ZAK
YOU'VE EARNED A FAR LESS MERCIFUL FINAL HOUR BATHED IN MY PERFECTLY ORCHESTRATED CHAOS.
SPLITTING YOUR ATOMS!
YERGHAH!
GAKK--!
KRAKOOOM
GHERAGHH--!
YOUR ONLY VALUE WAS TO OFFER INSIGHT THROUGH YOUR FAILINGS--AND YOU OUTLIVED EVEN THAT.
SAYS THE REJECTED SON, CAST DOWN FROM FATHER'S GRACE.
IF LIFE'S VALUE WAS MERELY DEFINED BY ITS GENETIC PERFECTION, LUMINOUS, HOW COULD IT RESULT IN SUCH A COLD MONSTER AS YOU?
ZAK
ZAK
SAYS SOMEONE WITH A DAMNED SOUL!
ZAP

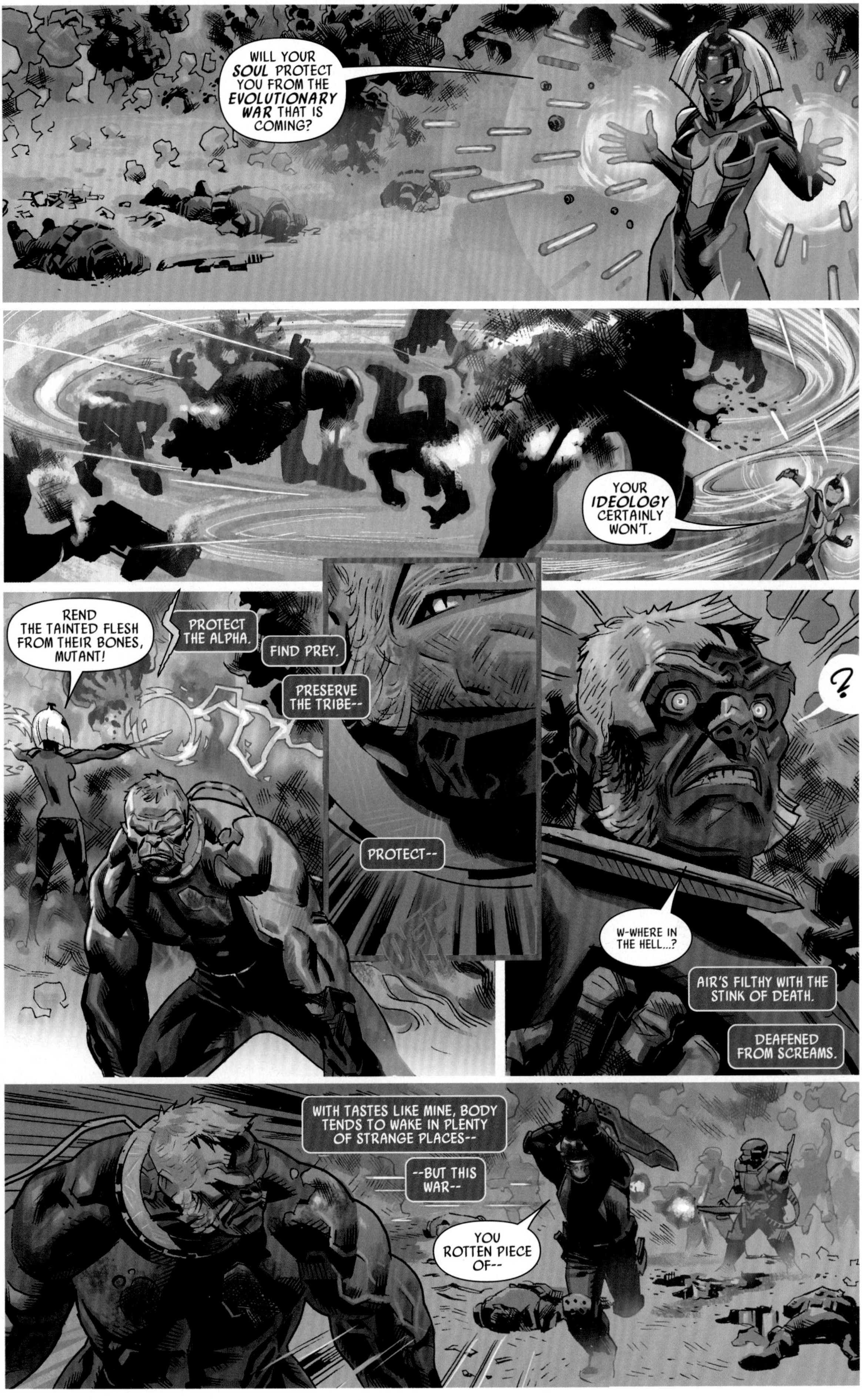
WILL YOUR SOUL PROTECT YOU FROM THE EVOLUTIONARY WAR THAT IS COMING?
YOUR IDEOLOGY CERTAINLY WON'T.
REND THE TAINTED FLESH FROM THEIR BONES, MUTANT!
PROTECT THE ALPHA.
FIND PREY.
PRESERVE THE TRIBE--
PROTECT--
?
W-WHERE IN THE HELL...?
AIR'S FILTHY WITH THE STINK OF DEATH.
DEAFENED FROM SCREAMS.
WITH TASTES LIKE MINE, BODY TENDS TO WAKE IN PLENTY OF STRANGE PLACES--
--BUT THIS WAR--
YOU ROTTEN PIECE OF--

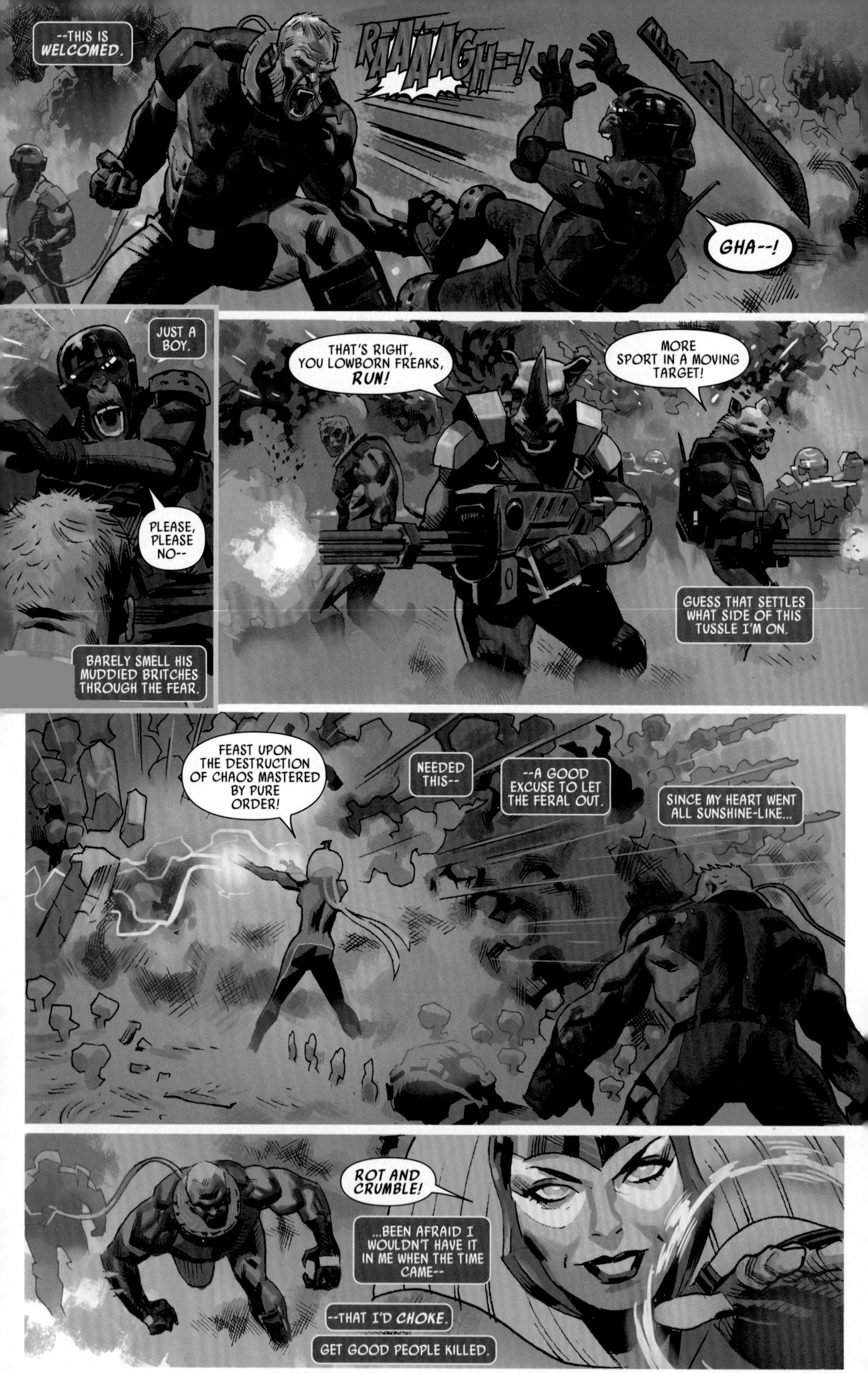
--THIS IS WELCOMED.
RAAAAGH--!
GHA--!
JUST A BOY.
PLEASE, PLEASE NO--
BARELY SMELL HIS MUDDIED BRITCHES THROUGH THE FEAR.
THAT'S RIGHT, YOU LOWBORN FREAKS, RUN!
MORE SPORT IN A MOVING TARGET!
GUESS THAT SETTLES WHAT SIDE OF THIS TUSSLE I'M ON.
FEAST UPON THE DESTRUCTION OF CHAOS MASTERED BY PURE ORDER!
NEEDED THIS--
--A GOOD EXCUSE TO LET THE FERAL OUT.
SINCE MY HEART WENT ALL SUNSHINE-LIKE...
ROT AND CRUMBLE!
...BEEN AFRAID I WOULDN'T HAVE IT IN ME WHEN THE TIME CAME--
--THAT I'D CHOKE.
GET GOOD PEOPLE KILLED.

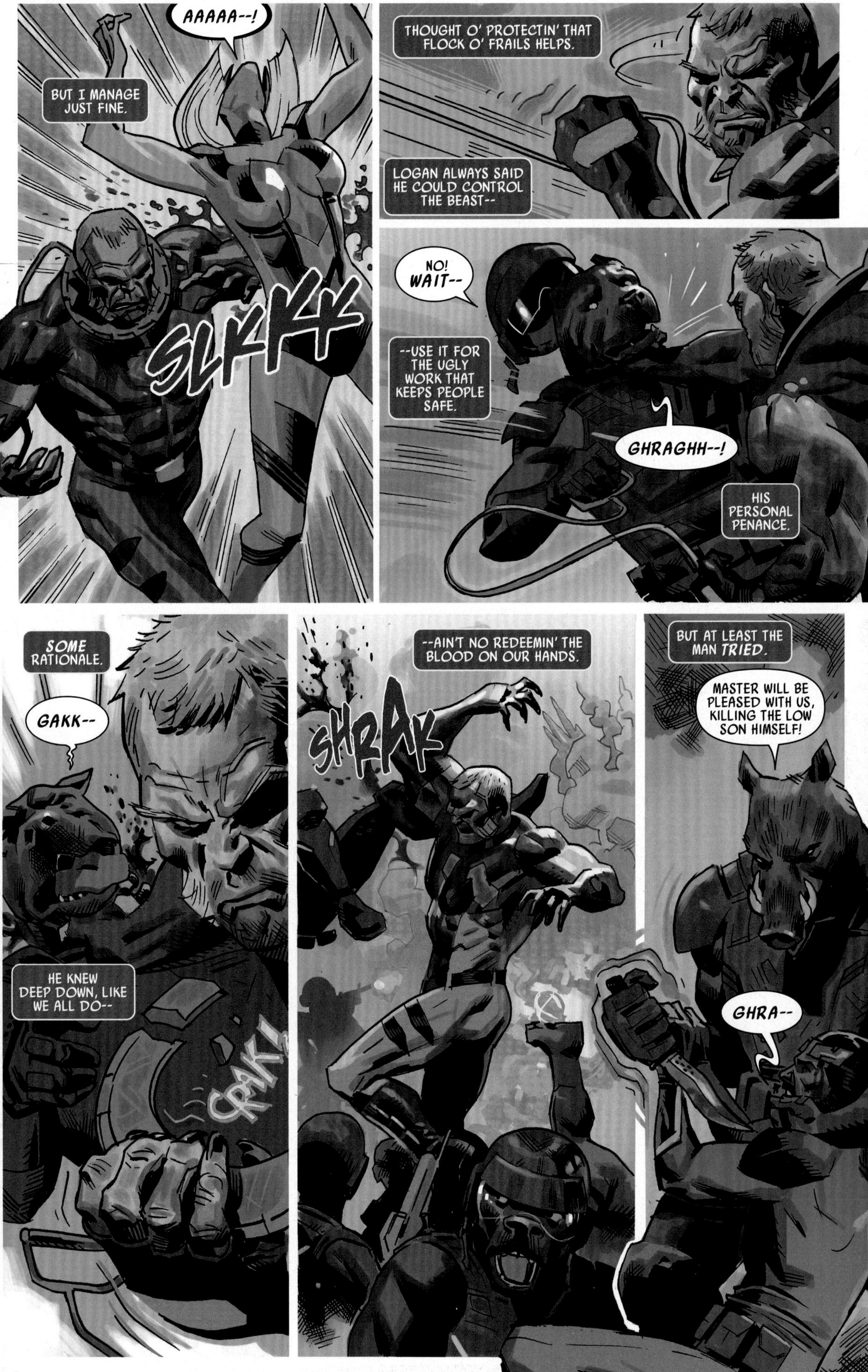
AAAAA--!
BUT I MANAGE JUST FINE.
SLKKK
THOUGHT O' PROTECTIN' THAT FLOCK O' FRAILS HELPS.
LOGAN ALWAYS SAID HE COULD CONTROL THE BEAST--
NO! WAIT--
--USE IT FOR THE UGLY WORK THAT KEEPS PEOPLE SAFE.
GHRAGHH--!
HIS PERSONAL PENANCE.
SOME RATIONALE.
GAKK--
HE KNEW DEEP DOWN, LIKE WE ALL DO--
--AIN'T NO REDEEMIN' THE BLOOD ON OUR HANDS.
SHRAK
BUT AT LEAST THE MAN TRIED.
MASTER WILL BE PLEASED WITH US, KILLING THE LOW SON HIMSELF!
GHRA--

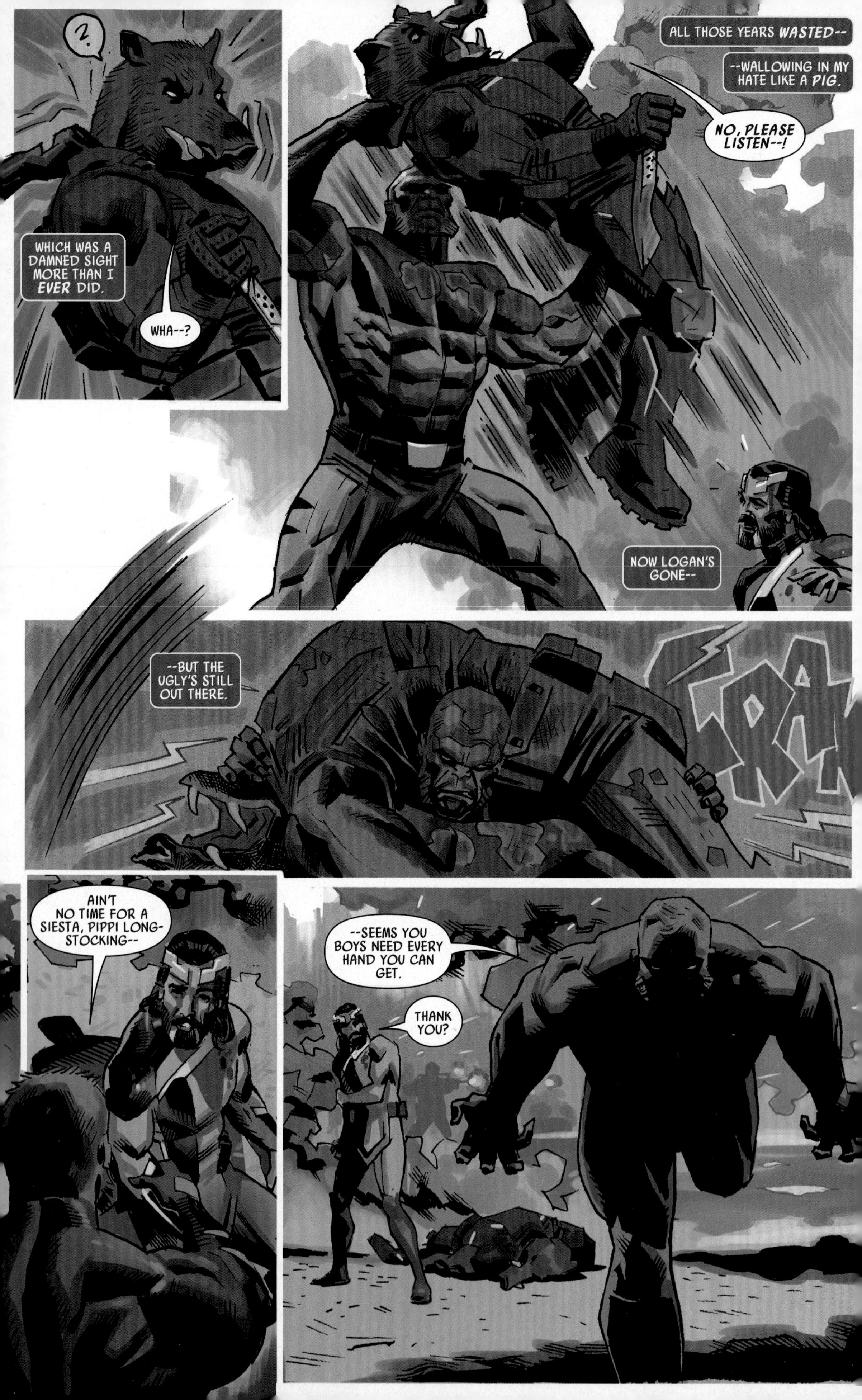
?
WHICH WAS A DAMNED SIGHT MORE THAN I EVER DID.
WHA--?
ALL THOSE YEARS WASTED--
--WALLOWING IN MY HATE LIKE A PIG.
NO, PLEASE LISTEN--!
NOW LOGAN'S GONE--
--BUT THE UGLY'S STILL OUT THERE.
AIN'T NO TIME FOR A SIESTA, PIPPI LONG-STOCKING--
--SEEMS YOU BOYS NEED EVERY HAND YOU CAN GET.
THANK YOU?

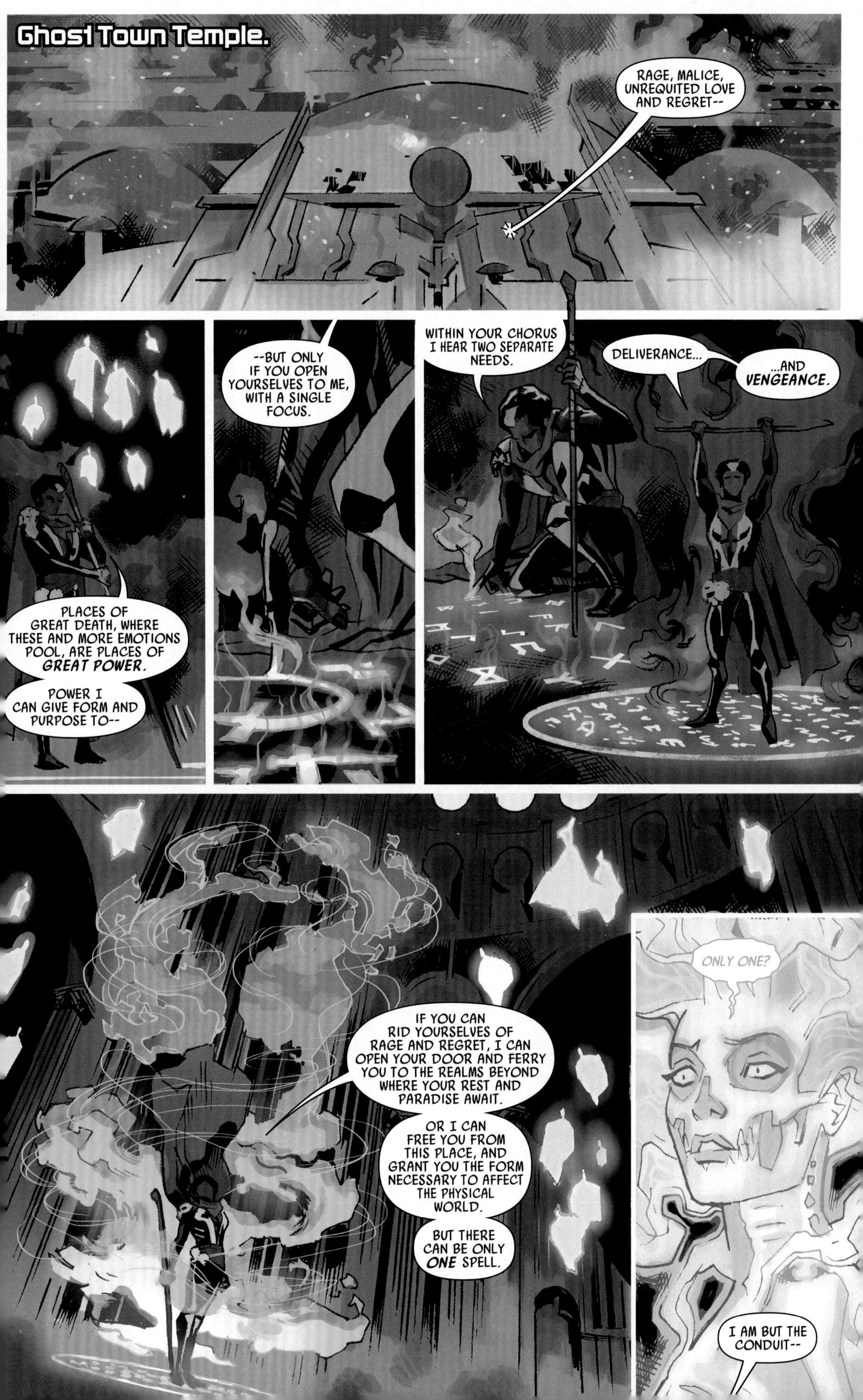
Ghost Town Temple.
RAGE, MALICE, UNREQUITED LOVE AND REGRET--
PLACES OF GREAT DEATH, WHERE THESE AND MORE EMOTIONS POOL, ARE PLACES OF GREAT POWER.
POWER I CAN GIVE FORM AND PURPOSE TO--
--BUT ONLY IF YOU OPEN YOURSELVES TO ME, WITH A SINGLE FOCUS.
WITHIN YOUR CHORUS I HEAR TWO SEPARATE NEEDS.
DELIVERANCE...
...AND VENGEANCE.
IF YOU CAN RID YOURSELVES OF RAGE AND REGRET, I CAN OPEN YOUR DOOR AND FERRY YOU TO THE REALMS BEYOND WHERE YOUR REST AND PARADISE AWAIT.
OR I CAN FREE YOU FROM THIS PLACE, AND GRANT YOU THE FORM NECESSARY TO AFFECT THE PHYSICAL WORLD.
BUT THERE CAN BE ONLY ONE SPELL.
ONLY ONE?
I AM BUT THE CONDUIT--

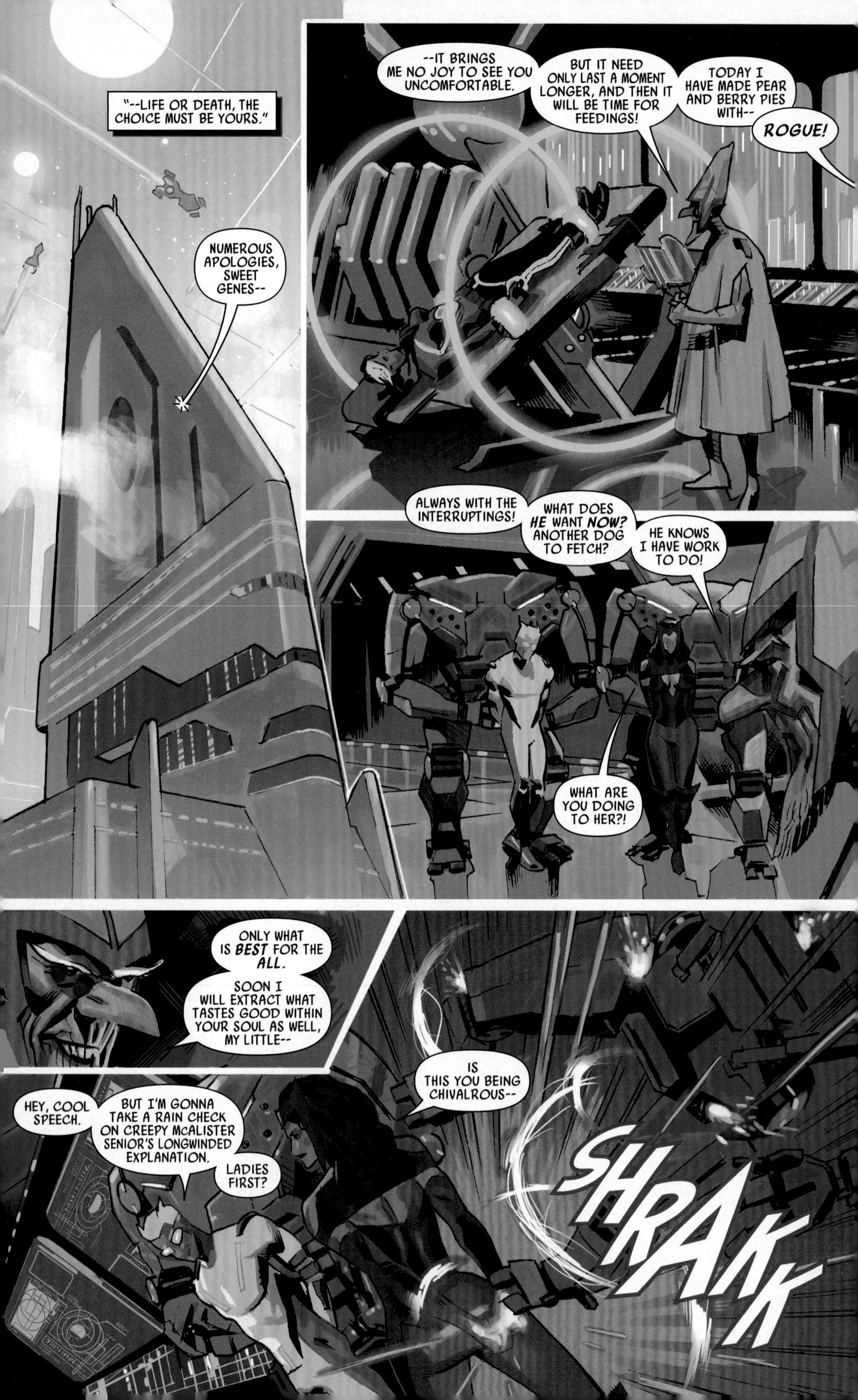
"--LIFE OR DEATH, THE CHOICE MUST BE YOURS."
NUMEROUS APOLOGIES, SWEET GENES--
--IT BRINGS ME NO JOY TO SEE YOU UNCOMFORTABLE.
BUT IT NEED ONLY LAST A MOMENT LONGER, AND THEN IT WILL BE TIME FOR FEEDINGS!
TODAY I HAVE MADE PEAR AND BERRY PIES WITH--
ROGUE!
ALWAYS WITH THE INTERRUPTINGS!
WHAT DOES HE WANT NOW? ANOTHER DOG TO FETCH?
HE KNOWS I HAVE WORK TO DO!
WHAT ARE YOU DOING TO HER?!
ONLY WHAT IS BEST FOR THE ALL.
SOON I WILL EXTRACT WHAT TASTES GOOD WITHIN YOUR SOUL AS WELL, MY LITTLE--
HEY, COOL SPEECH.
BUT I'M GONNA TAKE A RAIN CHECK ON CREEPY McALISTER SENIOR'S LONGWINDED EXPLANATION.
LADIES FIRST?
IS THIS YOU BEING CHIVALROUS--
SHRAKK

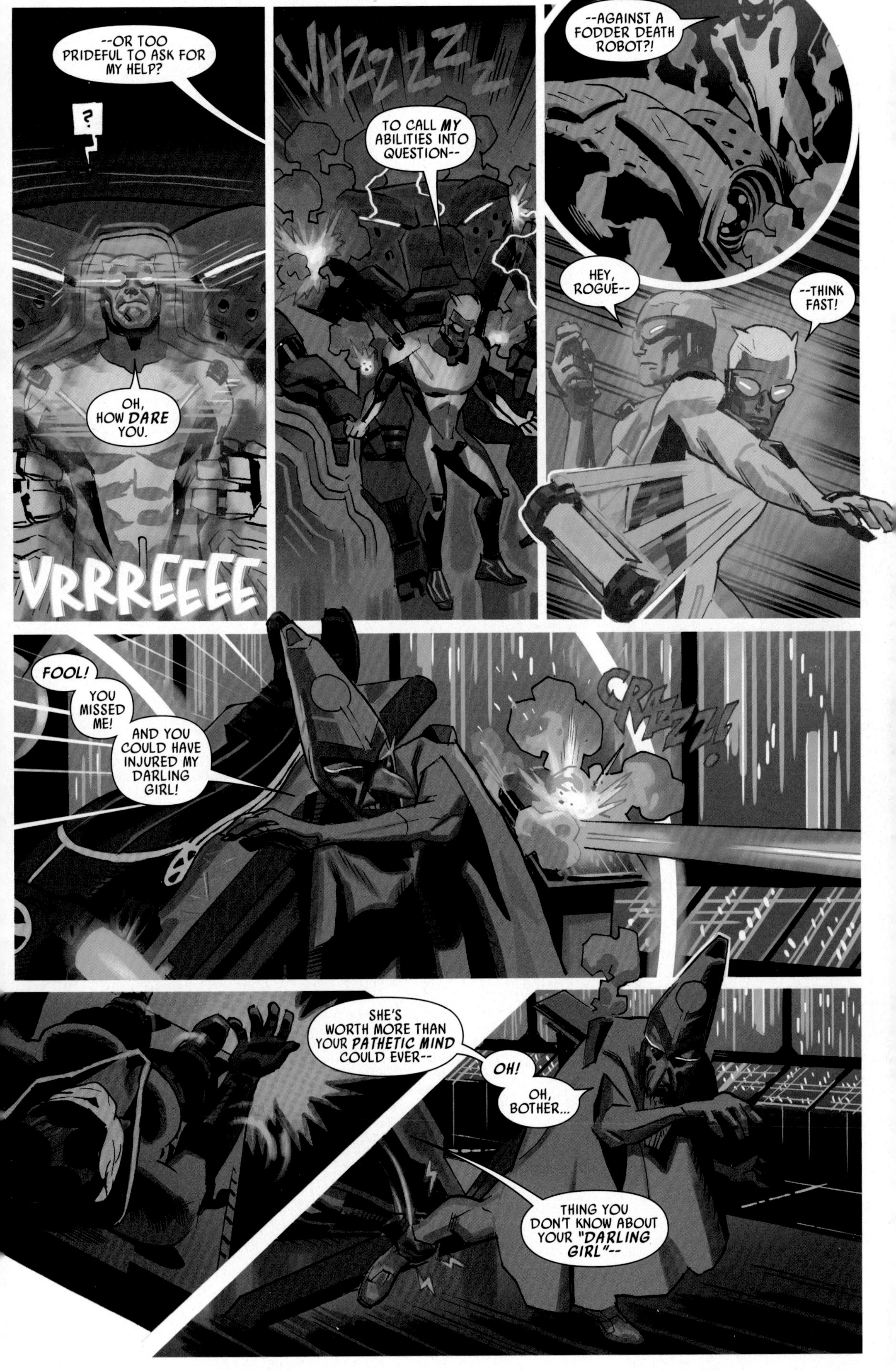
--OR TOO PRIDEFUL TO ASK FOR MY HELP?
?
OH, HOW DARE YOU.
VRRREEEE
WHZZZZZ
TO CALL MY ABILITIES INTO QUESTION--
--AGAINST A FODDER DEATH ROBOT?!
HEY, ROGUE--
--THINK FAST!
FOOL!
YOU MISSED ME!
AND YOU COULD HAVE INJURED MY DARLING GIRL!
SHE'S WORTH MORE THAN YOUR PATHETIC MIND COULD EVER--
OH!
OH, BOTHER...
THING YOU DON'T KNOW ABOUT YOUR "DARLING GIRL"--

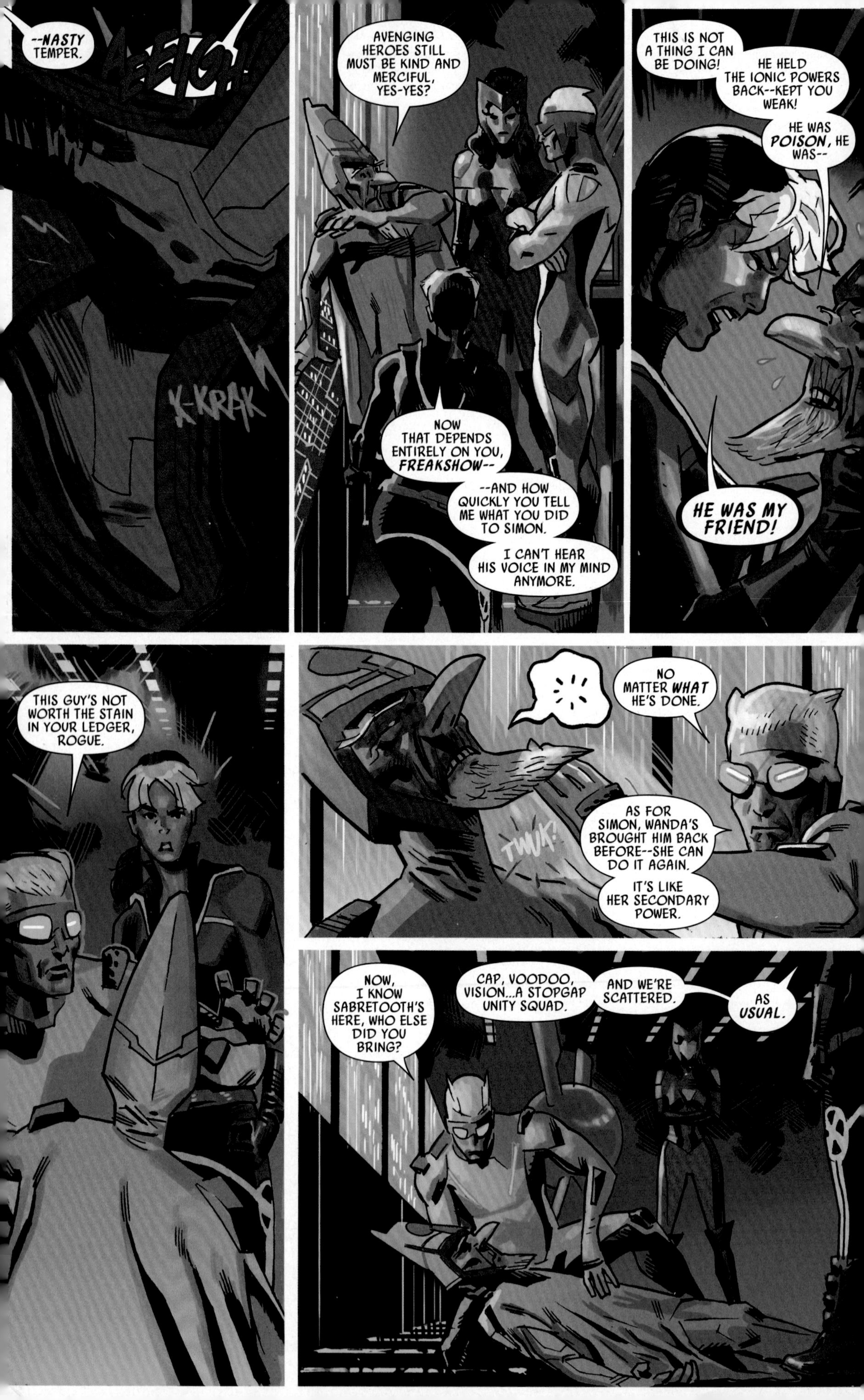
--NASTY TEMPER.
AEEIGH!
K-KRAK
AVENGING HEROES STILL MUST BE KIND AND MERCIFUL, YES-YES?
NOW THAT DEPENDS ENTIRELY ON YOU, FREAKSHOW--
--AND HOW QUICKLY YOU TELL ME WHAT YOU DID TO SIMON.
I CAN'T HEAR HIS VOICE IN MY MIND ANYMORE.
THIS IS NOT A THING I CAN BE DOING!
HE HELD THE IONIC POWERS BACK--KEPT YOU WEAK!
HE WAS POISON, HE WAS--
HE WAS MY FRIEND!
THIS GUY'S NOT WORTH THE STAIN IN YOUR LEDGER, ROGUE.
NO MATTER WHAT HE'S DONE.
TWUK!
AS FOR SIMON, WANDA'S BROUGHT HIM BACK BEFORE--SHE CAN DO IT AGAIN.
IT'S LIKE HER SECONDARY POWER.
NOW, I KNOW SABRETOOTH'S HERE, WHO ELSE DID YOU BRING?
CAP, VOODOO, VISION...A STOPGAP UNITY SQUAD.
AND WE'RE SCATTERED.
AS USUAL.

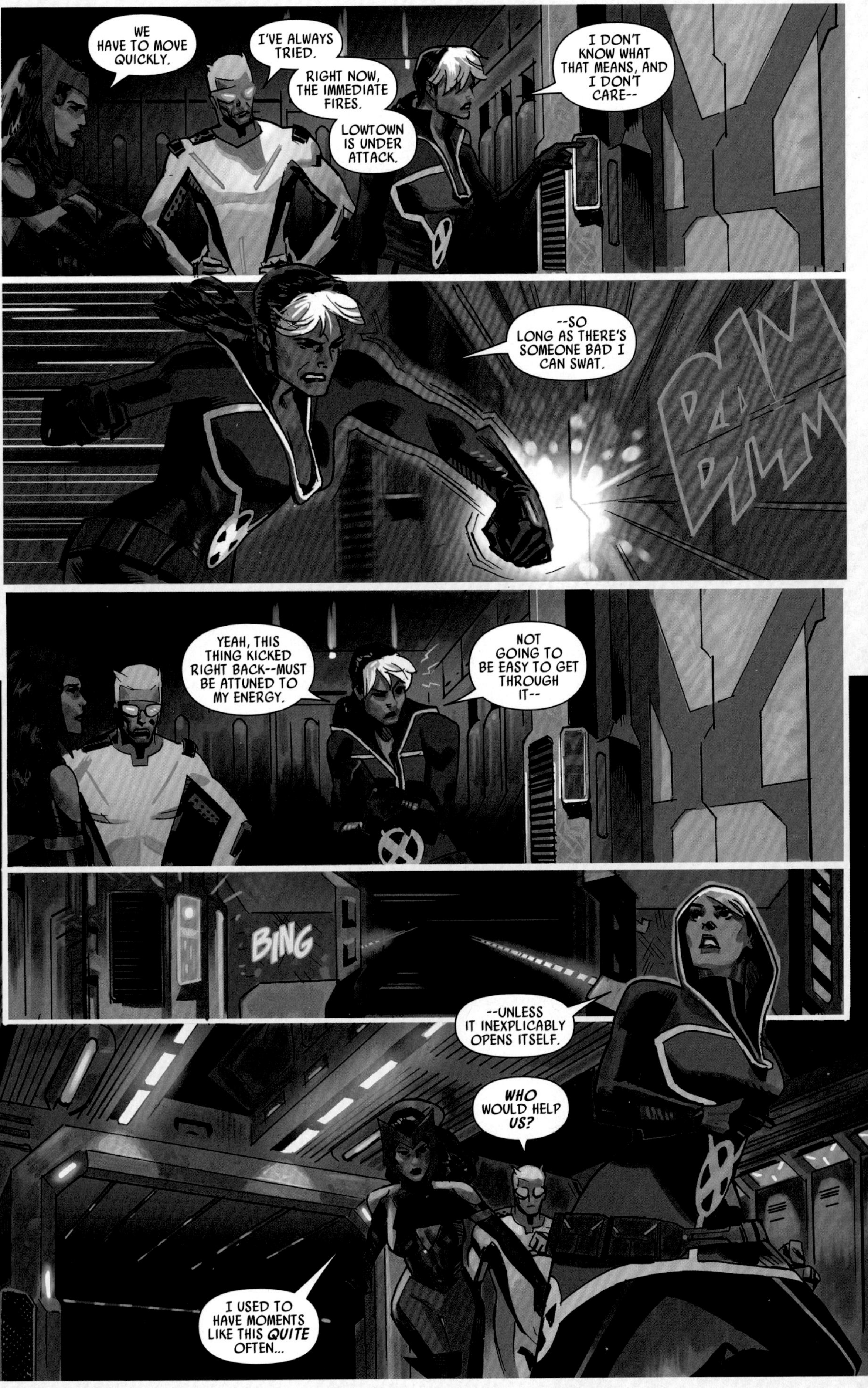
WE HAVE TO MOVE QUICKLY.
I'VE ALWAYS TRIED.
RIGHT NOW, THE IMMEDIATE FIRES.
LOWTOWN IS UNDER ATTACK.
I DON'T KNOW WHAT THAT MEANS, AND I DON'T CARE--
--SO LONG AS THERE'S SOMEONE BAD I CAN SWAT.
YEAH, THIS THING KICKED RIGHT BACK--MUST BE ATTUNED TO MY ENERGY.
NOT GOING TO BE EASY TO GET THROUGH IT--
BING
--UNLESS IT INEXPLICABLY OPENS ITSELF.
WHO WOULD HELP *US?*
I USED TO HAVE MOMENTS LIKE THIS *QUITE* OFTEN...

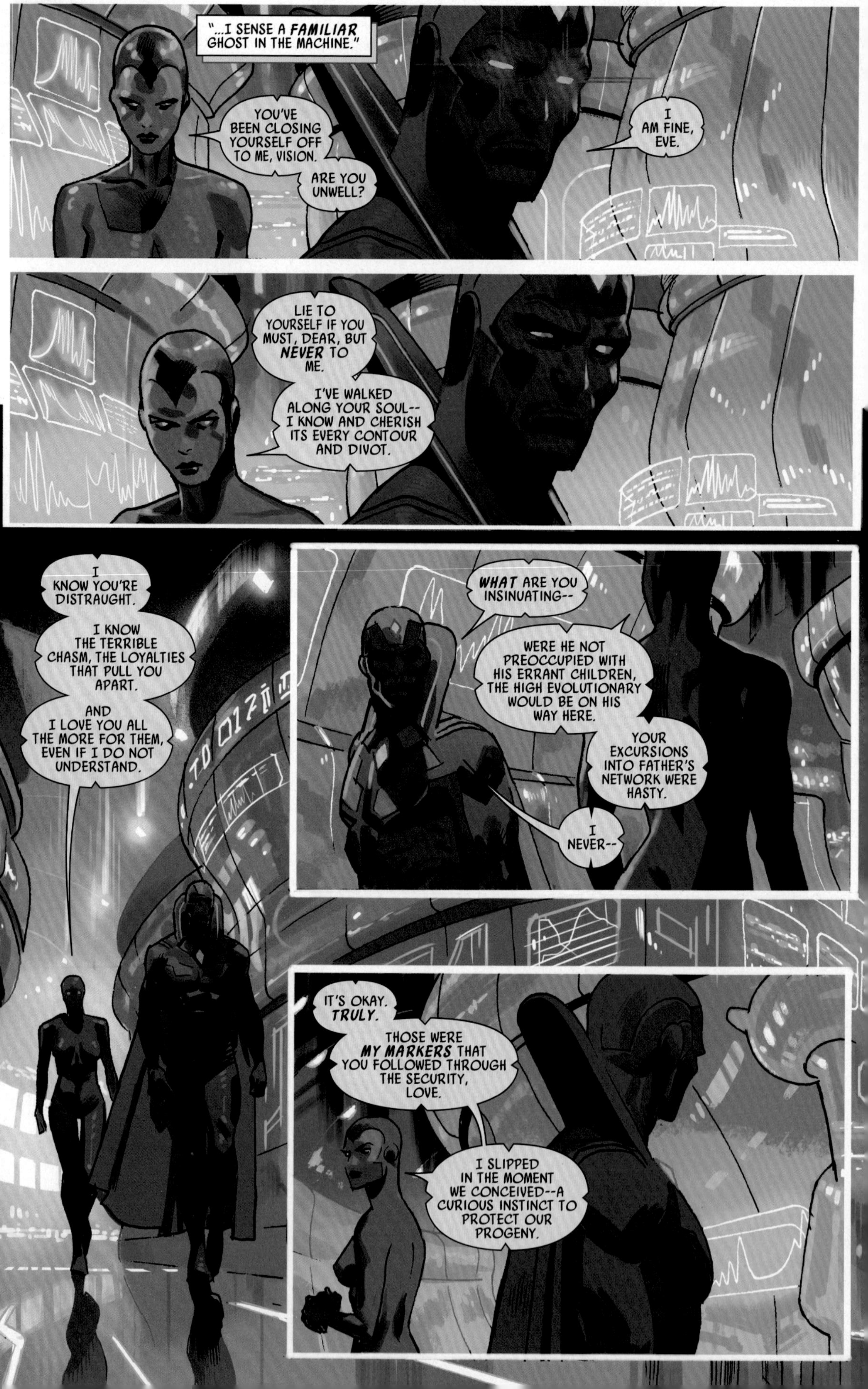
"...I SENSE A *FAMILIAR* GHOST IN THE MACHINE."
YOU'VE BEEN CLOSING YOURSELF OFF TO ME, VISION.
ARE YOU UNWELL?
I AM FINE, EVE.
LIE TO YOURSELF IF YOU MUST, DEAR, BUT *NEVER* TO ME.
I'VE WALKED ALONG YOUR SOUL-- I KNOW AND CHERISH ITS EVERY CONTOUR AND DIVOT.
I KNOW YOU'RE DISTRAUGHT.
I KNOW THE TERRIBLE CHASM, THE LOYALTIES THAT PULL YOU APART.
AND I LOVE YOU ALL THE MORE FOR THEM, EVEN IF I DO NOT UNDERSTAND.
WHAT ARE YOU INSINUATING--
WERE HE NOT PREOCCUPIED WITH HIS ERRANT CHILDREN, THE HIGH EVOLUTIONARY WOULD BE ON HIS WAY HERE.
YOUR EXCURSIONS INTO FATHER'S NETWORK WERE HASTY.
I NEVER--
IT'S OKAY. *TRULY.*
THOSE WERE *MY MARKERS* THAT YOU FOLLOWED THROUGH THE SECURITY, LOVE.
I SLIPPED IN THE MOMENT WE CONCEIVED--A CURIOUS INSTINCT TO PROTECT OUR PROGENY.

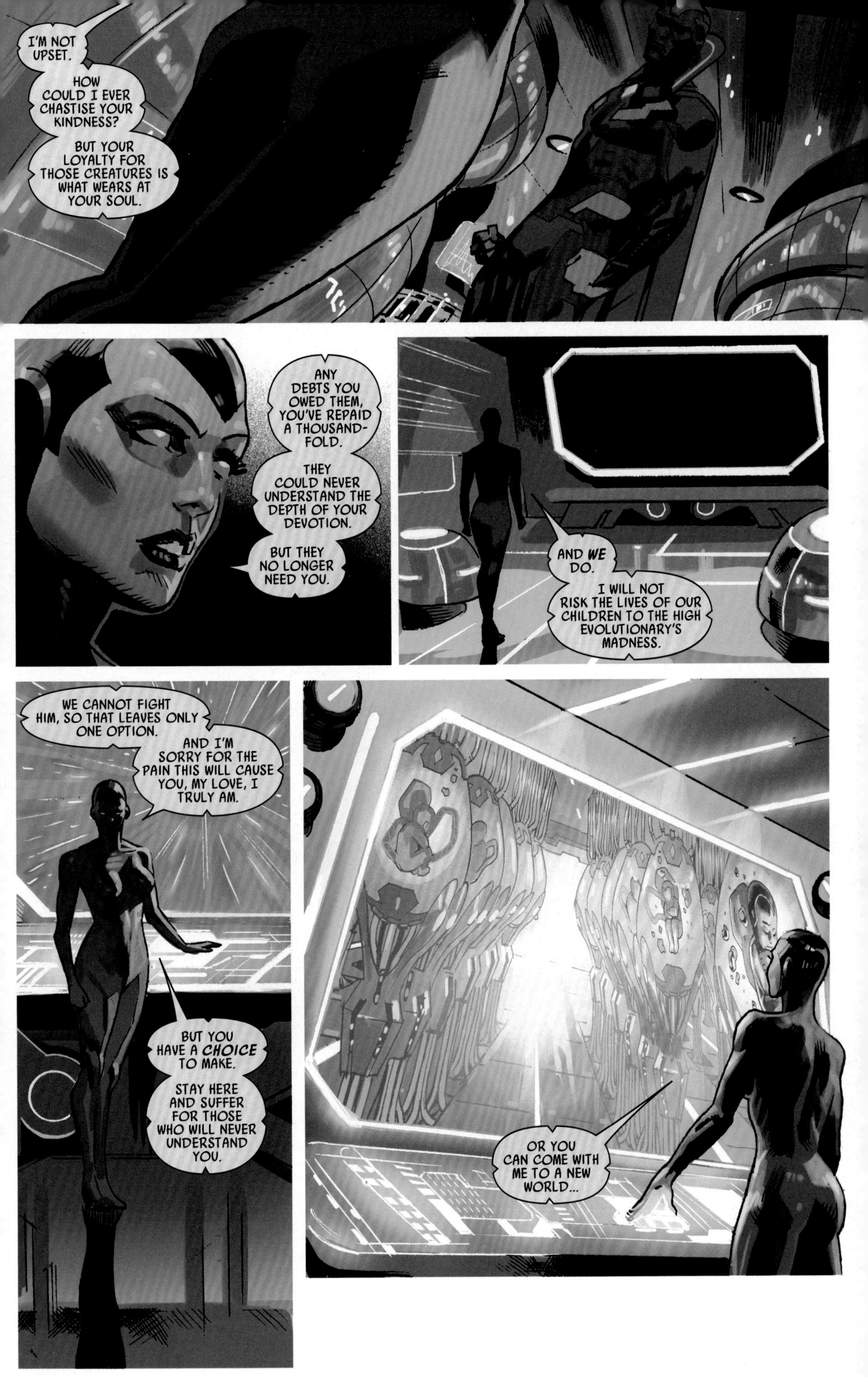

I'M NOT UPSET.
HOW COULD I EVER CHASTISE YOUR KINDNESS?
BUT YOUR LOYALTY FOR THOSE CREATURES IS WHAT WEARS AT YOUR SOUL.
ANY DEBTS YOU OWED THEM, YOU'VE REPAID A THOUSAND-FOLD.
THEY COULD NEVER UNDERSTAND THE DEPTH OF YOUR DEVOTION.
BUT THEY NO LONGER NEED YOU.
AND WE DO.
I WILL NOT RISK THE LIVES OF OUR CHILDREN TO THE HIGH EVOLUTIONARY'S MADNESS.
WE CANNOT FIGHT HIM, SO THAT LEAVES ONLY ONE OPTION.
AND I'M SORRY FOR THE PAIN THIS WILL CAUSE YOU, MY LOVE, I TRULY AM.
BUT YOU HAVE A CHOICE TO MAKE.
STAY HERE AND SUFFER FOR THOSE WHO WILL NEVER UNDERSTAND YOU.
OR YOU CAN COME WITH ME TO A NEW WORLD...

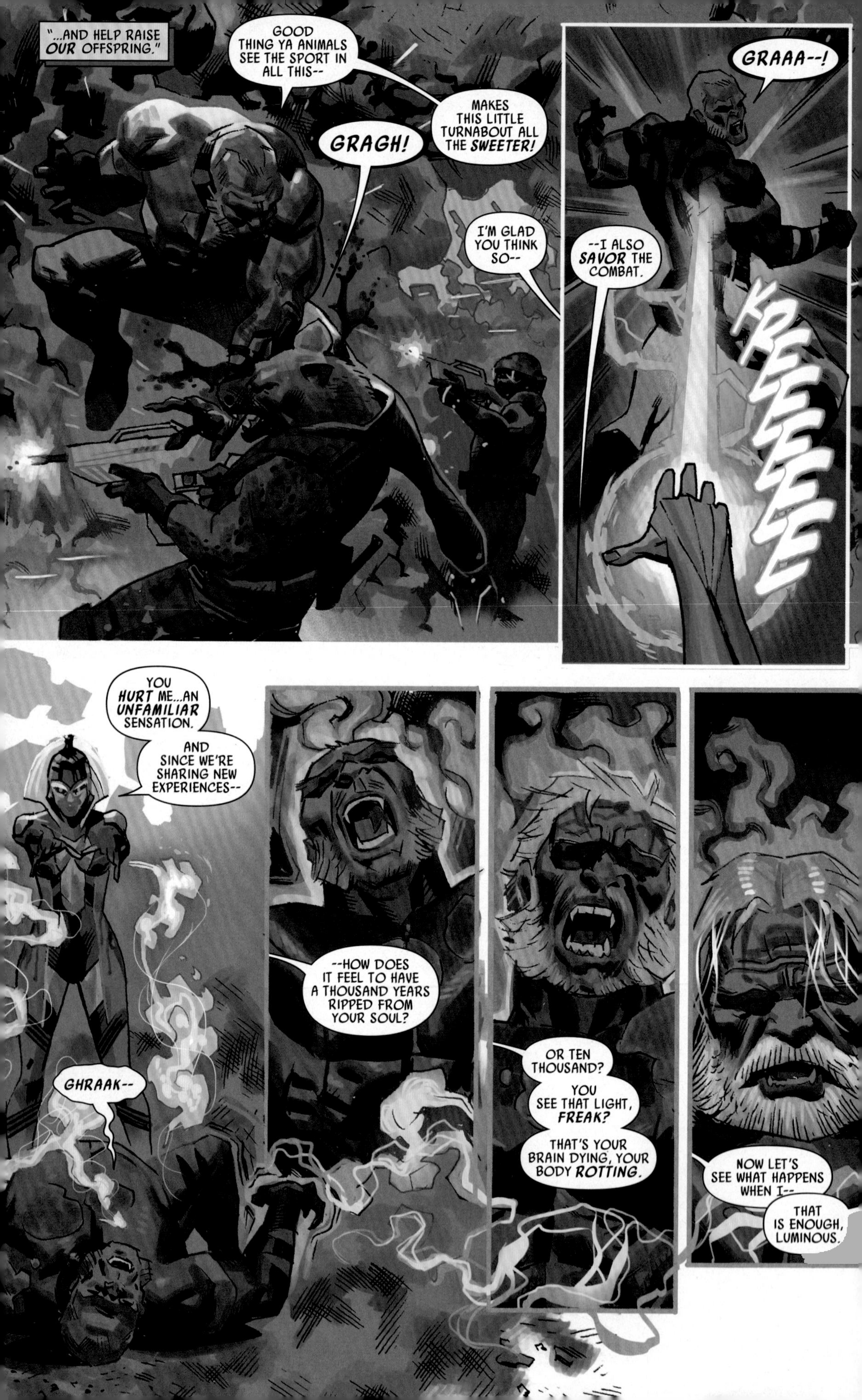
"...AND HELP RAISE OUR OFFSPRING."
GOOD THING YA ANIMALS SEE THE SPORT IN ALL THIS--
MAKES THIS LITTLE TURNABOUT ALL THE SWEETER!
GRAGH!
I'M GLAD YOU THINK SO--
--I ALSO SAVOR THE COMBAT.
GRAAA--!
KREEEEEE
YOU HURT ME...AN UNFAMILIAR SENSATION.
AND SINCE WE'RE SHARING NEW EXPERIENCES--
--HOW DOES IT FEEL TO HAVE A THOUSAND YEARS RIPPED FROM YOUR SOUL?
GHRAAK--
OR TEN THOUSAND?
YOU SEE THAT LIGHT, FREAK?
THAT'S YOUR BRAIN DYING, YOUR BODY ROTTING.
NOW LET'S SEE WHAT HAPPENS WHEN I--
THAT IS ENOUGH, LUMINOUS.

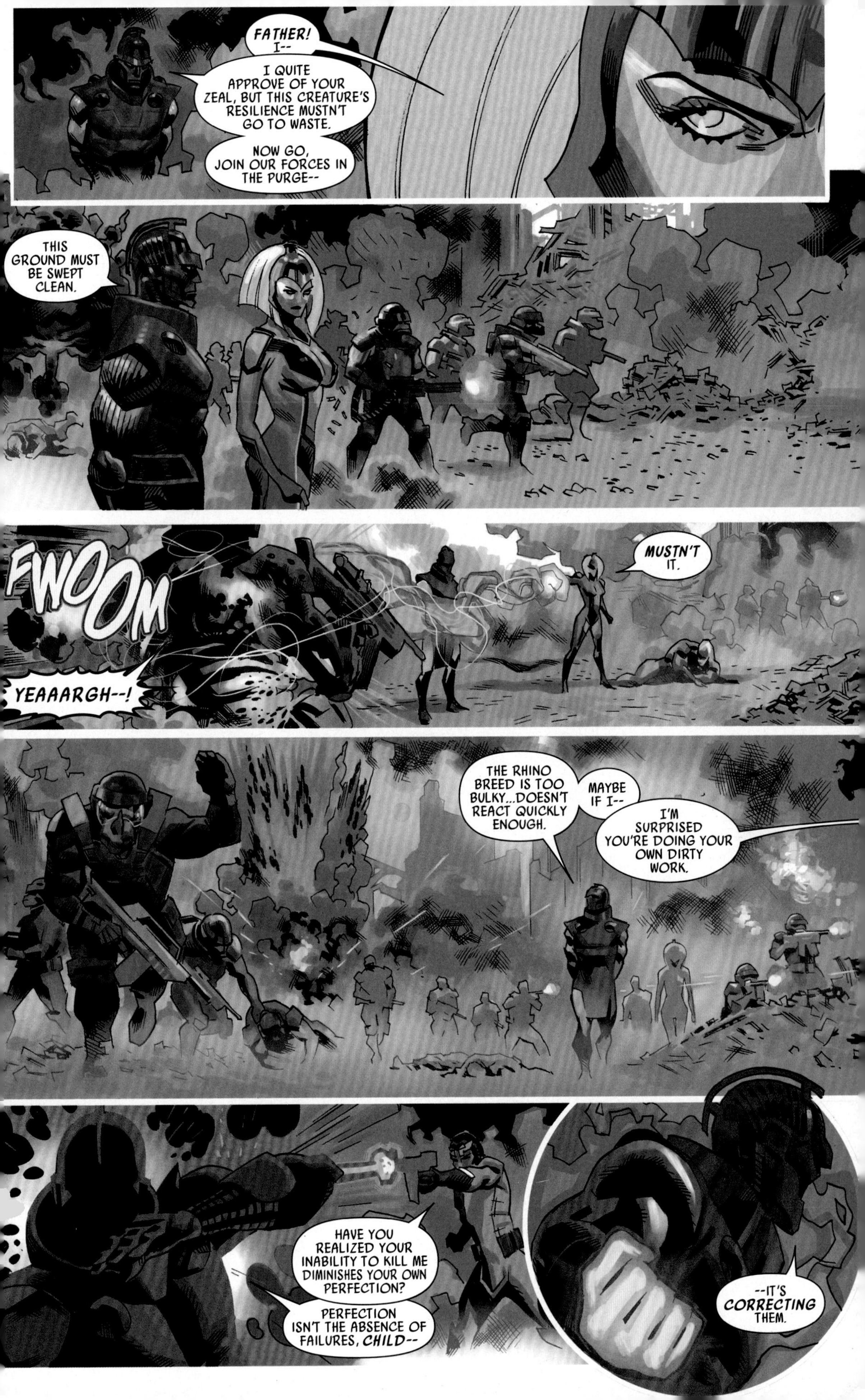
FATHER! I--
I QUITE APPROVE OF YOUR ZEAL, BUT THIS CREATURE'S RESILIENCE MUSTN'T GO TO WASTE.
NOW GO, JOIN OUR FORCES IN THE PURGE--
THIS GROUND MUST BE SWEPT CLEAN.
FWOOM
YEAAARGH--!
MUSTN'T IT.
THE RHINO BREED IS TOO BULKY...DOESN'T REACT QUICKLY ENOUGH.
MAYBE IF I--
I'M SURPRISED YOU'RE DOING YOUR OWN DIRTY WORK.
HAVE YOU REALIZED YOUR INABILITY TO KILL ME DIMINISHES YOUR OWN PERFECTION?
PERFECTION ISN'T THE ABSENCE OF FAILURES, CHILD--
--IT'S CORRECTING THEM.

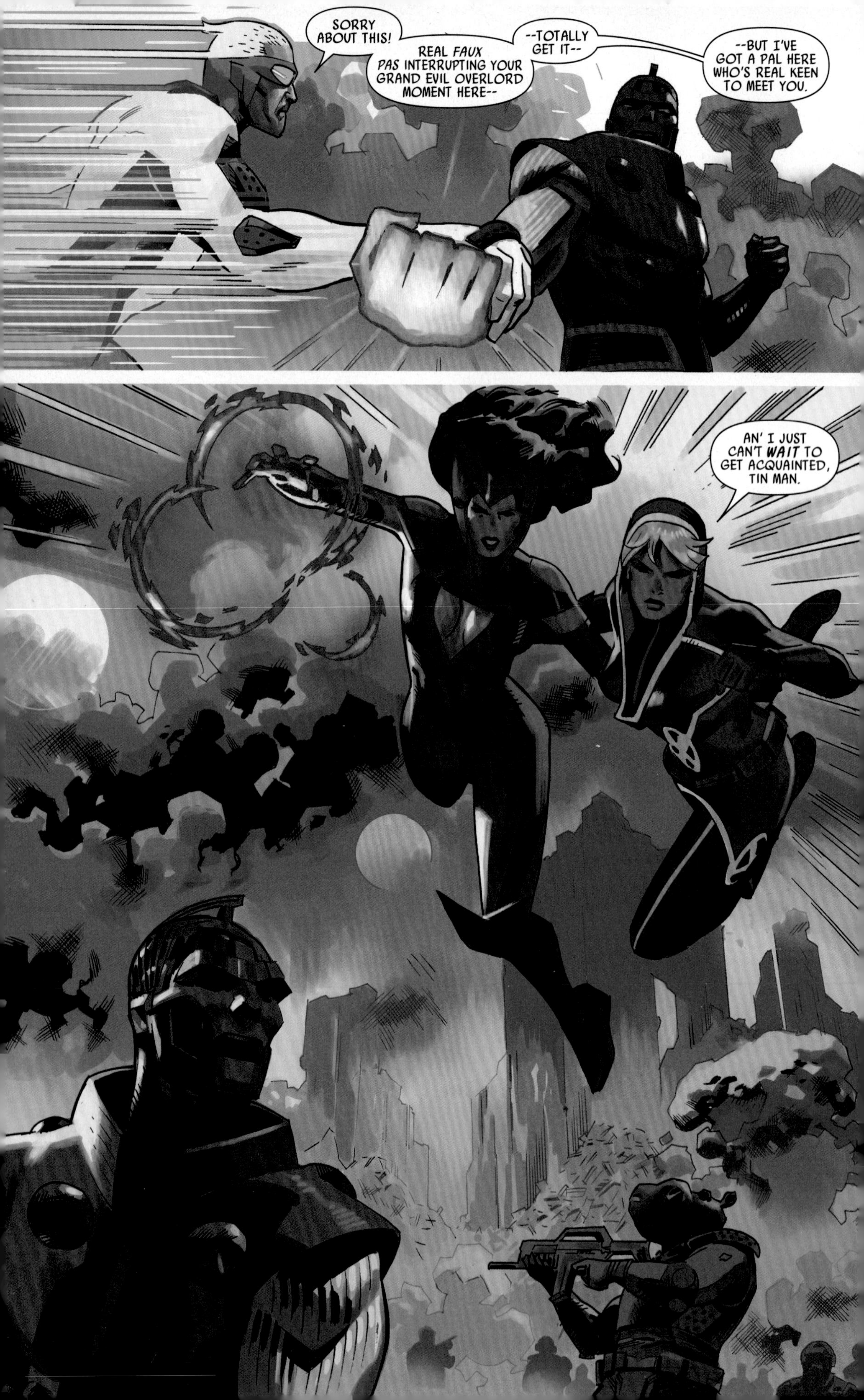
SORRY ABOUT THIS!
REAL *FAUX PAS* INTERRUPTING YOUR GRAND EVIL OVERLORD MOMENT HERE--
--TOTALLY GET IT--
--BUT I'VE GOT A PAL HERE WHO'S REAL KEEN TO MEET YOU.
AN' I JUST CAN'T ***WAIT*** TO GET ACQUAINTED, TIN MAN.

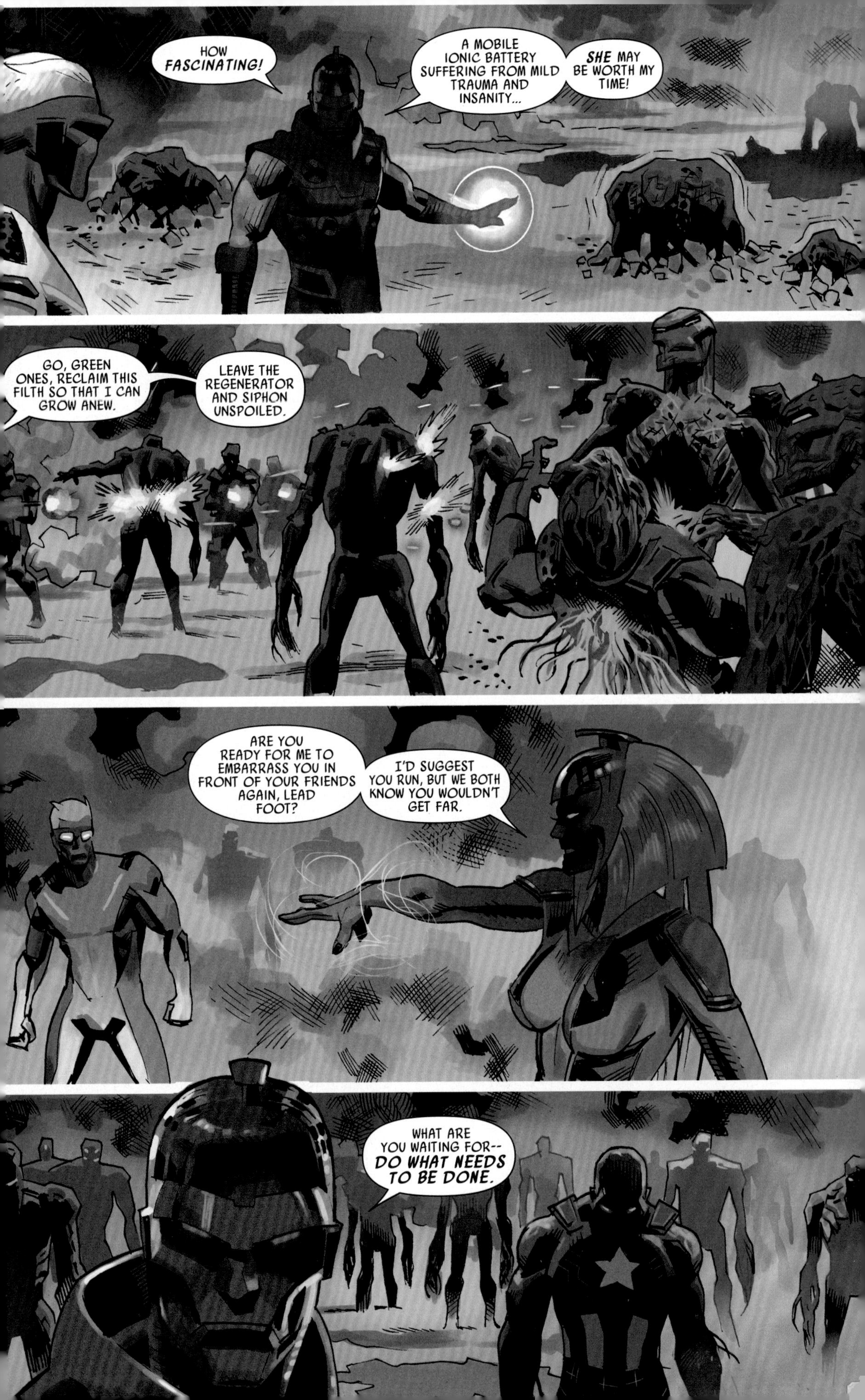
HOW FASCINATING!
A MOBILE IONIC BATTERY SUFFERING FROM MILD TRAUMA AND INSANITY...
SHE MAY BE WORTH MY TIME!
GO, GREEN ONES, RECLAIM THIS FILTH SO THAT I CAN GROW ANEW.
LEAVE THE REGENERATOR AND SIPHON UNSPOILED.
ARE YOU READY FOR ME TO EMBARRASS YOU IN FRONT OF YOUR FRIENDS AGAIN, LEAD FOOT?
I'D SUGGEST YOU RUN, BUT WE BOTH KNOW YOU WOULDN'T GET FAR.
WHAT ARE YOU WAITING FOR-- DO WHAT NEEDS TO BE DONE.

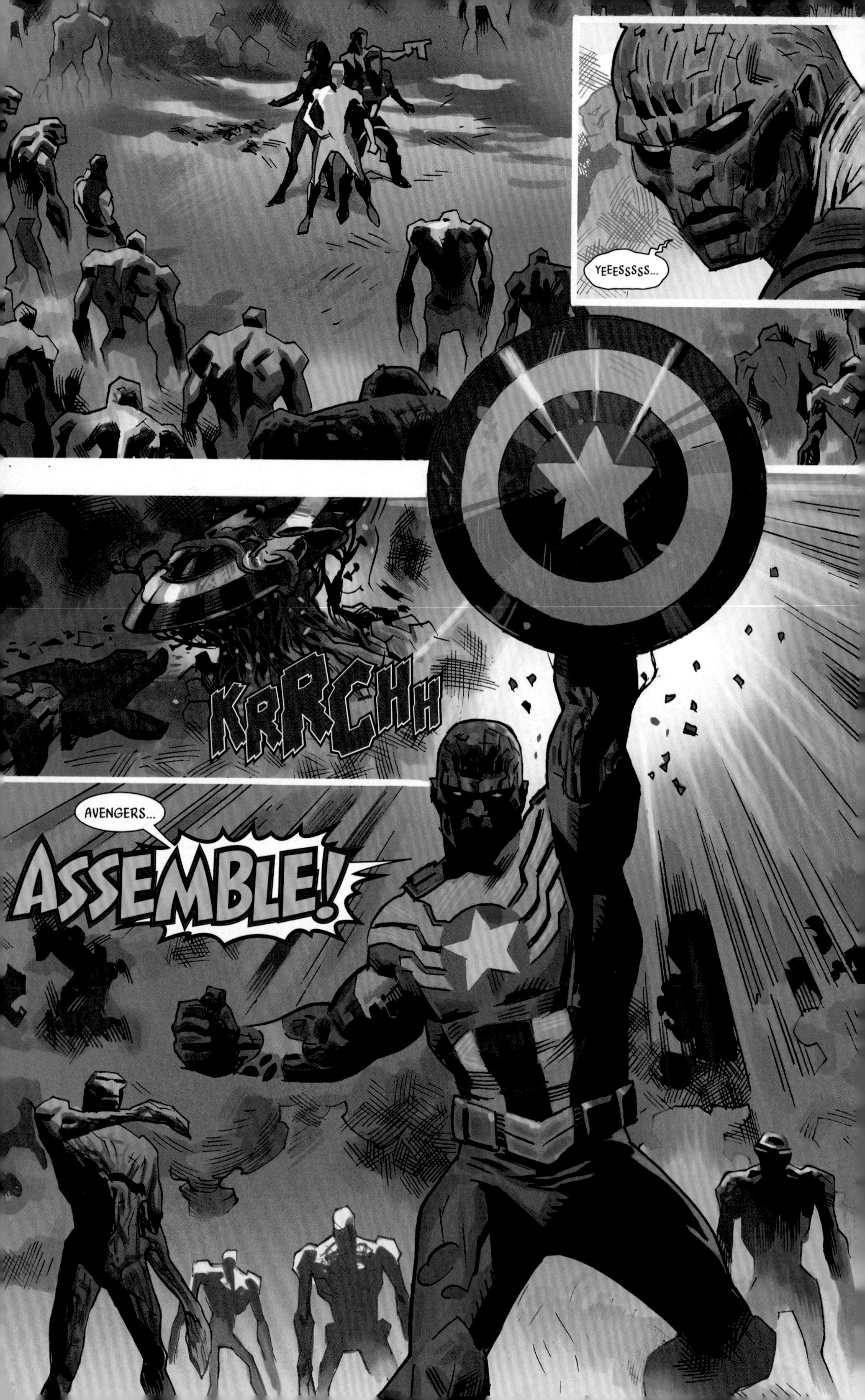
YEEESSSSS...
KRRCHH
AVENGERS...
ASSEMBLE!

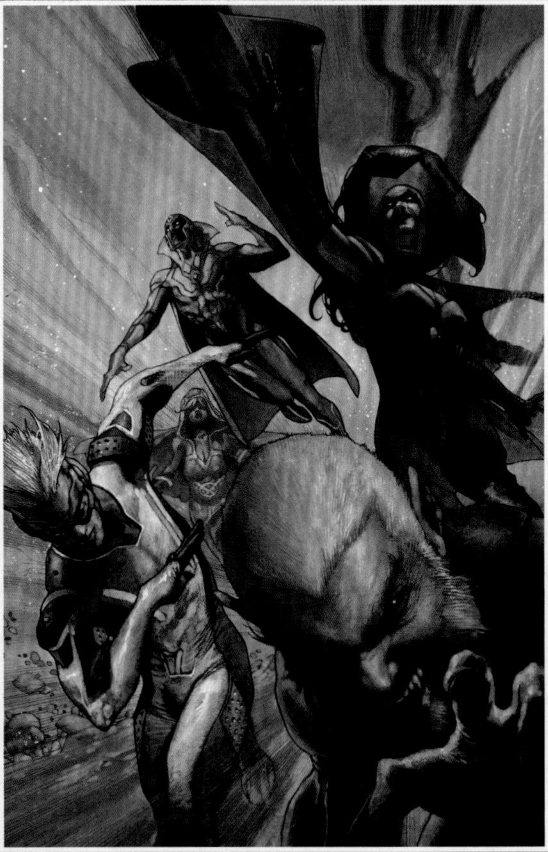

ISSUE #2 VARIANT
BY SIMONE BIANCHI

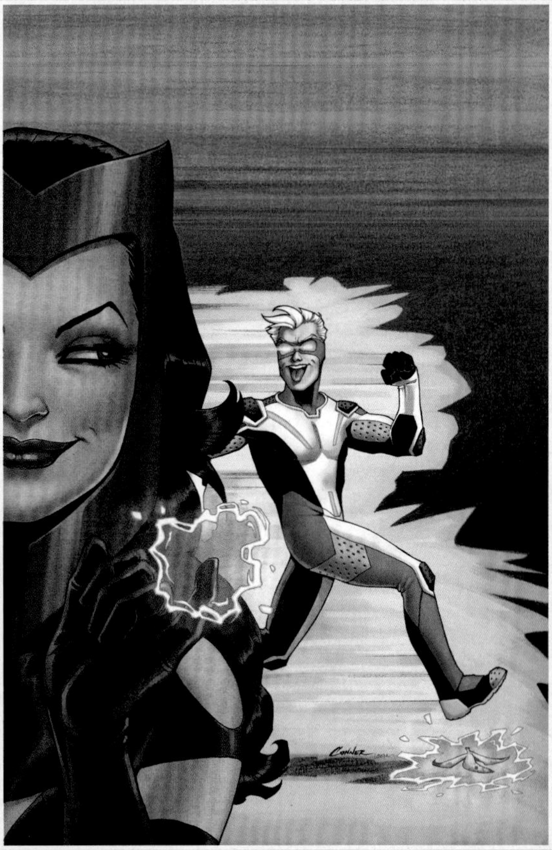

ISSUE #3 VARIANT
BY AMANDA CONNER & LAURA MARTIN

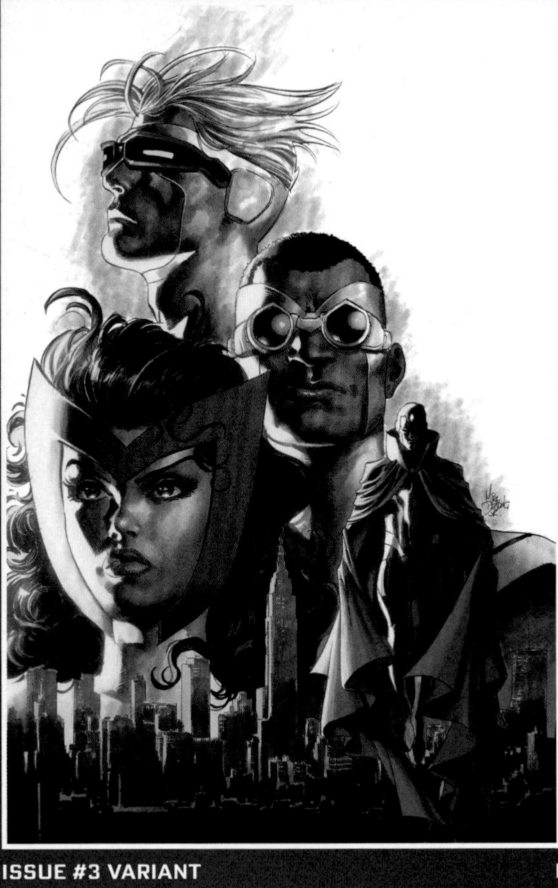

ISSUE #3 VARIANT
BY MIKE DEDDATO & FRANK MARTIN

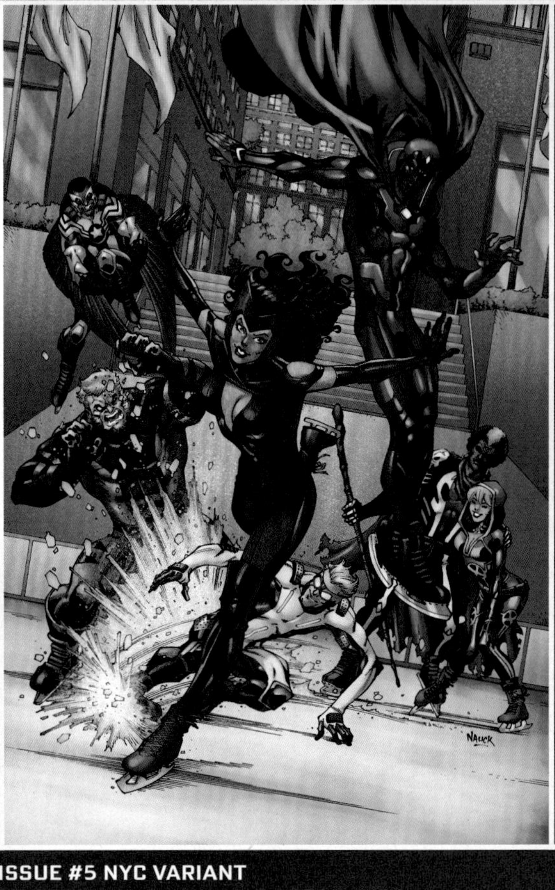

ISSUE #5 NYC VARIANT
BY TODD NAUCK & CHRIS SOTOMAYOR

UNCANNY AVENGERS #5

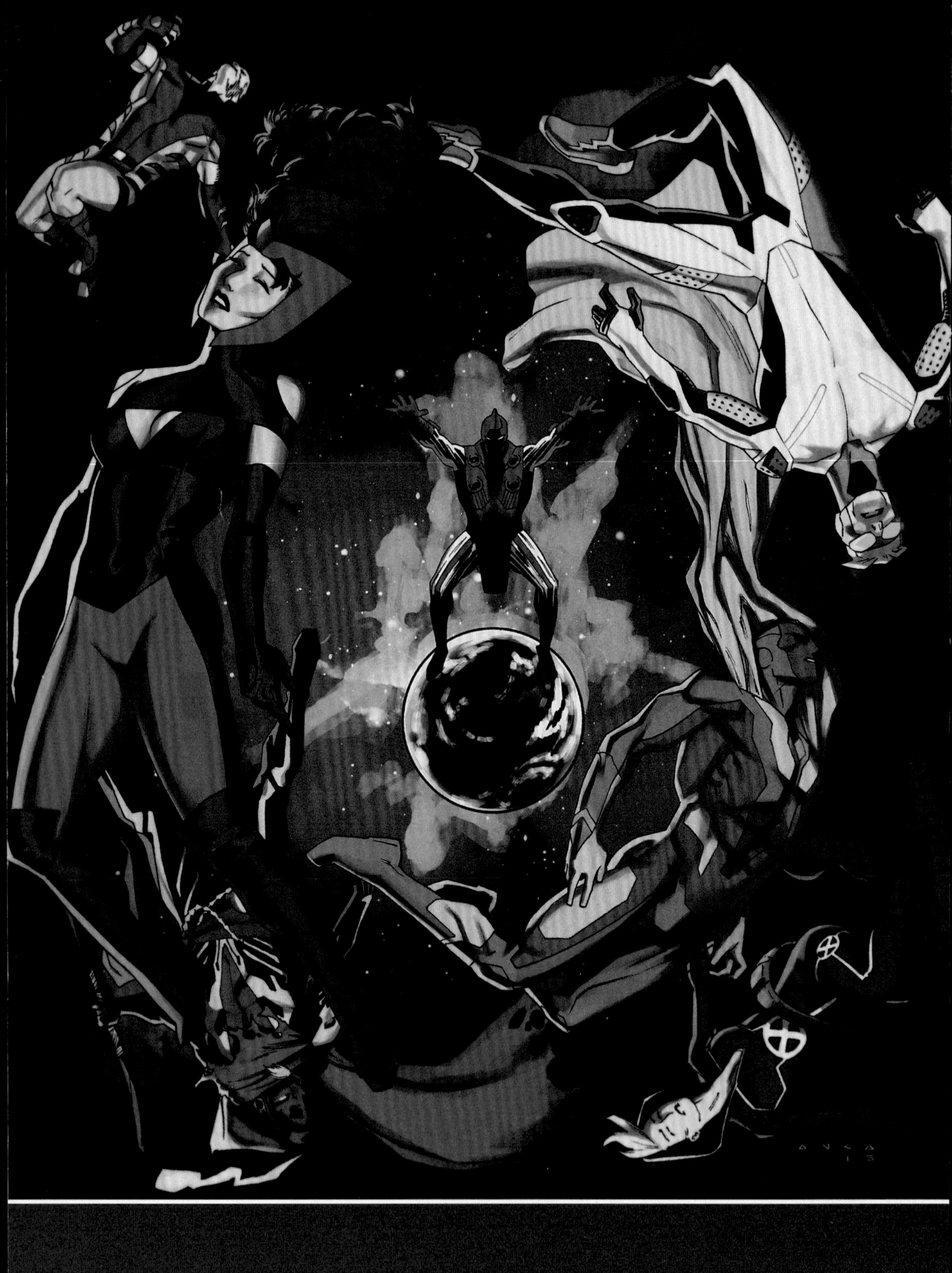

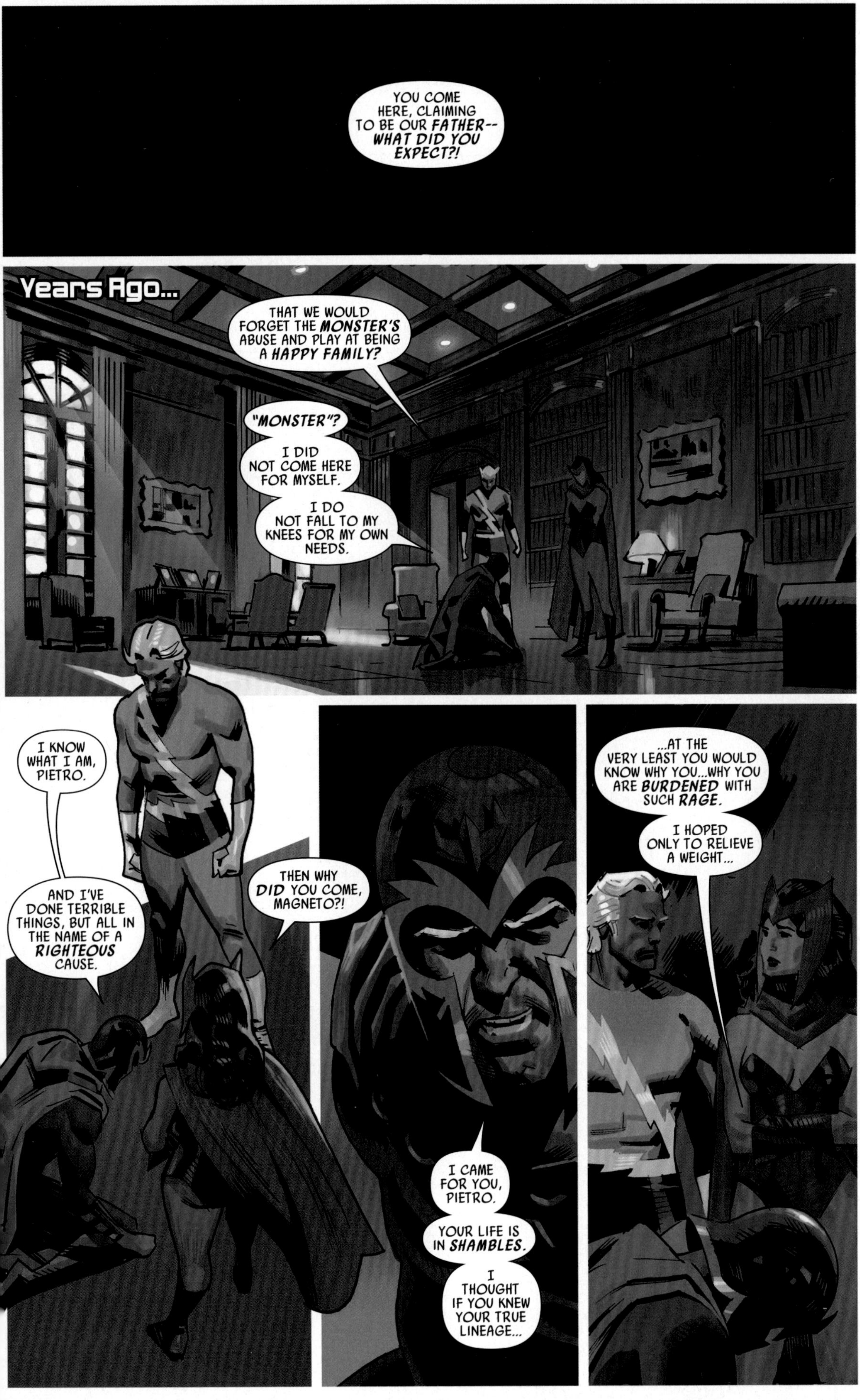
YOU COME HERE, CLAIMING TO BE OUR FATHER-- WHAT DID YOU EXPECT?!
Years Ago...
THAT WE WOULD FORGET THE MONSTER'S ABUSE AND PLAY AT BEING A HAPPY FAMILY?
"MONSTER"?
I DID NOT COME HERE FOR MYSELF.
I DO NOT FALL TO MY KNEES FOR MY OWN NEEDS.
I KNOW WHAT I AM, PIETRO.
AND I'VE DONE TERRIBLE THINGS, BUT ALL IN THE NAME OF A RIGHTEOUS CAUSE.
THEN WHY DID YOU COME, MAGNETO?!
I CAME FOR YOU, PIETRO.
YOUR LIFE IS IN SHAMBLES.
I THOUGHT IF YOU KNEW YOUR TRUE LINEAGE...
...AT THE VERY LEAST YOU WOULD KNOW WHY YOU...WHY YOU ARE BURDENED WITH SUCH RAGE.
I HOPED ONLY TO RELIEVE A WEIGHT...

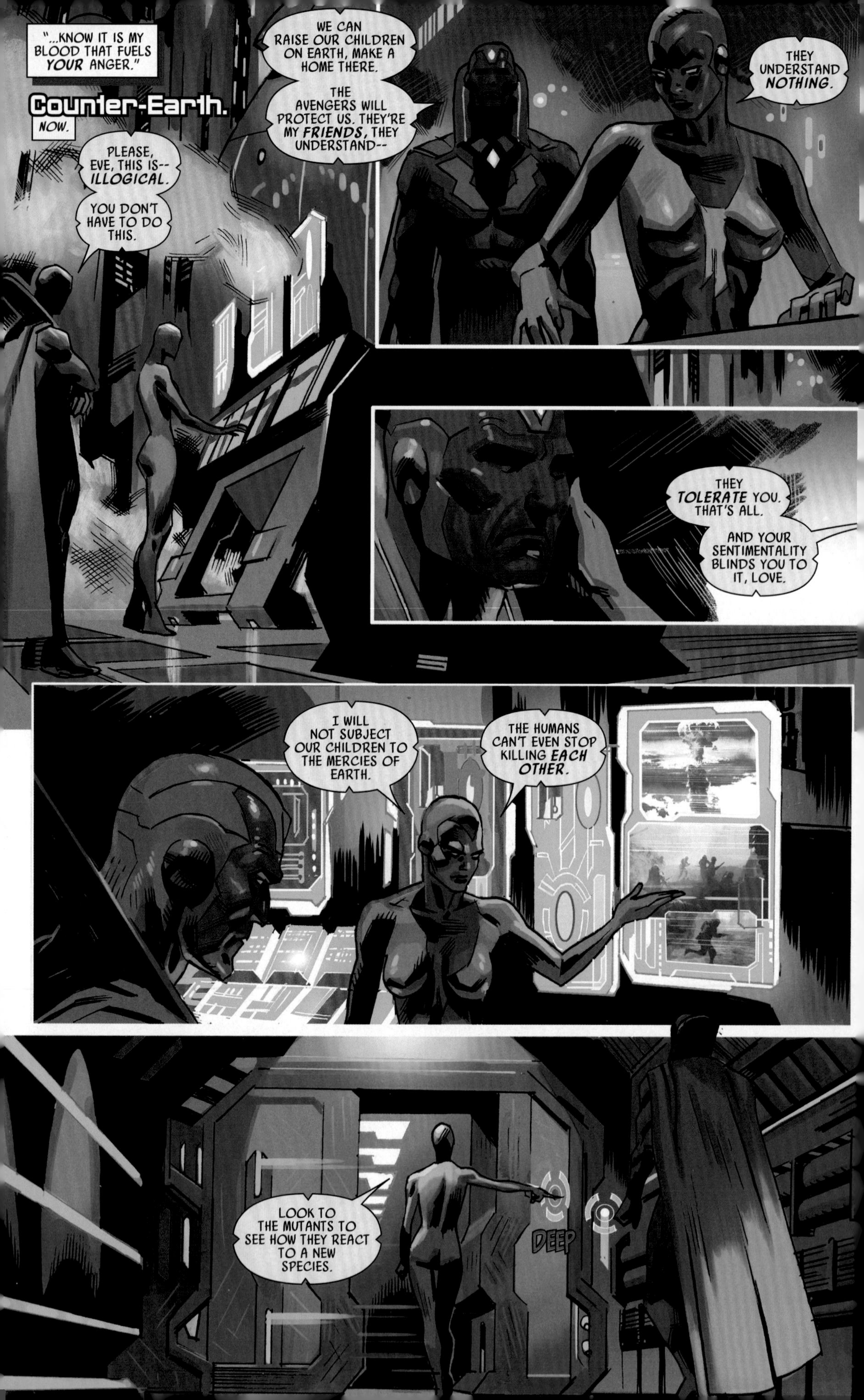
"...KNOW IT IS MY BLOOD THAT FUELS YOUR ANGER."
Counter-Earth.
NOW.
PLEASE, EVE, THIS IS-- ILLOGICAL.
YOU DON'T HAVE TO DO THIS.
WE CAN RAISE OUR CHILDREN ON EARTH, MAKE A HOME THERE.
THE AVENGERS WILL PROTECT US. THEY'RE MY FRIENDS, THEY UNDERSTAND--
THEY UNDERSTAND NOTHING.
THEY TOLERATE YOU. THAT'S ALL.
AND YOUR SENTIMENTALITY BLINDS YOU TO IT, LOVE.
I WILL NOT SUBJECT OUR CHILDREN TO THE MERCIES OF EARTH.
THE HUMANS CAN'T EVEN STOP KILLING EACH OTHER.
LOOK TO THE MUTANTS TO SEE HOW THEY REACT TO A NEW SPECIES.
DEEP

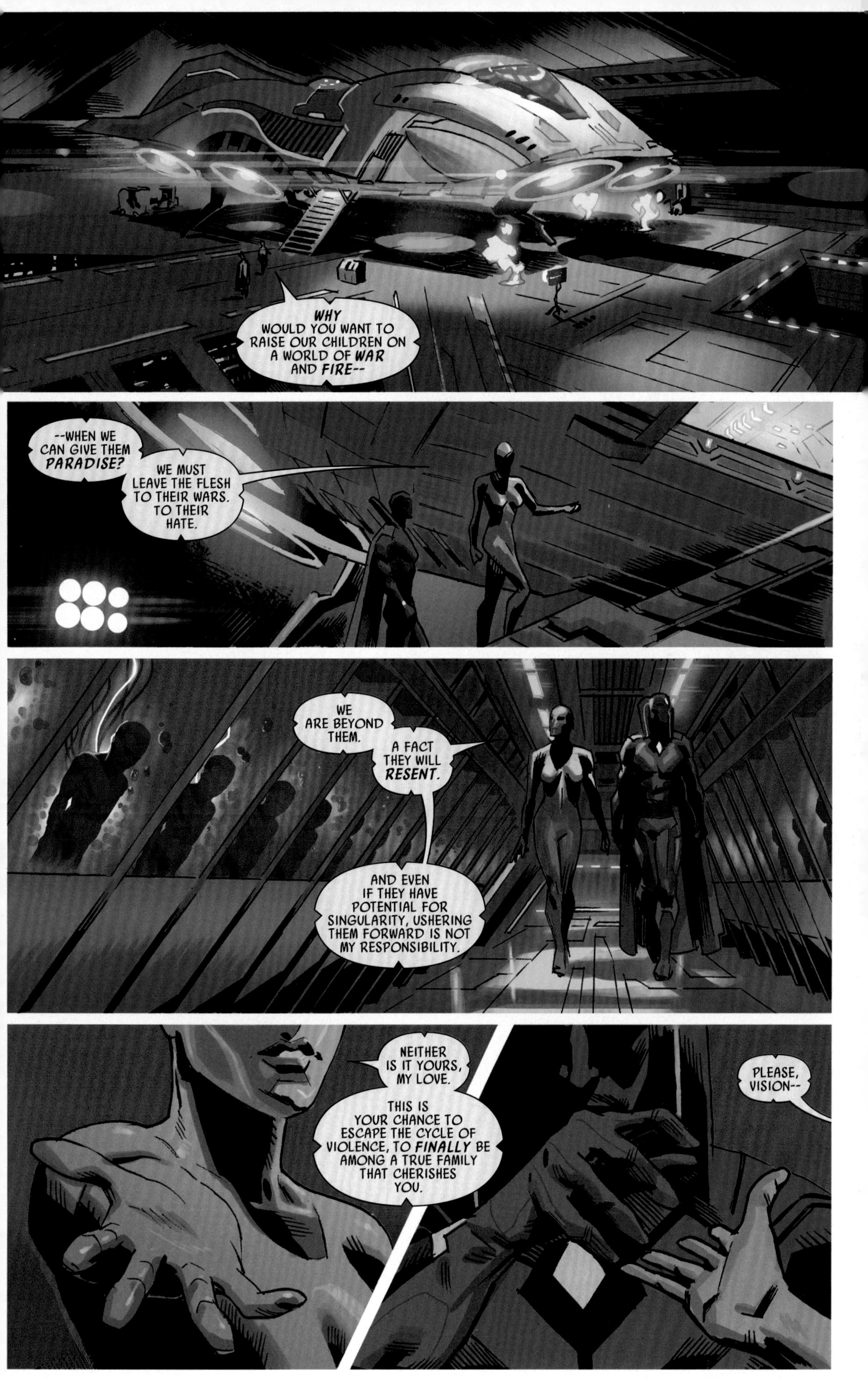
WHY WOULD YOU WANT TO RAISE OUR CHILDREN ON A WORLD OF WAR AND FIRE--
--WHEN WE CAN GIVE THEM PARADISE?
WE MUST LEAVE THE FLESH TO THEIR WARS. TO THEIR HATE.
WE ARE BEYOND THEM.
A FACT THEY WILL RESENT.
AND EVEN IF THEY HAVE POTENTIAL FOR SINGULARITY, USHERING THEM FORWARD IS NOT MY RESPONSIBILITY.
NEITHER IS IT YOURS, MY LOVE.
THIS IS YOUR CHANCE TO ESCAPE THE CYCLE OF VIOLENCE, TO FINALLY BE AMONG A TRUE FAMILY THAT CHERISHES YOU.
PLEASE, VISION--

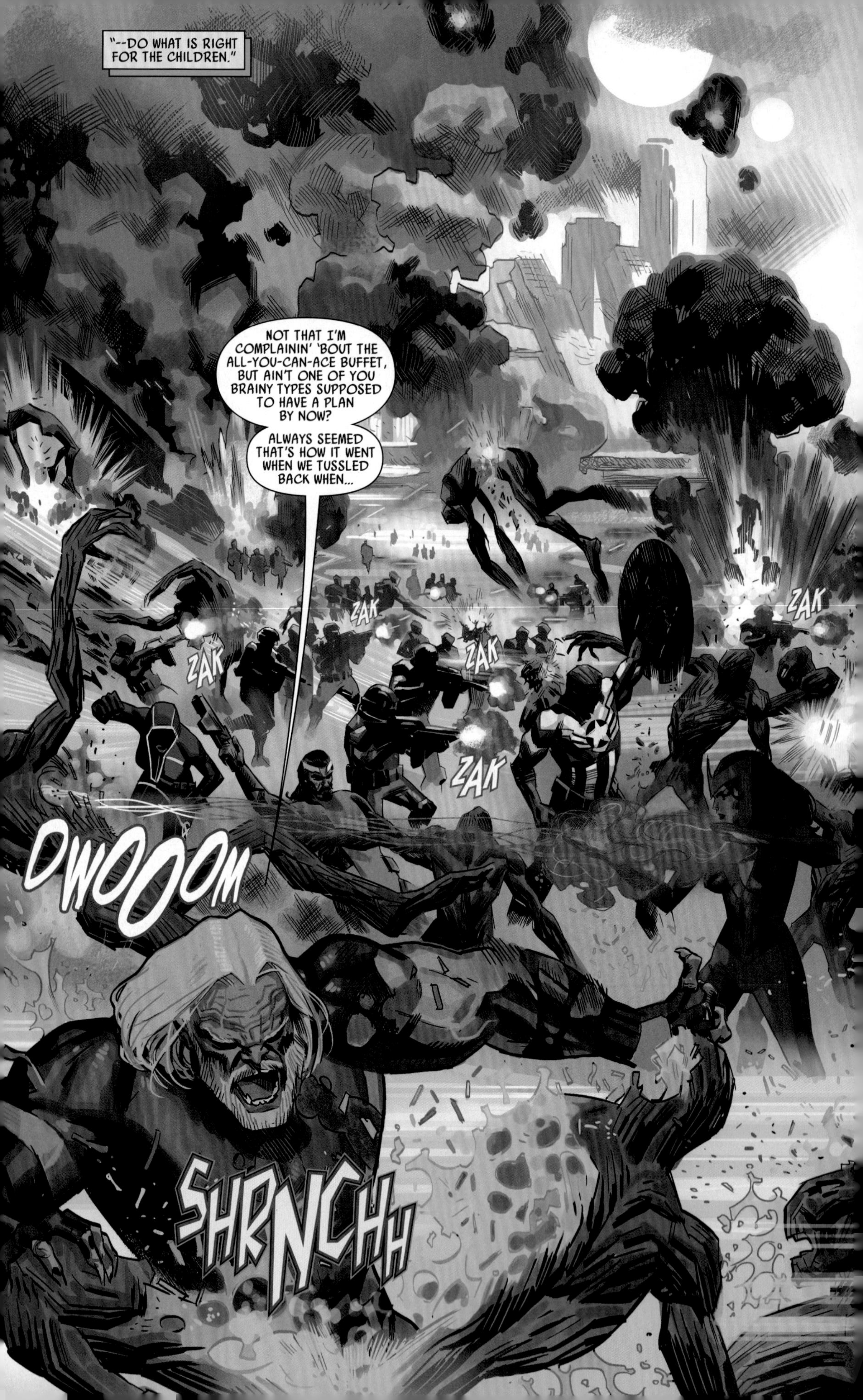
"--DO WHAT IS RIGHT FOR THE CHILDREN."
NOT THAT I'M COMPLAININ' 'BOUT THE ALL-YOU-CAN-ACE BUFFET, BUT AIN'T ONE OF YOU BRAINY TYPES SUPPOSED TO HAVE A PLAN BY NOW?
ALWAYS SEEMED THAT'S HOW IT WENT WHEN WE TUSSLED BACK WHEN...
ZAK
ZAK
ZAK
ZAK
ZAK
DWOOOOM
SHRNCHH

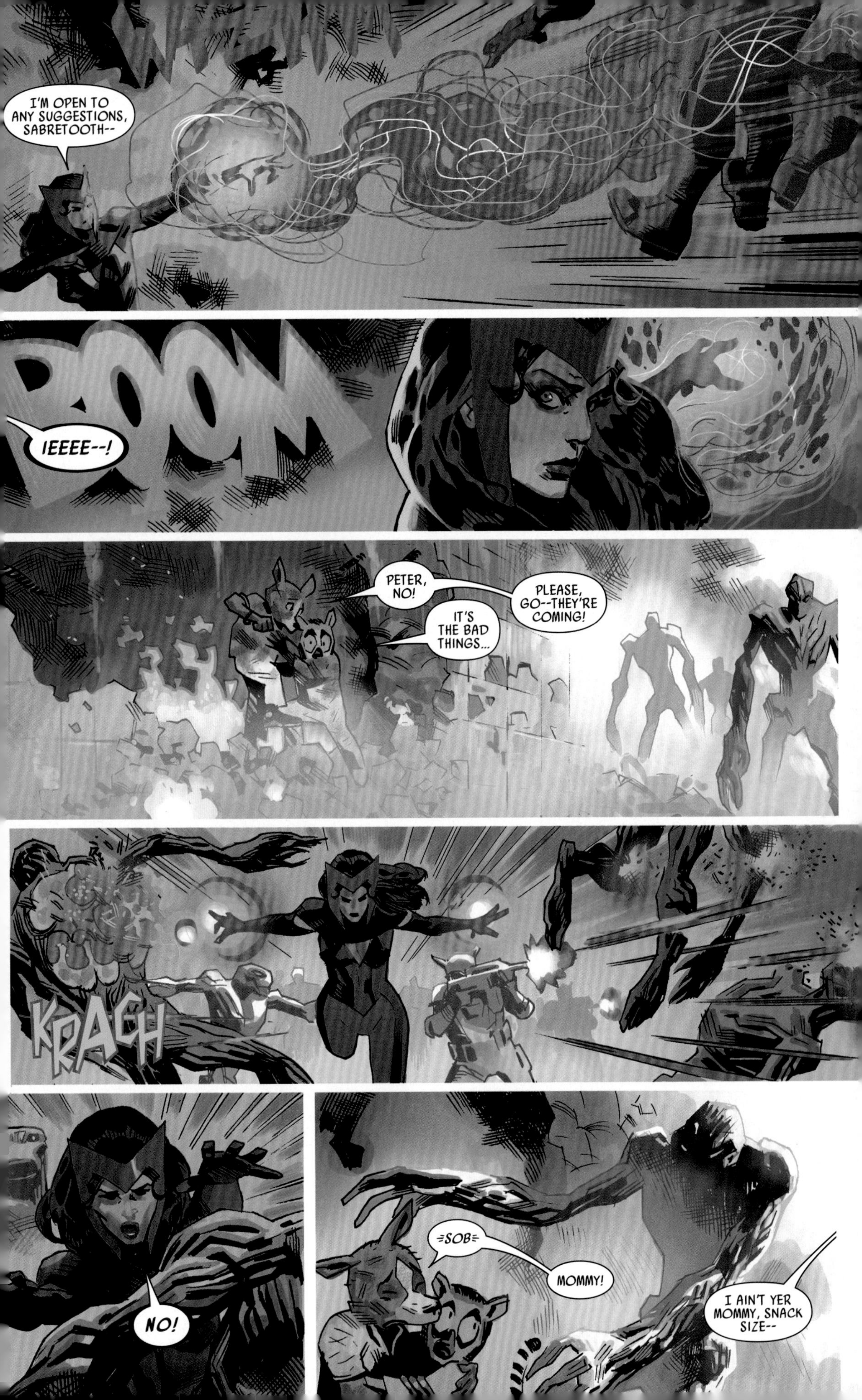
I'M OPEN TO ANY SUGGESTIONS, SABRETOOTH--
BOOM
IEEEE--!
PETER, NO!
IT'S THE BAD THINGS...
PLEASE, GO--THEY'RE COMING!
KRACH
NO!
SOB
MOMMY!
I AIN'T YER MOMMY, SNACK SIZE--

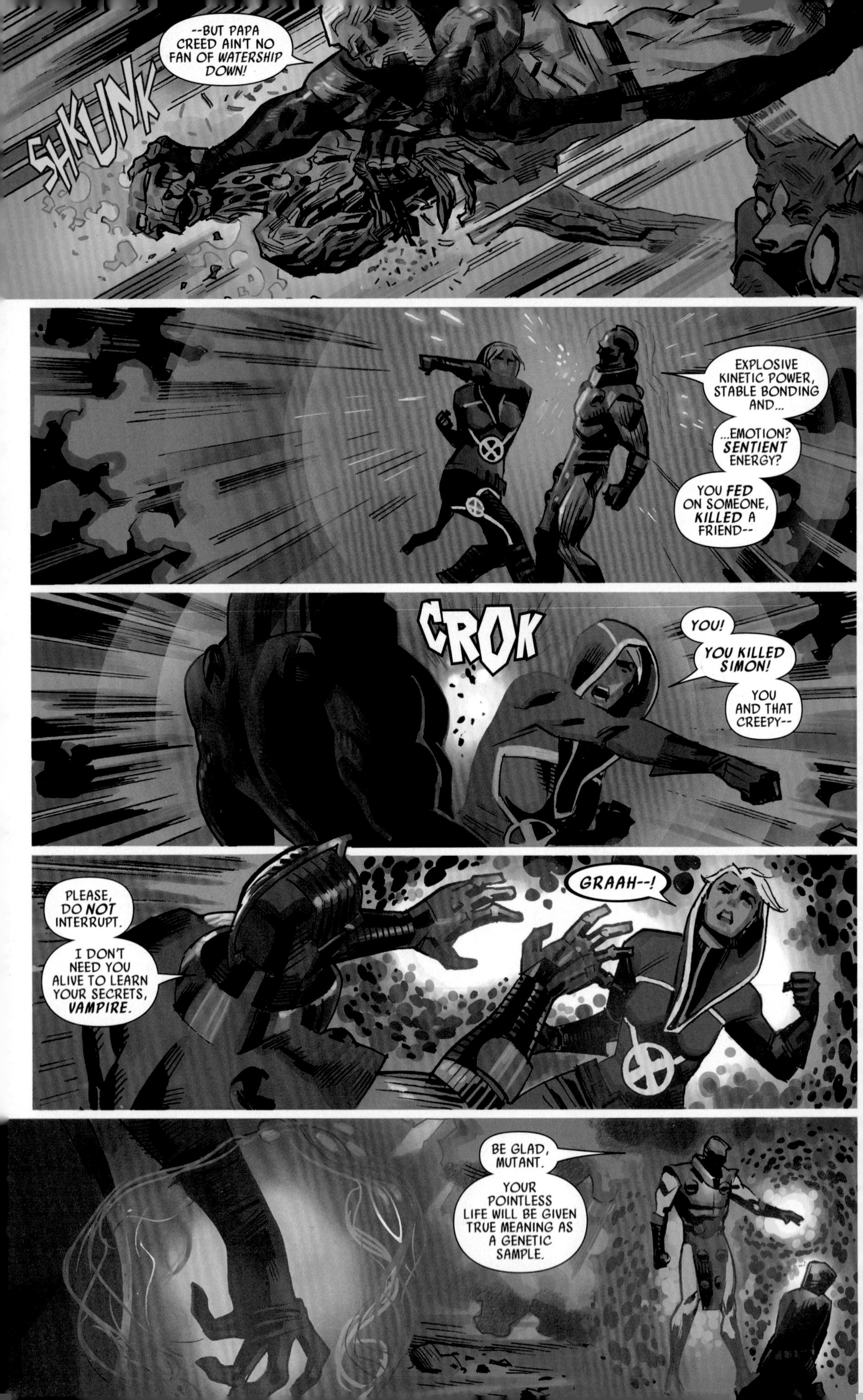
--BUT PAPA CREED AIN'T NO FAN OF WATERSHIP DOWN!
SHKUNK
EXPLOSIVE KINETIC POWER, STABLE BONDING AND...
...EMOTION? SENTIENT ENERGY?
YOU FED ON SOMEONE, KILLED A FRIEND--
CROK
YOU!
YOU KILLED SIMON!
YOU AND THAT CREEPY--
PLEASE, DO NOT INTERRUPT.
I DON'T NEED YOU ALIVE TO LEARN YOUR SECRETS, VAMPIRE.
GRAAH--!
BE GLAD, MUTANT.
YOUR POINTLESS LIFE WILL BE GIVEN TRUE MEANING AS A GENETIC SAMPLE.

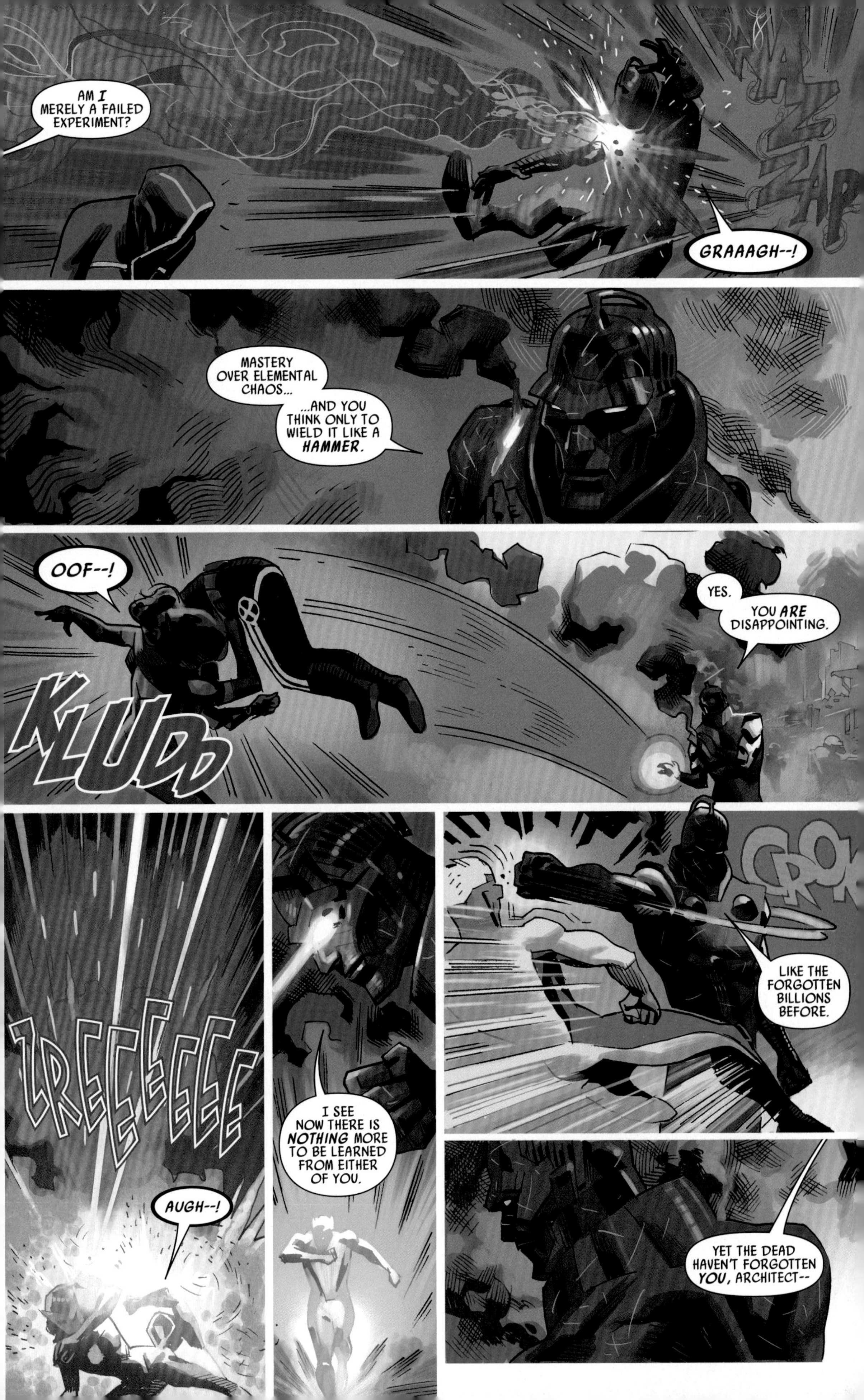

AM I MERELY A FAILED EXPERIMENT?
ZAP
GRAAAGH--!
MASTERY OVER ELEMENTAL CHAOS...
...AND YOU THINK ONLY TO WIELD IT LIKE A HAMMER.
OOF--!
YES.
YOU ARE DISAPPOINTING.
KLUDD
ZREEEEEEE
AUGH--!
I SEE NOW THERE IS NOTHING MORE TO BE LEARNED FROM EITHER OF YOU.
LIKE THE FORGOTTEN BILLIONS BEFORE.
YET THE DEAD HAVEN'T FORGOTTEN YOU, ARCHITECT--

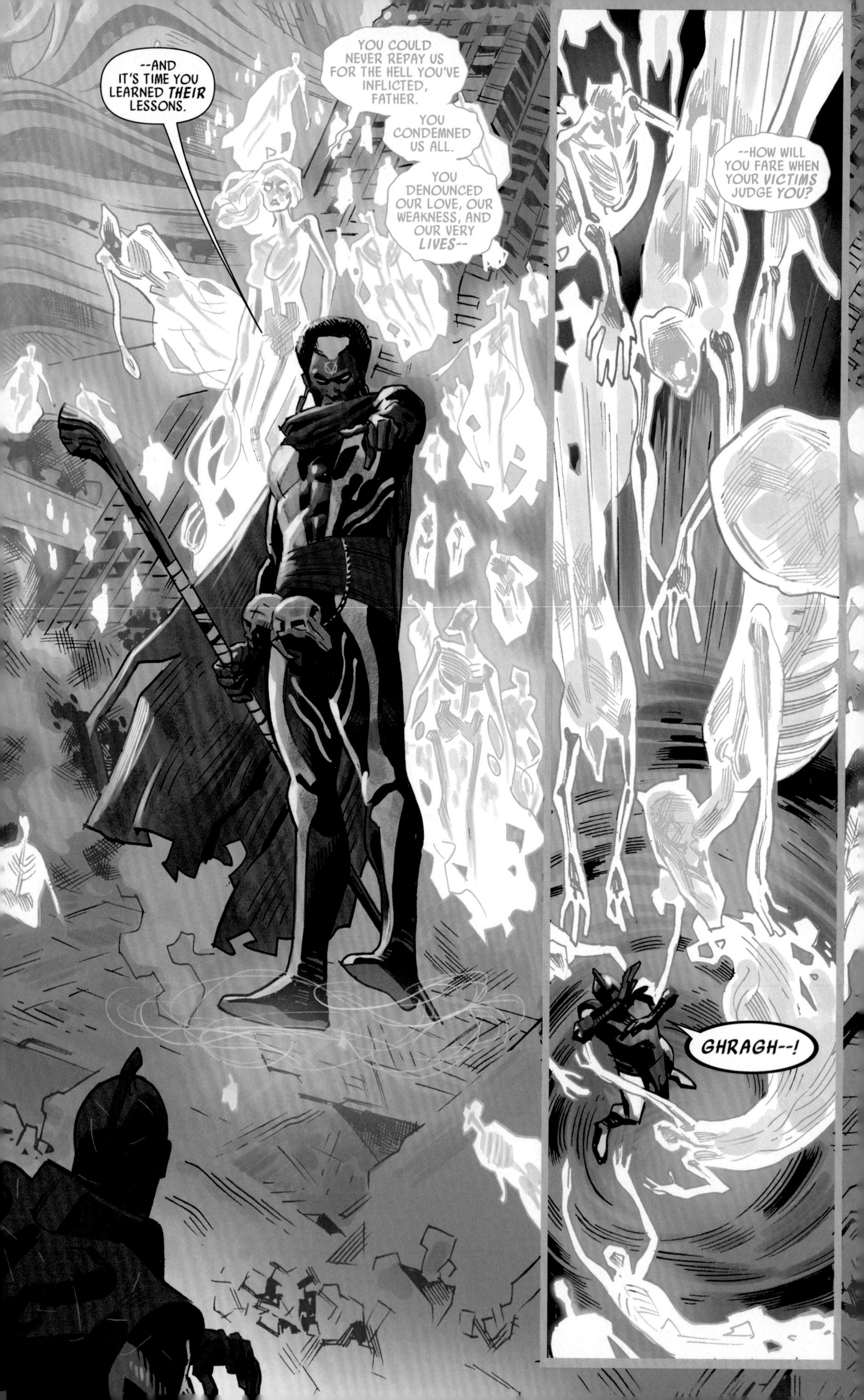

--AND IT'S TIME YOU LEARNED THEIR LESSONS.
YOU COULD NEVER REPAY US FOR THE HELL YOU'VE INFLICTED, FATHER.
YOU CONDEMNED US ALL.
YOU DENOUNCED OUR LOVE, OUR WEAKNESS, AND OUR VERY LIVES--
--HOW WILL YOU FARE WHEN YOUR VICTIMS JUDGE YOU?
GHRAGH--!

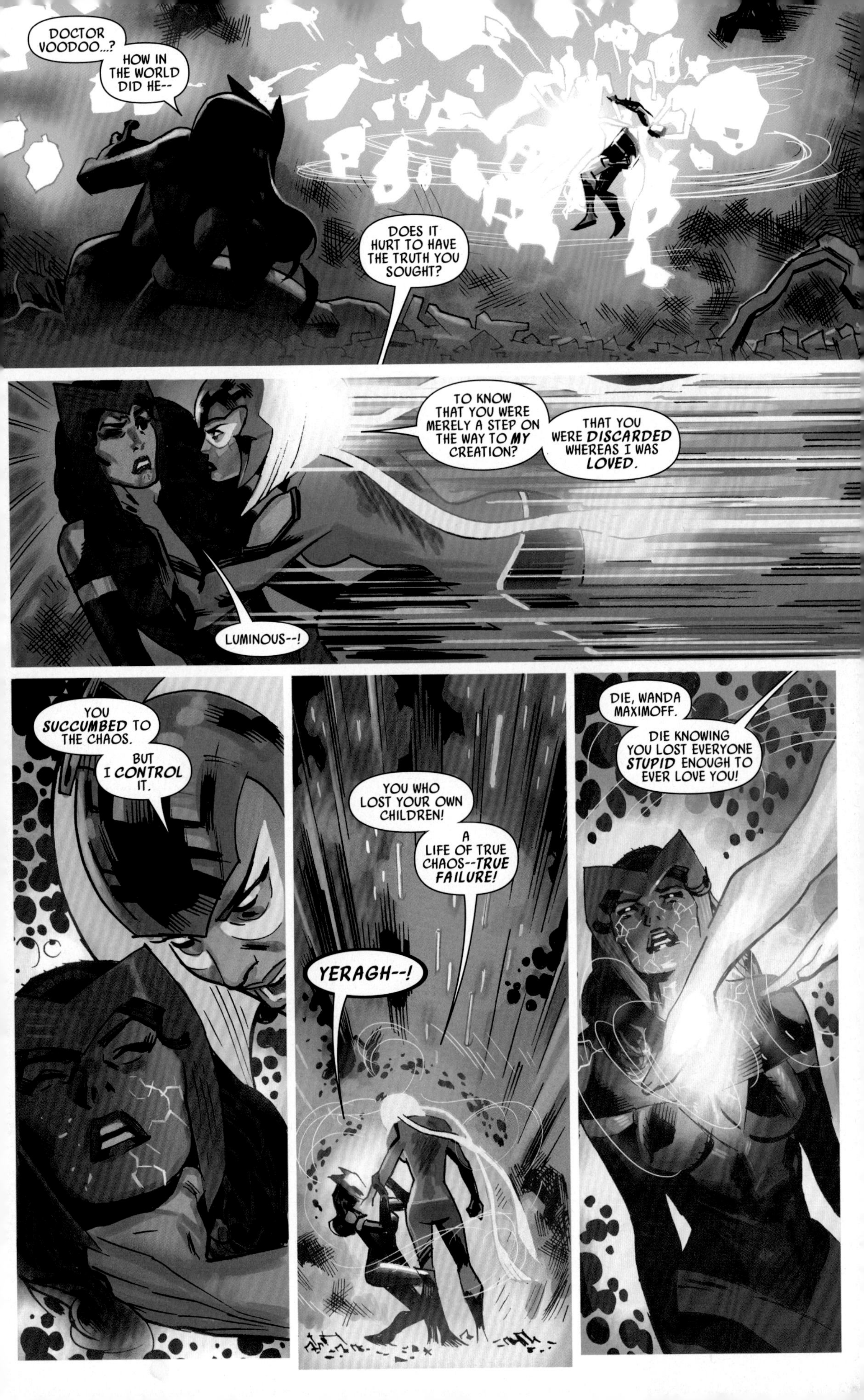
DOCTOR VOODOO...?
HOW IN THE WORLD DID HE--
DOES IT HURT TO HAVE THE TRUTH YOU SOUGHT?
TO KNOW THAT YOU WERE MERELY A STEP ON THE WAY TO MY CREATION?
THAT YOU WERE DISCARDED WHEREAS I WAS LOVED.
LUMINOUS--!
YOU SUCCUMBED TO THE CHAOS.
BUT I CONTROL IT.
YOU WHO LOST YOUR OWN CHILDREN!
A LIFE OF TRUE CHAOS--TRUE FAILURE!
YERAGH--!
DIE, WANDA MAXIMOFF.
DIE KNOWING YOU LOST EVERYONE STUPID ENOUGH TO EVER LOVE YOU!

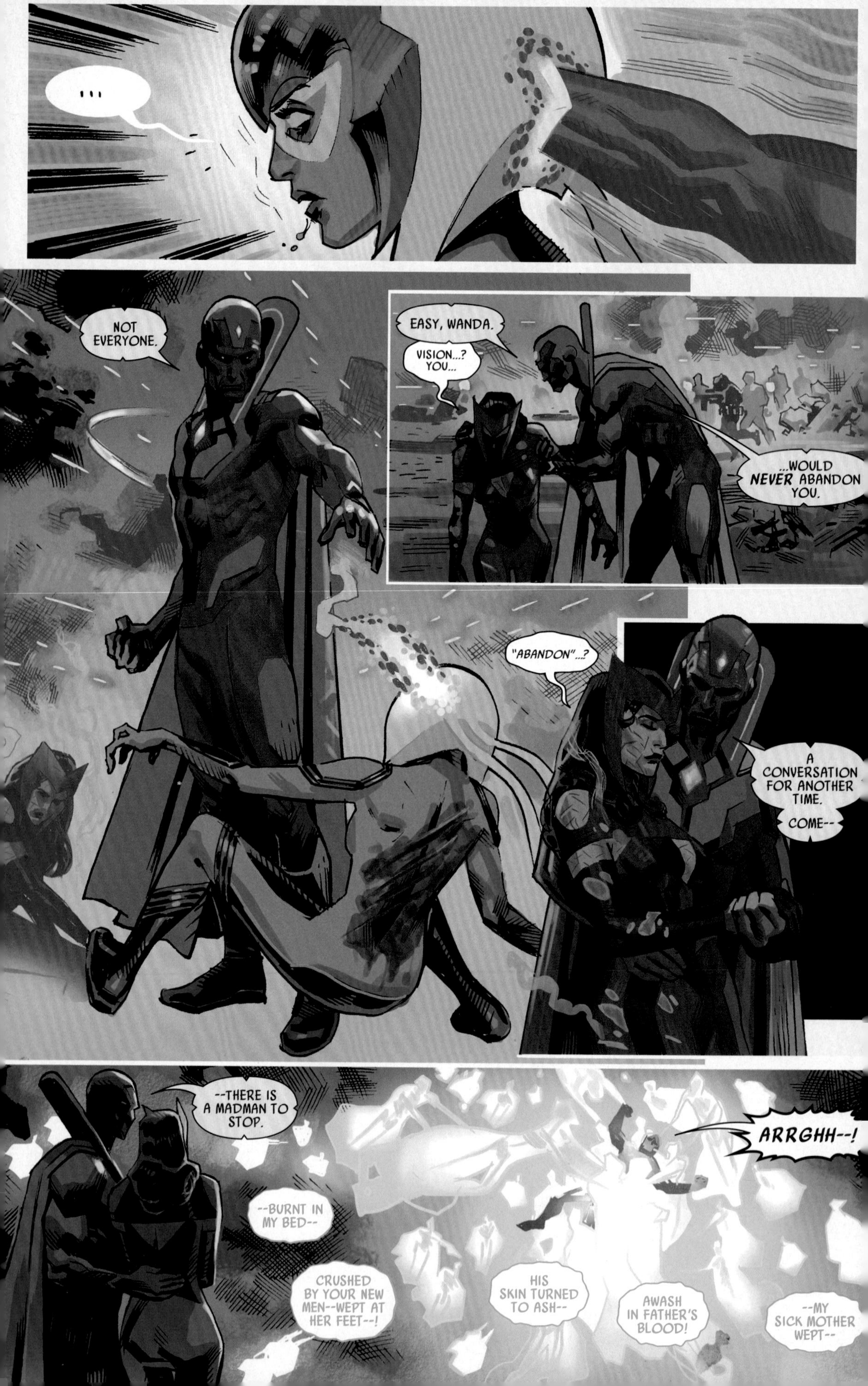
...
NOT EVERYONE.
EASY, WANDA.
VISION...? YOU...
...WOULD NEVER ABANDON YOU.
"ABANDON"...?
A CONVERSATION FOR ANOTHER TIME.
COME--
--THERE IS A MADMAN TO STOP.
ARRGHH--!
--BURNT IN MY BED--
CRUSHED BY YOUR NEW MEN--WEPT AT HER FEET--!
HIS SKIN TURNED TO ASH--
AWASH IN FATHER'S BLOOD!
--MY SICK MOTHER WEPT--

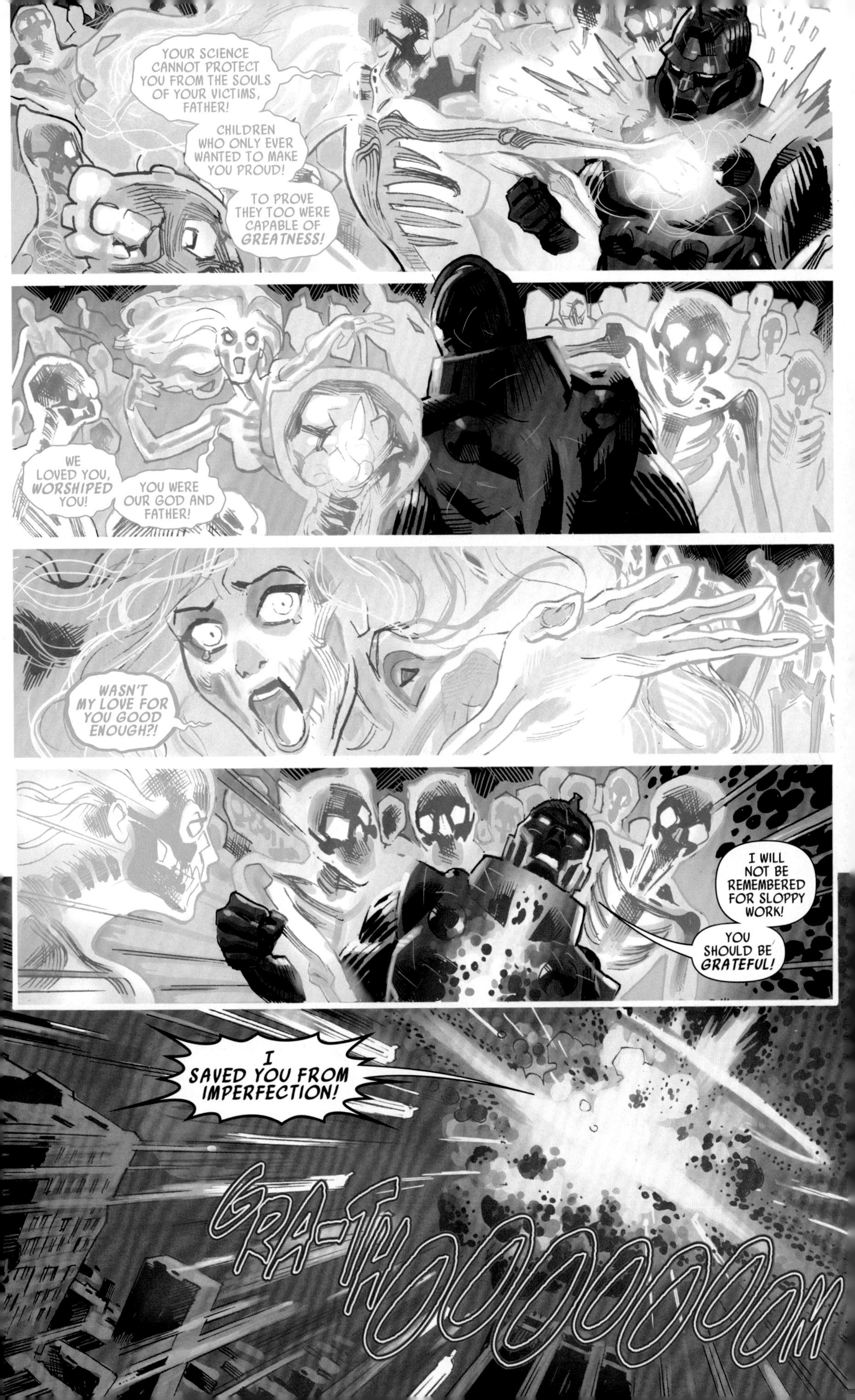
YOUR SCIENCE CANNOT PROTECT YOU FROM THE SOULS OF YOUR VICTIMS, FATHER!
CHILDREN WHO ONLY EVER WANTED TO MAKE YOU PROUD!
TO PROVE THEY TOO WERE CAPABLE OF GREATNESS!
WE LOVED YOU, WORSHIPED YOU!
YOU WERE OUR GOD AND FATHER!
WASN'T MY LOVE FOR YOU GOOD ENOUGH?!
I WILL NOT BE REMEMBERED FOR SLOPPY WORK!
YOU SHOULD BE GRATEFUL!
I SAVED YOU FROM IMPERFECTION!
GRA-THOOOOOOOOM

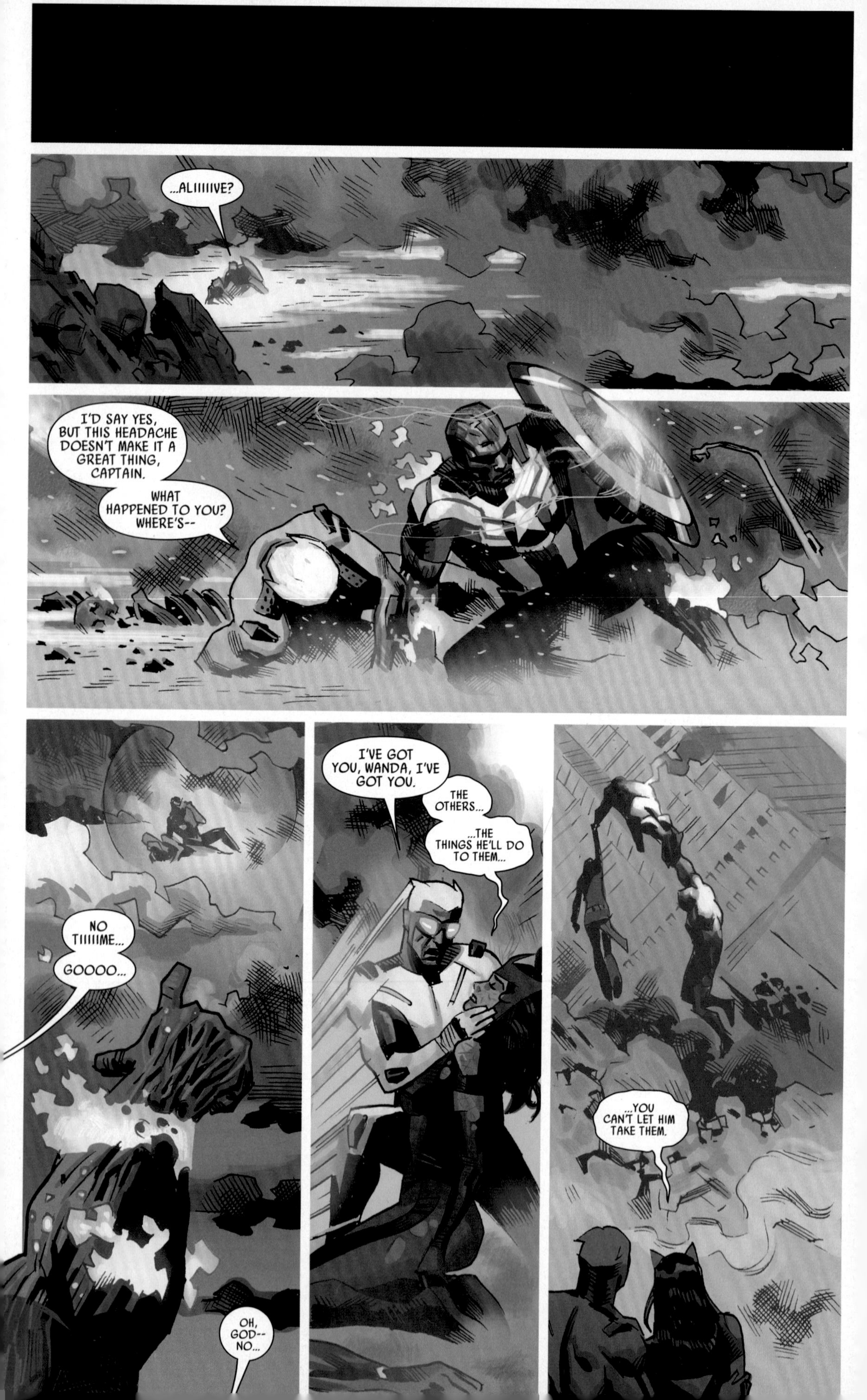
...ALIIIIIVE?
I'D SAY YES, BUT THIS HEADACHE DOESN'T MAKE IT A GREAT THING, CAPTAIN.
WHAT HAPPENED TO YOU? WHERE'S--
NO TIIIIIME...
GOOOO...
OH, GOD-- NO...
I'VE GOT YOU, WANDA, I'VE GOT YOU.
THE OTHERS...
...THE THINGS HE'LL DO TO THEM...
...YOU CAN'T LET HIM TAKE THEM.

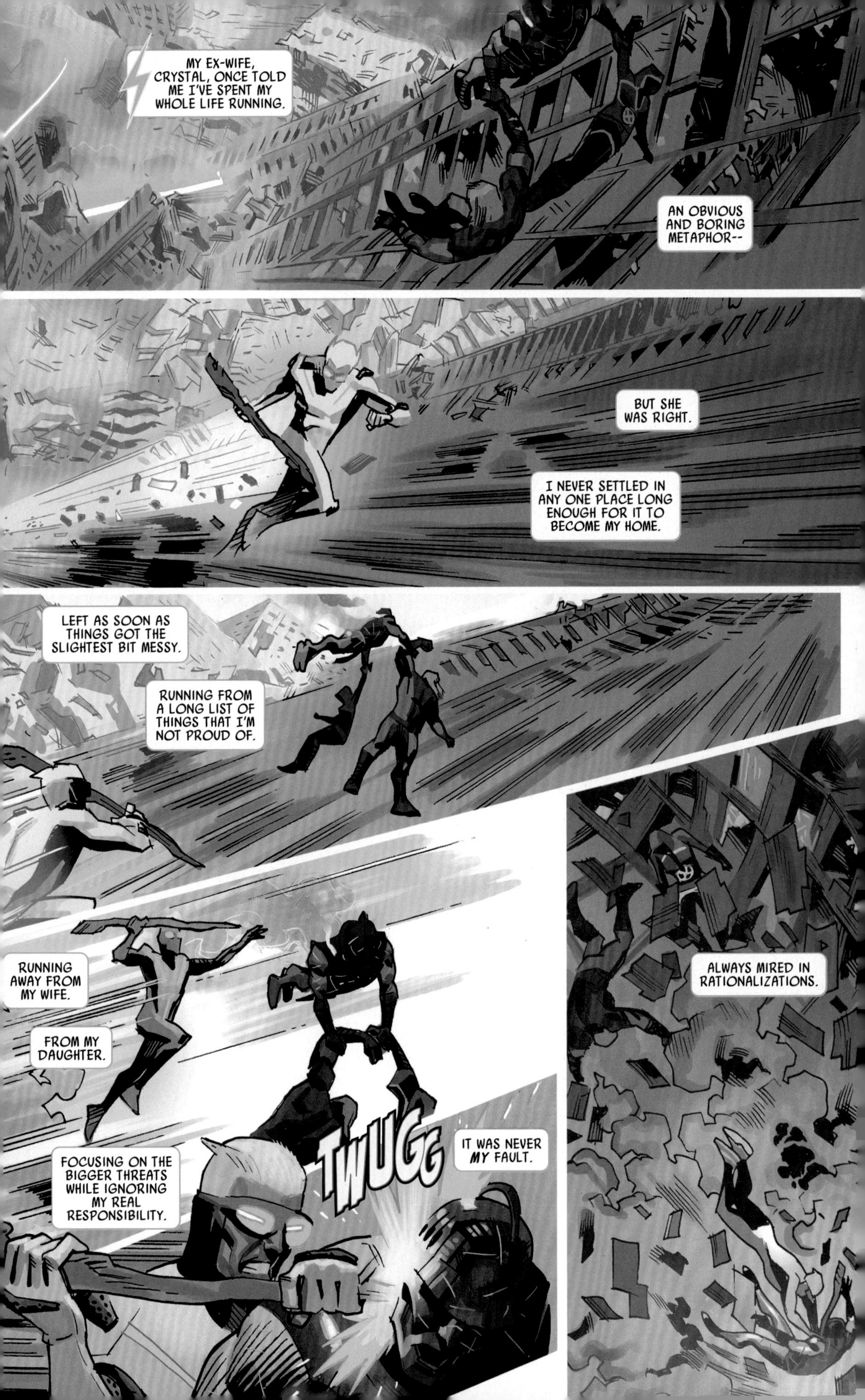
MY EX-WIFE, CRYSTAL, ONCE TOLD ME I'VE SPENT MY WHOLE LIFE RUNNING.
AN OBVIOUS AND BORING METAPHOR--
BUT SHE WAS RIGHT.
I NEVER SETTLED IN ANY ONE PLACE LONG ENOUGH FOR IT TO BECOME MY HOME.
LEFT AS SOON AS THINGS GOT THE SLIGHTEST BIT MESSY.
RUNNING FROM A LONG LIST OF THINGS THAT I'M NOT PROUD OF.
RUNNING AWAY FROM MY WIFE.
FROM MY DAUGHTER.
FOCUSING ON THE BIGGER THREATS WHILE IGNORING MY REAL RESPONSIBILITY.
TWUGG
IT WAS NEVER MY FAULT.
ALWAYS MIRED IN RATIONALIZATIONS.

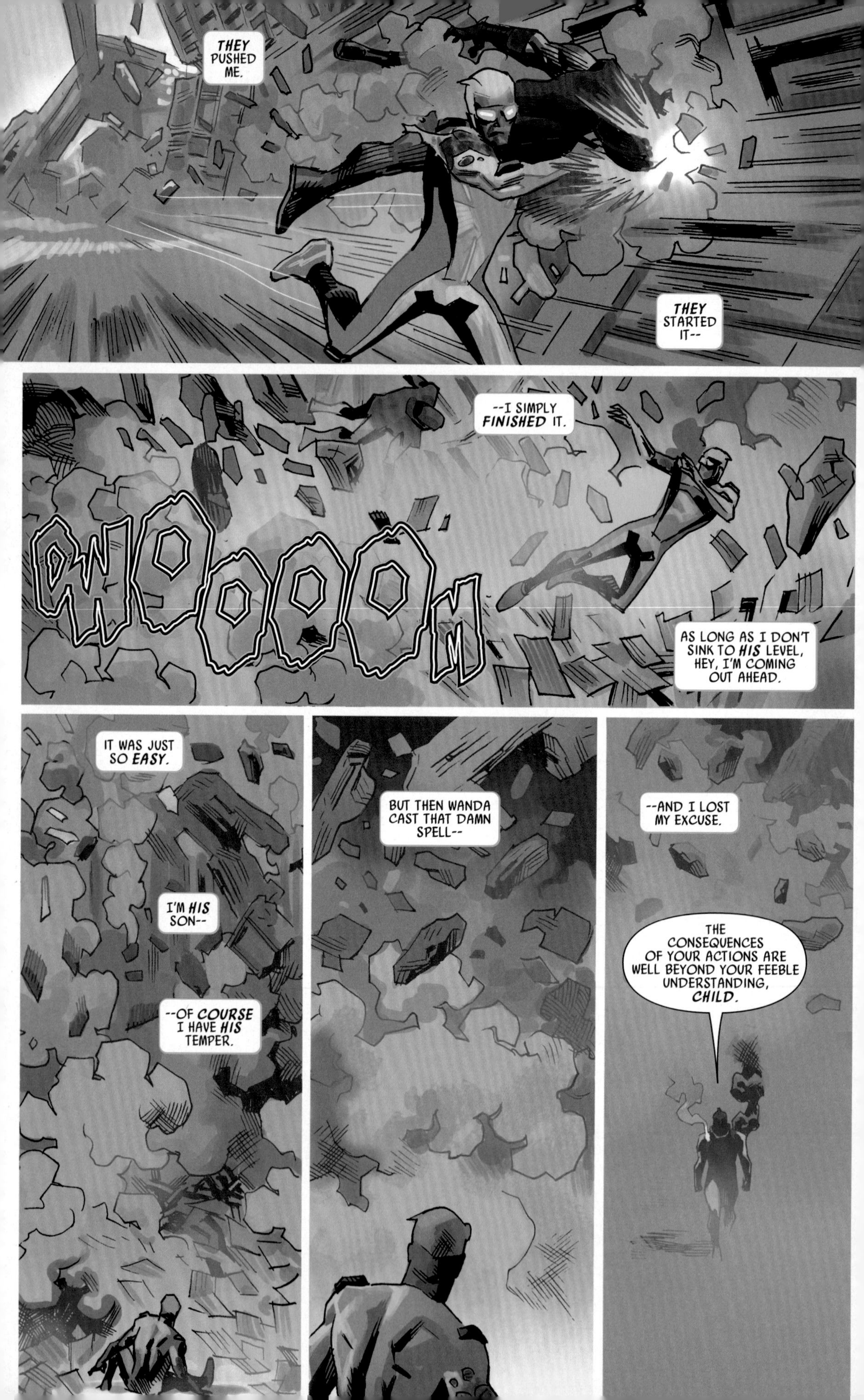
THEY PUSHED ME.
THEY STARTED IT--
--I SIMPLY FINISHED IT.
WOOOOOM
AS LONG AS I DON'T SINK TO HIS LEVEL, HEY, I'M COMING OUT AHEAD.
IT WAS JUST SO EASY.
I'M HIS SON--
--OF COURSE I HAVE HIS TEMPER.
BUT THEN WANDA CAST THAT DAMN SPELL--
--AND I LOST MY EXCUSE.
THE CONSEQUENCES OF YOUR ACTIONS ARE WELL BEYOND YOUR FEEBLE UNDERSTANDING, CHILD.

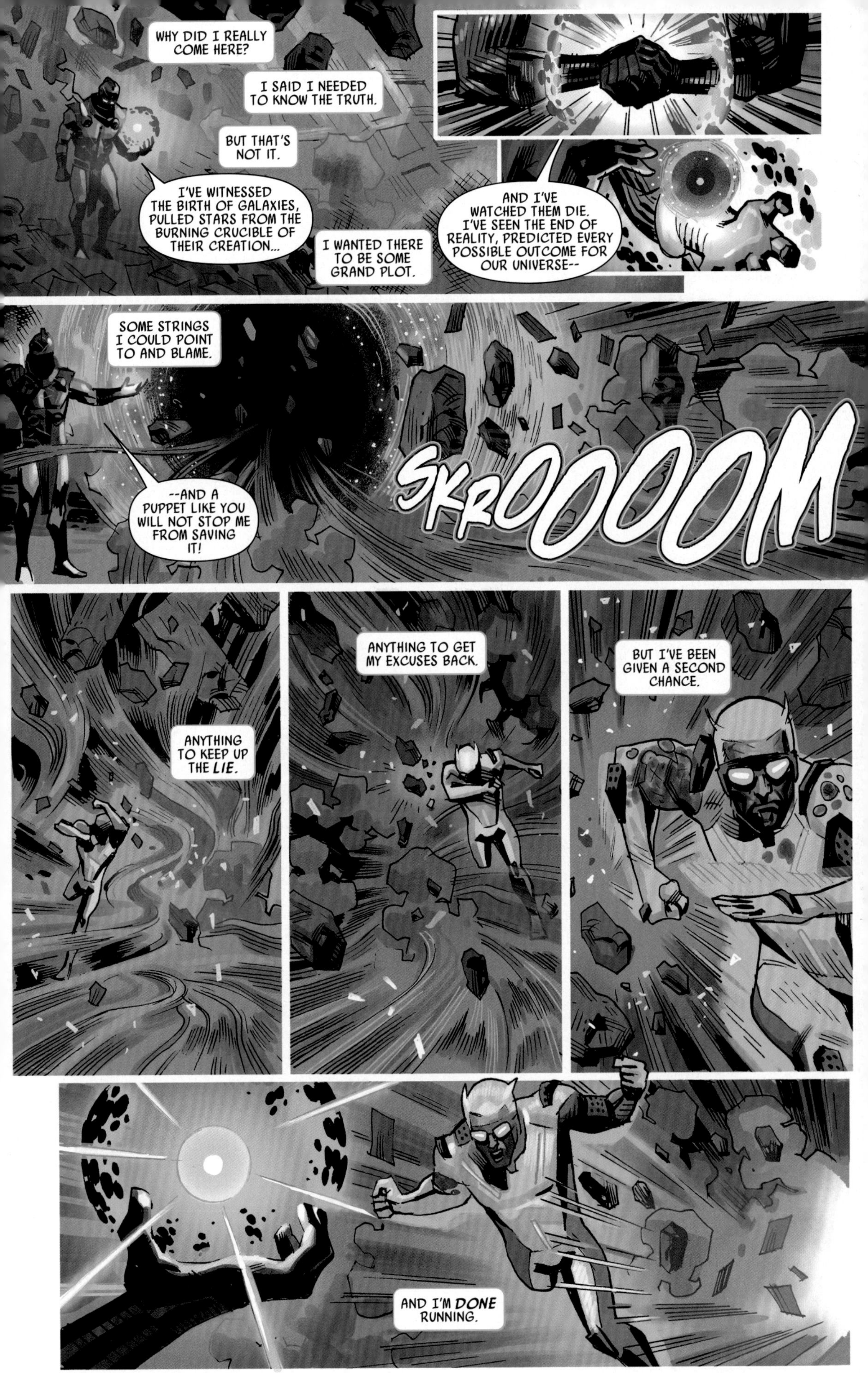
WHY DID I REALLY COME HERE?
I SAID I NEEDED TO KNOW THE TRUTH.
BUT THAT'S NOT IT.
I'VE WITNESSED THE BIRTH OF GALAXIES, PULLED STARS FROM THE BURNING CRUCIBLE OF THEIR CREATION...
I WANTED THERE TO BE SOME GRAND PLOT.
AND I'VE WATCHED THEM DIE. I'VE SEEN THE END OF REALITY, PREDICTED EVERY POSSIBLE OUTCOME FOR OUR UNIVERSE--
SOME STRINGS I COULD POINT TO AND BLAME.
--AND A PUPPET LIKE YOU WILL NOT STOP ME FROM SAVING IT!
SKROOOOOM
ANYTHING TO KEEP UP THE LIE.
ANYTHING TO GET MY EXCUSES BACK.
BUT I'VE BEEN GIVEN A SECOND CHANCE.
AND I'M DONE RUNNING.

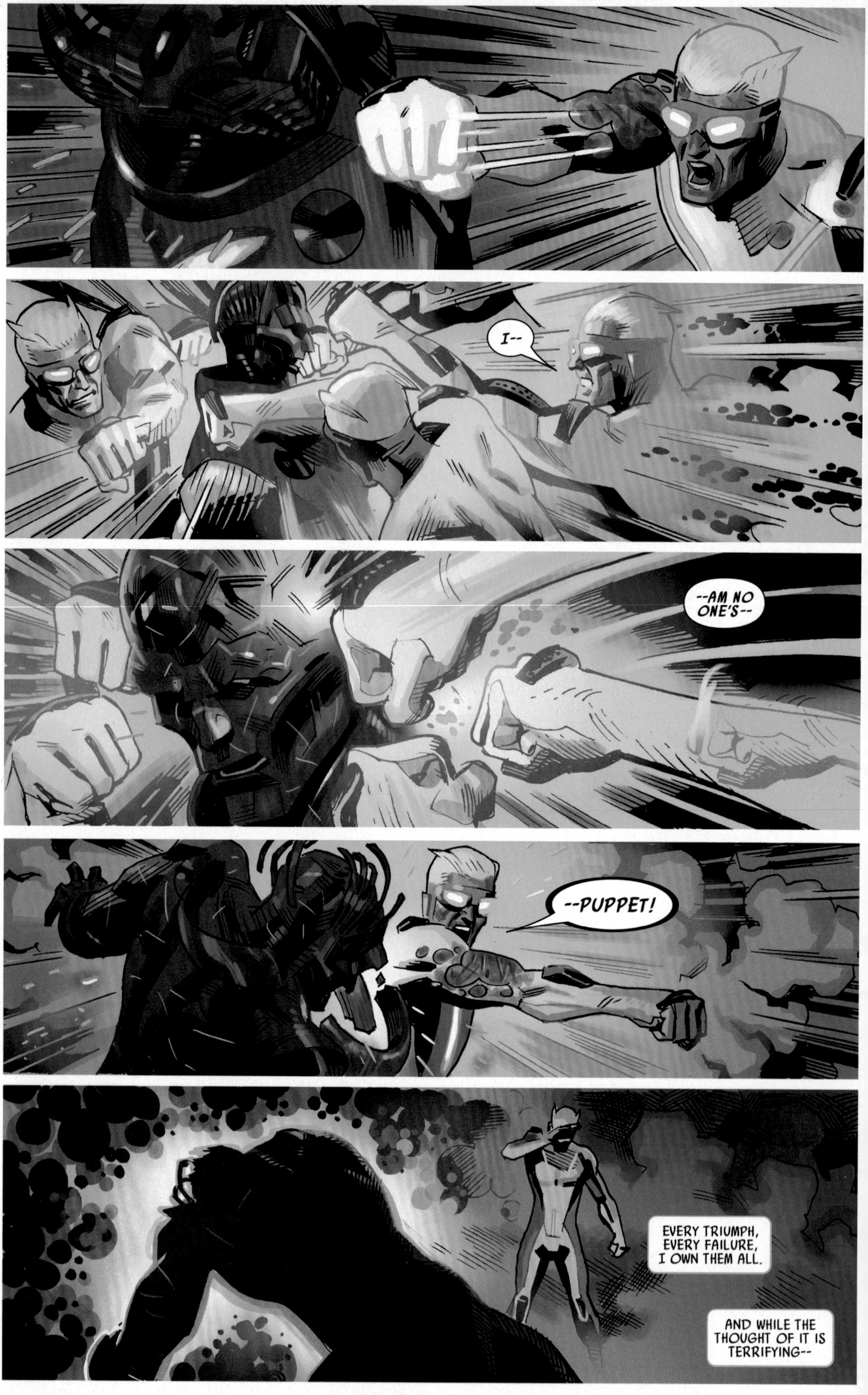
I--
--AM NO ONE'S--
--PUPPET!
EVERY TRIUMPH, EVERY FAILURE, I OWN THEM ALL.
AND WHILE THE THOUGHT OF IT IS TERRIFYING--

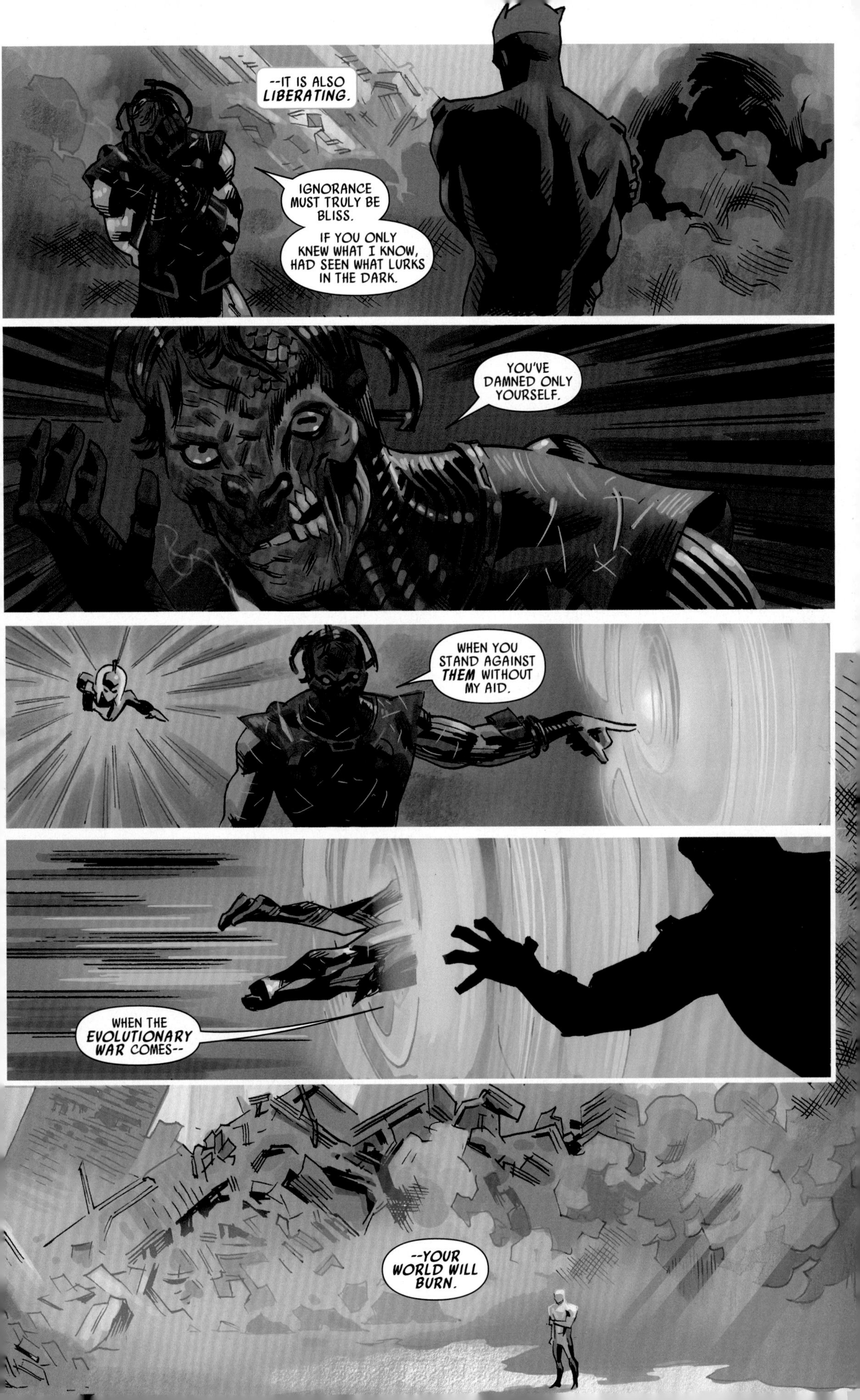
--IT IS ALSO LIBERATING.
IGNORANCE MUST TRULY BE BLISS.
IF YOU ONLY KNEW WHAT I KNOW, HAD SEEN WHAT LURKS IN THE DARK.
YOU'VE DAMNED ONLY YOURSELF.
WHEN YOU STAND AGAINST THEM WITHOUT MY AID.
WHEN THE EVOLUTIONARY WAR COMES--
--YOUR WORLD WILL BURN.

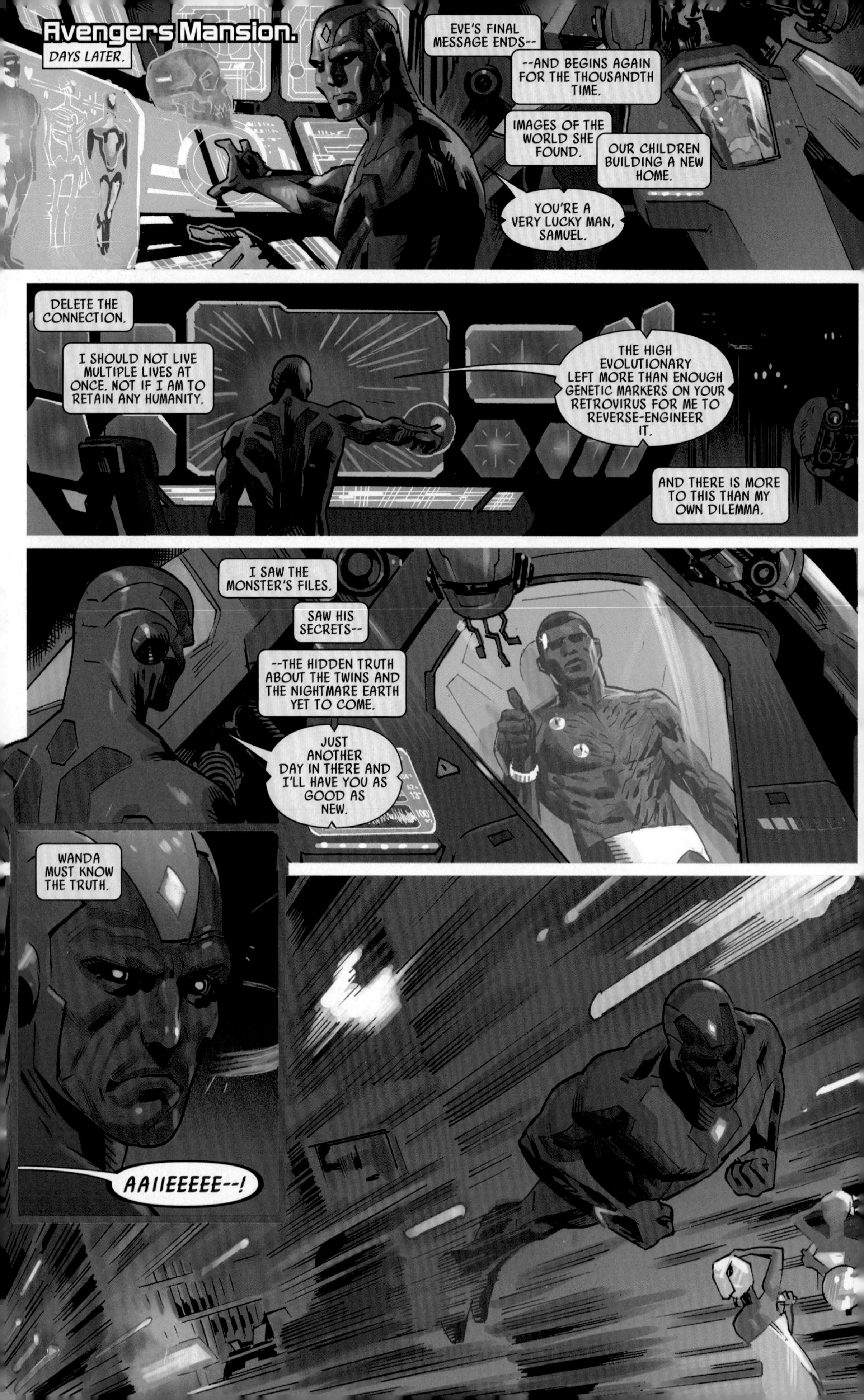
Avengers Mansion.
DAYS LATER.
EVE'S FINAL MESSAGE ENDS--
--AND BEGINS AGAIN FOR THE THOUSANDTH TIME.
IMAGES OF THE WORLD SHE FOUND.
OUR CHILDREN BUILDING A NEW HOME.
YOU'RE A VERY LUCKY MAN, SAMUEL.
DELETE THE CONNECTION.
I SHOULD NOT LIVE MULTIPLE LIVES AT ONCE. NOT IF I AM TO RETAIN ANY HUMANITY.
THE HIGH EVOLUTIONARY LEFT MORE THAN ENOUGH GENETIC MARKERS ON YOUR RETROVIRUS FOR ME TO REVERSE-ENGINEER IT.
AND THERE IS MORE TO THIS THAN MY OWN DILEMMA.
I SAW THE MONSTER'S FILES.
SAW HIS SECRETS--
--THE HIDDEN TRUTH ABOUT THE TWINS AND THE NIGHTMARE EARTH YET TO COME.
JUST ANOTHER DAY IN THERE AND I'LL HAVE YOU AS GOOD AS NEW.
WANDA MUST KNOW THE TRUTH.
AAIIEEEEE--!

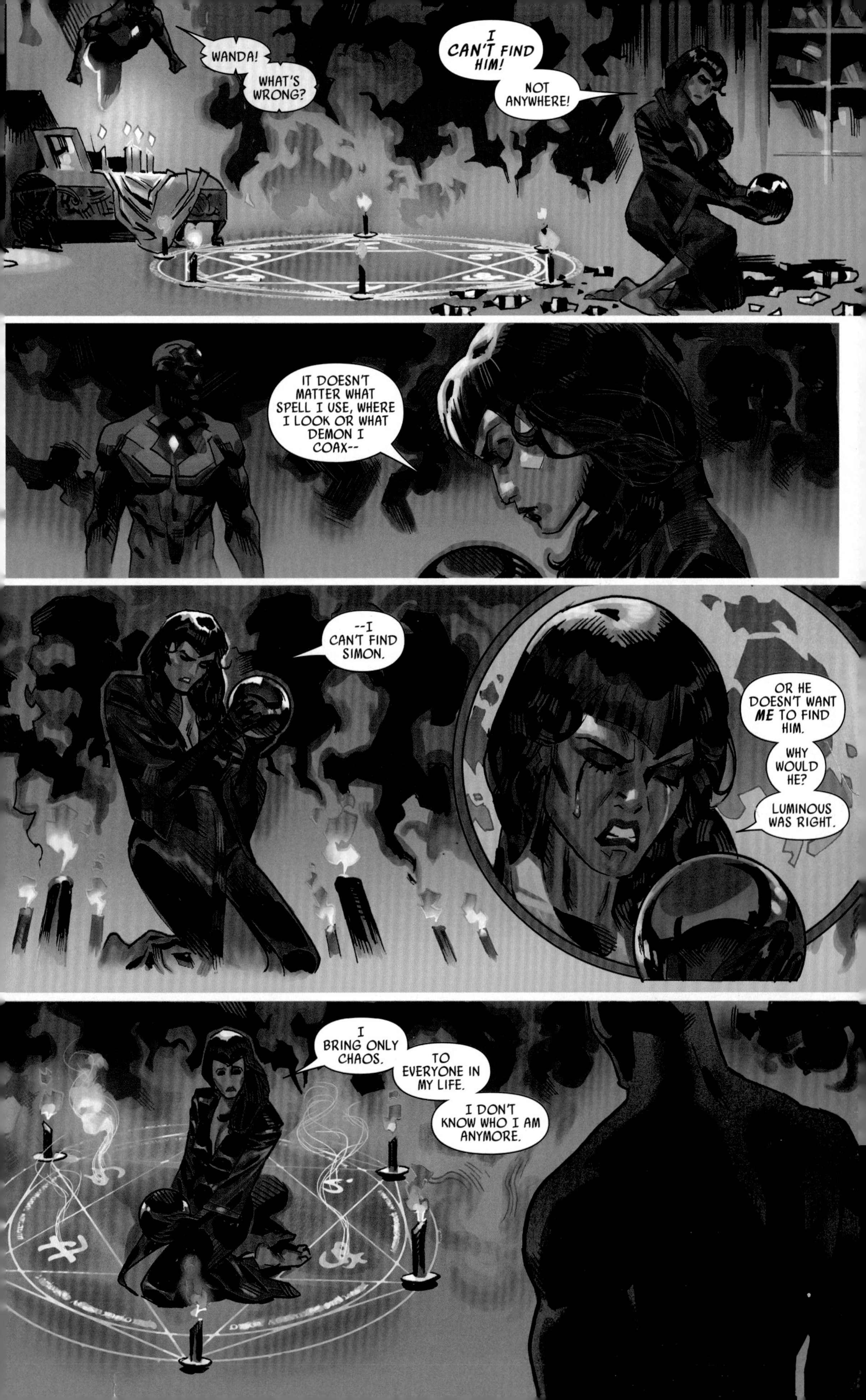
WANDA!
WHAT'S WRONG?
I CAN'T FIND HIM!
NOT ANYWHERE!
IT DOESN'T MATTER WHAT SPELL I USE, WHERE I LOOK OR WHAT DEMON I COAX--
--I CAN'T FIND SIMON.
OR HE DOESN'T WANT ME TO FIND HIM.
WHY WOULD HE?
LUMINOUS WAS RIGHT.
I BRING ONLY CHAOS.
TO EVERYONE IN MY LIFE.
I DON'T KNOW WHO I AM ANYMORE.

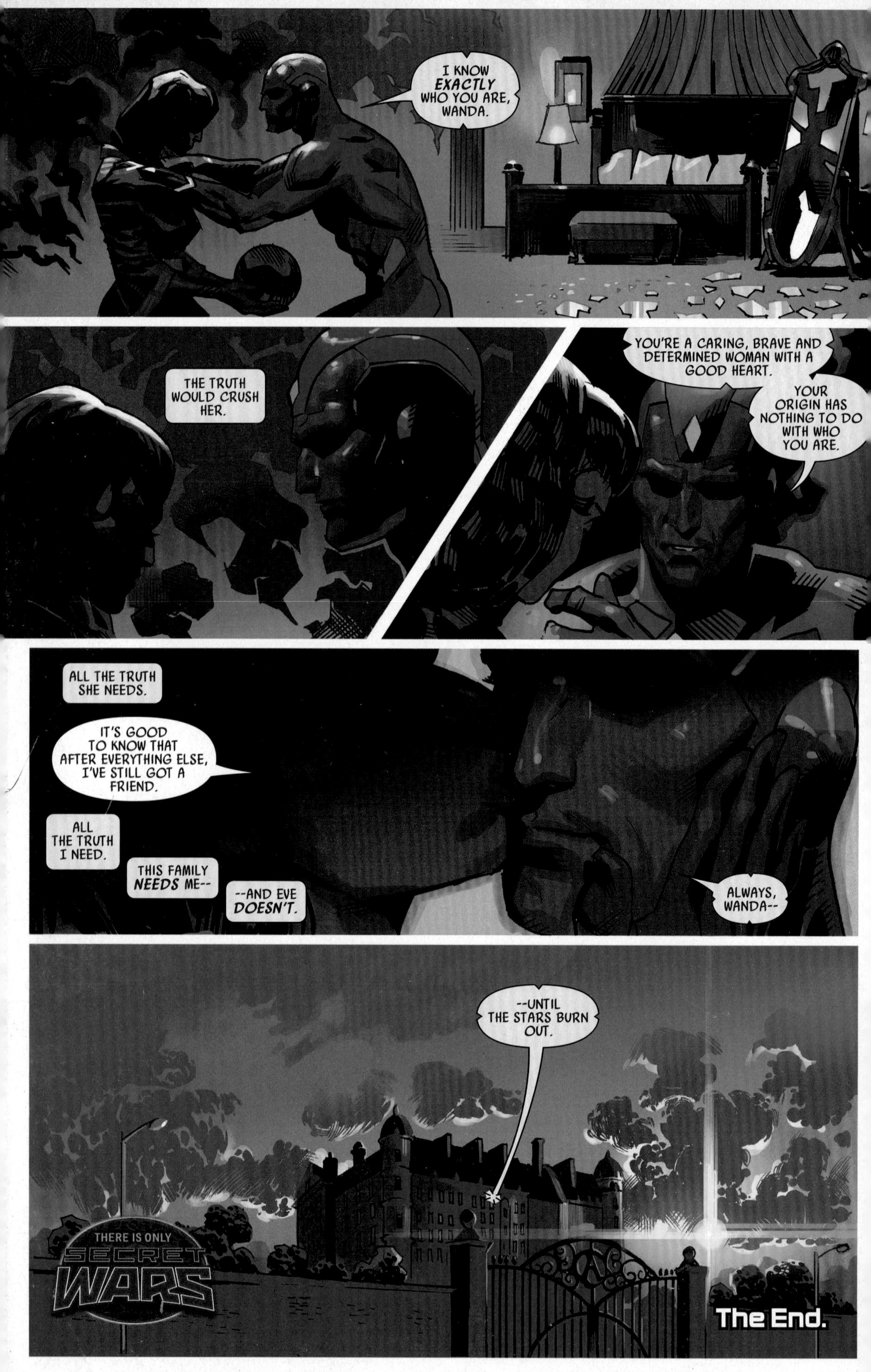
I KNOW EXACTLY WHO YOU ARE, WANDA.
THE TRUTH WOULD CRUSH HER.
YOU'RE A CARING, BRAVE AND DETERMINED WOMAN WITH A GOOD HEART.
YOUR ORIGIN HAS NOTHING TO DO WITH WHO YOU ARE.
ALL THE TRUTH SHE NEEDS.
IT'S GOOD TO KNOW THAT AFTER EVERYTHING ELSE, I'VE STILL GOT A FRIEND.
ALL THE TRUTH I NEED.
THIS FAMILY NEEDS ME--
--AND EVE DOESN'T.
ALWAYS, WANDA--
--UNTIL THE STARS BURN OUT.
THERE IS ONLY SECRET WARS
The End.